CHARTING TWENTIETH-CENTURY MONETARY POLICY

Recent Titles in
Contributions in Economics and Economic History

Inequality and Equity: Economics of Greed, Politics of Envy, Ethics of Equality
Charles T. Stewart, Jr.

Democracy in Desperation: The Depression of 1893
Douglas Steeples and David O. Whitten

The Origins of American Public Finance: Debates over Money, Debt, and Taxes in the
Constitutional Era, 1776–1836
Donald R. Stabile

The Pillage of Sustainability in Eritrea, 1600s–1990s: Rural Communities
and the Creeping Shadows of Hegemony
Niaz Murtaza

Opening the West: Federal Internal Improvements Before 1860
Laurence J. Malone

Oil and Coffee: Latin American Merchant Shipping from the Imperial Era to the 1950s
René De La Pedraja

The American Peasantry
Southern Agricultural Labor and Its Legacy, 1850–1995: A Study in Political Economy
Ronald E. Seavoy

Keynes: A Critical Life
David Felix

Treasure from the Painted Hills: A History of Calico, California, 1882–1907
Douglas Steeples

Ecology and the World-System
Walter L. Goldfrank, David Goodman, and Andrew Szasz, editors

Latin American Merchant Shipping in the Age of Global Competition
René De La Pedraja

Maritime Sector, Institutions, and Sea Power of Premodern China
Gang Deng

CHARTING TWENTIETH-CENTURY MONETARY POLICY

Herbert Hoover and Benjamin Strong, 1917–1927

SILVANO A. WUESCHNER

Foreword by Ellis W. Hawley

Contributions in Economics and Economic History, Number 210
David O. Whitten, *Series Adviser*

GREENWOOD PRESS
Westport, Connecticut • London

Library of Congress Cataloging-in-Publication Data

Wueschner, Silvano A. (Silvano Alfons), 1950–
　　Charting twentieth-century monetary policy : Herbert Hoover and
　Benjamin Strong, 1917–1927 / Silvano A. Wueschner.
　　　　p.　cm.—(Contributions in economics and economic history,
　ISSN 0084–9235 ; no. 210)
　　Includes bibliographical references and index.
　　ISBN 0–313–30978–7 (alk. paper)
　　1. Monetary policy—United States—History—20th century.
　2. Hoover, Herbert, 1874–1964.　3. Strong, Benjamin, 1872–1928.
　4. Board of Governors of the Federal Reserve System (U.S.)　5. Banks
　and banking—United States—History—20th century.　I. Title.
　II. Series.
　HC538.W94　1999
　332.4′973—dc21　　　98–44219

British Library Cataloguing in Publication Data is available.

Copyright © 1999 by Silvano A. Wueschner

Library of Congress Catalog Card Number: 98–44219
ISBN: 0–313–30978–7
ISSN: 0084–9235

First published in 1999

Greenwood Press, 88 Post Road West, Westport, CT 06881
An imprint of Greenwood Publishing Group, Inc.

Printed in the United States of America

The paper used in this book complies with the
Permanent Paper Standard issued by the National
Information Standards Organization (Z39.48–1984).

10　9　8　7　6　5　4　3　2　1

To my family

Contents

Foreword

In today's America the delegation of monetary policy making to the peculiar complex of governmental and private institutions known as the Federal Reserve System appears at long last to be paying substantial dividends. Under the unifying leadership of Alan Greenspan, the "Fed" has largely displaced the Office of Management and Budget and the Council of Economic Advisers as the nation's major instrument of economic fine tuning, has received credit for the "soft landings," sustained economic growth, and remarkable price stability of recent years, and seems to have all but silenced calls for equipping the country with new economic planning and monetary management institutions. At last, it seems, a combination of piecemeal reform, economic learning, and institutional evolution has produced something approaching what the system's champions have long envisioned for it. At least it was winning the kind of accolades that had been notably absent during much of its history.

That history, however, deserves fuller and more detailed study, both to help us explain why such success was so long deferred and as an aid to understanding the tensions within and pressures upon the system that may eventually reemerge and prevent it from taking the actions required for continuing economic stability. It is only in recent years that historians of the system have begun viewing its policy output as a product of interest group and bureaucratic interaction rather than decisions generated by the search of disinterested and independent experts for a socio-economic optimum. And while it has become clear that its history has been a troubled one, involving periods of marginalization and domination by outside agencies as well as factional strife and protracted struggles for liberation from its would-be masters, we still know relatively little about these periods and struggles or about the external pressures, internal dynamics, and individual policy makers that have shaped the course of events. A new history of the system, in which its changing fortunes and efforts to serve different masters are more fully explored and accounted for, is clearly needed.

What is true of the system's history as a whole, moreover, is even more true of its history during the 1920s. Although customarily skipped over as a "quiet period" during which little of significance occurred, the decade was actually one in which the system's structural weaknesses and difficulties in achieving policy coherence were highlighted and in which its future struggles for liberation, both against the Treasury and against the New York banking establishment, were anticipated. In addition, one can find in the period the beginnings of three kinds of institutional reform initiatives that would continue to threaten the system's status as an independent agency, one coming from the heirs of an agrarian populism, a second from believers in the subordination of monetary to fiscal policy, and a third from would-be subordinators of monetary action to the development of a new capitalism managed through expert commissions and public-spirited associations. These would become greater threats during the New Deal era, when the Fed's glaring failure as an economic manager led not only to internal structural changes but also to support for subordinating it to designs stressing currency manipulation, compensatory public spending, and detailed codes of fair competition. And in its later history threats of this sort, leading to intermittent calls for new monetary, fiscal, and industrial policy agencies, continued to play a role. In them one can discern a pattern of challenge and response about which we know too little and the origins of which have remained particularly murky.

In the study that follows, Silvano Wueschner makes an important contribution to the fuller and more politically oriented history now needed if we are to understand the workings and capabilities of what has become our central institution of macroeconomic management. Focusing on particular aspects of Federal Reserve policy making in the 1920s, his study highlights not only the system's structural peculiarities and their early consequences but also the emergence and maneuvering of rival factions having differing priorities and goals, the responsiveness of policy makers to special interests and encroaching bureaucratic domains, the persisting disagreements concerning the system's regulatory and administrative capacities, and the resulting failure to arrive at a coherent policy capable of meeting both international and domestic needs. It tells a story that says much about why the system initially failed to meet the expectations of its creators and how the stage was set for its woeful failures, diminished standing, and subordination to other agencies of economic management in the 1930s and 1940s.

In addition, the study sheds much new light on the debates that swirled around the system's international actions and the "easy money" policy that it adopted to facilitate and sustain them. And by focusing on Benjamin Strong and Herbert Hoover, it highlights the system's need for and failure to find a unifying leader and brings out, much more fully and clearly than others have done, the extent to which Hoover's vision of a progressive capitalism differed from

Strong's and the ways in which the former tried to bring monetary policy into line with his efforts to turn the Department of Commerce into the nation's center for economic development and management. These years, Professor Wueschner argues, were anything but "quiet years." They were noisy and filled with portentous events, and a fuller knowledge and understanding of them can enhance our understanding of the Federal Reserve System as a political entity and help us to explain both its subsequent history and its current achievements and vulnerabilities.

Some may also be intrigued by the striking parallels between certain developments today and those of the period upon which Professor Wueschner has focused. Again there are those who hail the coming of a "new era," ushered in by technological and organizational advances that have rendered invalid our established wisdom concerning overpriced stocks, inflationary wage levels, maximum employment, and cyclical fluctuations. Again there is concern with the "demon" of irrational speculation and the consequences that it could have for the economic system as a whole. Again the difficulties and conflicting pressures inherent in achieving both international and domestic stabilization are apparent. And again, if the current success story has an unhappy ending, there is a potential for shifting managerial duties to other agencies and toppling the tool of monetary policy from the high perch it now enjoys.

Whether fuller study of policy making and implementation in the earlier period can help us to avoid its major errors seems debatable. But it can provide much food for thought. And in any event, a study that moves us closer to the history needed for assessing a bureaucratic complex now entrusted with immense power and accorded great deference is a welcome addition to the available literature.

Ellis W. Hawley

Introduction

Federal Reserve Board decisions and pronouncements were read by very few. Bank officers who would be obliged to conform to them. Among businessmen, a small proportion who were aware that Federal Reserve Board actions would affect business, in some cases powerfully. A few scholars in monetary theory and economics. Of reading by the general public, there was almost literally none.

Mark Sullivan[1]

The focus of this work is on American monetary policy formulation during the 1920s and how this was affected by Herbert Hoover as Secretary of Commerce and Benjamin Strong as Governor of the Federal Reserve Bank of New York (FRBNY). The aim is both to shed new light on their roles in policy making and to relate these roles to larger conflicts over where policy should be made, how the Federal Reserve System should be structured and used, and what balance should be struck between international, national, and regional considerations.

In exploring these subjects the study also examines the roles played by the colleagues and professional acquaintances who comprised the frequently adversarial factions led by Strong and directed by Hoover. In these clashes Strong usually played a tough and, for the most part, open leadership role, while Hoover chose to exercise his influence behind the scenes. Too often he was reluctant to engage in public debates regarding government policy and at times opted to engage the opposition through carefully selected proxies.

The Hoover and Strong collaboration began in 1918 when Herbert Hoover sought the Federal Reserve System's assistance in dealing with the Cuban Sugar

---

1. Mark Sullivan. Unpublished Manuscript, in Mark Sullivan File, Post Presidential Individual (hereafter PPI), Herbert Hoover Presidential Library (hereafter HHPL).

Crisis. There were also official contacts during the early years of the Harding Administration, especially in regard to questions dealing with European financial stability. Hoover and Strong both wished to develop trade, and the latter maintained that such efforts would meet with far greater success if they resulted from an organized plan, ergo a concerted policy, as opposed to individual efforts.

Hoover believed in governmental cooperation with the private sector, and in May 1921, he and Secretary of the Treasury Andrew Mellon arranged for an informal conference between bankers and government officials at the White House. The intention was to reconcile foreign and domestic demands for American capital, and in this informal consultation Strong participated. In addition, Hoover co-operated with Strong when the latter sought written permission from the State Department to participate in financial negotiations involving European governments. This request, however, was denied by Secretary of State Charles Evans Hughes, who feared that Strong's actions, despite the best intentions, might lead to moral commitments that could prove to be embarrassing.

Hoover and Strong also agreed on the need for stabilizing exchange rates. Both believed that England's return to the gold standard was requisite to monetary stabilization in that country and that European economic stabilization was dependent on England's success in bringing her economy under control. They agreed, moreover, on a variety of other matters, and until 1923 Hoover and Strong enjoyed a cordial relationship. The disagreement came from 1923 on, primarily over such issues as the supervision of foreign loans, easy money policy, and the establishment of effective controls to ensure the use of credit for commercial, industrial, and agricultural purposes instead of underwriting speculation. By 1924 Hoover was becoming one of Strong's sharpest critics. He later referred to Strong as a "mental annex to Europe" and talked about "Strong and his European Allies," and as their relationship deteriorated factions developed.

In examining the resulting controversy, a number of "sub-themes" will be developed. One important area was European monetary stabilization, an area in which Strong argued that all "trade" had become subject to the possibility of large exchange losses and would benefit from stable exchange rates, which could be achieved only by England's return to the gold standard. On this most bankers, economists, and leading government figures, including Herbert Hoover, were in agreement, and in 1924 a banking group led by Strong devised a scheme to facilitate this action by extending a credit of $200 million to the Bank of England.[2] In January 1925, Strong and Montagu Norman of the Bank of England met with Secretary of the Treasury Andrew Mellon to sell him on the plan, and the latter promptly sanctioned Federal Reserve participation.

The plan, however, drew immediate criticism from Oscar T. Crosby, former Assistant Secretary of the Treasury during the Wilson Administration. In an article published by the *New York Times* on May 5, 1925, Crosby questioned

---

2. At the same time a credit, to be provided by J.P. Morgan et al., in the amount of $100 million was arranged for the English government.

both the legality and the propriety of the plan, and in so doing infuriated Strong. The latter believed that Reserve Board member Adolph Miller,[3] a close friend and neighbor of Hoover had incited the attack by leaking confidential information to Crosby. He considered this a serious breach of ethics and suggested that the matter be brought to the attention of President Coolidge for possible legal action. Mellon, though, urged caution in the matter and suggested that he could set the matter straight. He talked to Miller, but, as could be expected, Miller denied any complicity and argued that the information upon which the attack was based came from statements made by Strong to the press and by Winston Churchill in the House of Commons. There were, however, others who opposed the plan. Strong had issued a brief statement about the loan on April 29. This announcement drew an immediate inquiry from C.E. Mitchell of the National City Bank of New York, who was also concerned about the legality of the Federal Reserve Board's action.[4] This resulted in a considerable debate in the media concerning the powers and proper role of the Federal Reserve System. One aspect of the Hoover-Strong relationship would be a continuing struggle to define these.

In 1925 this renewed debate about the Federal Reserve System quickly moved from the public media into Congress, the result being committee hearings on a variety of bills to define more clearly the purpose of the system. In 1926 both Miller and Strong testified, and, although Hoover did not, he was quoted by other witnesses on several occasions. One feature of the hearings was a divergence of opinion between bankers and economists over the methods that should be used to improve the functioning of the monetary system. Some bankers argued that the regulation of the domestic economy should not depend to any great extent upon Reserve banks, while a number of economists argued that it was the duty of the Federal Reserve System to regulate the money supply in order to accommodate business and commerce. In addition, concern was expressed as to why the Federal Reserve Board was dominated by bankers. One witness, George Shibley, pointed out that "the board of the bank of England is composed wholly of big merchants, men who are interested in business. They do not permit on the board a banker who deals in checks."[5] And, according to Berkley Williams, a Richmond, Virginia, banker, Herbert Hoover had made a similar observation to his advisory committee of businessmen in 1921. Hoover had wanted to liberalize financial control and sought to have the secretaries of commerce and agriculture placed, ex officio, on the Federal Reserve Board. Subsequently, though, other witnesses noted that in England the merchants were

3. Adolph Miller, an economist, was one of the original Wilson appointees to the Federal Reserve Board. The son of a retail grocer in San Francisco he originally attended the University of California but completed his economics training at Harvard University after the Harvard Club of San Francisco established a scholarship fund to send him there.

4. Charles Mitchell to Benjamin Strong, May 8, 1925, in Strong Papers, FRBNY.

5. House Committee on Banking and Currency, *Stabilization, H.R. 7895*, 69th Cong., 1st Sess., 1926, p. 290.

the equivalent of American bankers and that in 1925 only one of the six appointees to the Federal Reserve Board was a banker.

Another area of concern at the time was the balance to be struck between domestic needs and foreign considerations. London had returned to the gold standard at an exchange rate of $4.86 to the pound, a rate that required continuing support from New York, and in the words of Charles S. Maier, "made greater demands on domestic economic policies than its pre-war counterpart." In effect, it required "more austerity in Britain and militated for a low-interest policy in New York which contributed to superheated stock speculation."[6] Moreover, it called for a joint Anglo-American monetary policy even though their domestic requirements were not the same. Its real beneficiaries were the central bankers and leading banking institutions whose influence and prestige were enhanced. But Strong insisted that this was justified. He repeatedly argued that bankers should maintain their independence from national treasuries, which were prone to inflation or exchange controls. He also maintained that a country that ensured the sovereignty of its central bank made itself a safe haven for long-term investment and that any adverse domestic effects from the new exchange rate were more than offset by its beneficial effects on convertibility, banking leadership and international commerce.[7]

Herbert Hoover, however, was concerned about the nature of American loans abroad and argued that they should be confined to reproductive purposes. He maintained that they should not be dissipated in propping up deflated currencies or squandered in countries with deficient budgets. And of still greater concern to Hoover was the continued expansion of lending for speculation on the New York Stock Exchange. This, he argued, stemmed from cheap money caused by the low interest policy, and beginning in 1925 he used a number of interviews and speeches to urge restraint on speculation and overexpansion. Adolph Miller and several economic and banking journals were also urging caution by late 1925, but were largely being ignored.

Publicly, to be sure, Hoover continued to say that economic conditions were the best that they had ever been and that the economy was basically sound. Though, privately, he feared that expansion of credit and speculation would have an adverse effect on the credit fund of the country, and that the speculative fever might extend into commodities and bring about a collapse that would affect every part of the nation. He also insisted that it was important to keep the Federal Reserve System from contributing to the growth of speculation, either directly or indirectly. He was especially concerned with the fact that there was a noticeable increase in the growth of the bill and security holdings of the Federal Reserve System, which appeared to parallel the growth of speculation on Wall

---

6. Charles S. Maier, *Recasting Bourgeois Europe: Stabilization in France, Germany and Italy in the Decade after World War I* (Princeton: Princeton University Press, 1975), p. 589.

7. Strong insisted during August 1925 that the international situation was of primary importance.

Street. There was, he suspected, a connection between the credit released by the Federal Reserve System and the increase of credit apparent in street loans.

Hoover's concern about street loans turned to alarm in late 1925. He believed now that the volume of these loans, which had increased to nearly two billion seven hundred million dollars, was of great importance to the whole country, and he made his concerns known to Governor Daniel Crissinger of the Federal Reserve Board, only to be chided for being "parochial minded."[8] He then appealed to President Coolidge, urging the president to summon Crissinger and "to express alarm over the board's policy."[9] But Coolidge refused to intervene, saying that the Administration should not attempt to influence the policy of the Federal Reserve Board. He said nothing about Mellon's earlier role in sanctioning the action of the FRBNY.

Whether the president should keep his distance from the board had been a matter of debate from the beginning. During Wilson's administration he had been criticized by two Federal Reserve Board members for his failure to become involved and had replied that this was a deliberately chosen policy because he wanted it to be able to pursue its course freely, without "any constraint or restraint from the Executive." Moreover, Wilson argued, "The very moment that I should attempt to establish close relations with the board, that moment I would be accused of trying to bring political pressure to bear."[10] Coolidge could argue similarly and could, as Carter Glass described Wilson's view, take the position that all matters relating to banking and commercial credits ought to be "removed from all sinister influences as one pole is from the other."[11]

As Hoover saw it, however, the sinister influence now threatening commercial credits was not the executive branch but the increasingly dominant leadership of the FRBNY in the person of Benjamin Strong. Consequently, with the help of Adolph Miller and Senator Irvine Lenroot of Wisconsin, he continued to make his views known to the board. His strategy now became a behind-the-scenes approach, deliberately chosen because he felt that as a member of the Administration he should refrain from publicly criticizing official policy. Instead, Lenroot sent a number of letters to the Federal Reserve Board, signed by him but at Hoover's "suggestion and under his collaboration" and conveying Hoover's messages concerning "the dangers of inflation and the desirability of raising the discount rates of the Federal Reserve Bank of New York."[12] The correspondence resulted in a personal visit from Benjamin Strong that lasted over two hours. But Strong, as did Governor Crissinger, maintained that there

8. Mark Sullivan, Unpublished Manuscript p. 41, in Mark Sullivan File, PPI, HHPL.
9. Ibid.
10. Carter Glass, *An Adventure in Constructive Finance* (Garden City, NY: Doubleday, Page, 1927), p. 272.
11. Ibid.
12. Irvine Lenroot to Mark Sullivan, November 6, 1947, reproduced from Library of Congress Manuscript Division, in General Accession 516, Irvine Lenroot, HHPL.

was "no danger in the financial situation" and in the end nothing was accomplished by the correspondence.[13]

In Hoover's view, the Federal Reserve Board had been established to control the amount of credit in the country during "boom" and "deflationary" periods by slowing up its increase during the former and by reducing the speed and extent of the decrease during the latter. The board could control the amount of credit by regulating interest rates, and in essence it had three methods of doing so. Through its Open Market Operations, it could increase or reduce the reserves of member banks, thereby influencing their lending capacity and the interest rate at which credit was available. It could raise or lower the "rediscount rate" paid by member banks for loans from the reserve banks. And it could apply "direct pressure" on member banks to limit or reduce their loans to customers, thereby limiting the quantity of available credit. These were powers, Hoover believed, that should be used in circumstances like those of 1925, and if it took "pressure" on the board to secure their use then pressure should be applied.

Involved here was not only a debate about the appropriateness of Federal Reserve policy but also a larger struggle for dominance over the Reserve Board. As it shaped up, it became a conflict between Benjamin Strong, supported by Mellon and the New York establishment, on the one side, and Adolph Miller, close friend and confidante of Herbert Hoover, on the other. In 1926 the contest of wills had reached such proportions that Strong kept track of the testimony given by Miller before the House Committee on Banking and Currency and deliberately tailored his own testimony so as to minimize any influence that Miller might have gained. At the same time he exerted his influence to have a portion of Miller's testimony excluded from the *Congressional Record*. Subsequently, Strong threatened to resign if Miller were not forced off the Federal Reserve Board. He tended to see Miller's opposition as a part of a larger pattern that also involved opposition from Midwestern bankers and disagreements with Governor Crissinger. The latter had not been physically well for some time, and Strong commented to Mellon that if Crissinger could not be forced from the board perhaps nature would lend a helping hand. It did not, but in 1927, amid a controversy over a forced rate reduction in the Chicago Federal Reserve district, Crissinger decided to resign.

Also complicating this battle between Strong and his critics were continuing charges of regional bias. Farm leaders and spokesmen continued to argue that the Federal Reserve System favored Wall Street at the expense of farmers in the Midwest and the South and that money was unavailable for farm loans because it had been diverted to the stock and commodities markets. In 1922 the congressional "farm bloc" had tried to remedy this bias through a law stipulating that there should be a farmer member on the Federal Reserve Board, a position that had gone to Milo D. Campbell of Michigan. In addition farm interests had welcomed the appointment of Crissinger a farmer from Ohio. But in the eyes of many, bias had persisted. In particular, the efforts of the Federal Reserve Act's authors to limit the influence of the New York Federal Reserve district had been

---

13. Ibid.

thwarted, and New York had again achieved dominant status through the Open Market Committee and other innovations.

Finally, the battle was also complicated by Strong's awareness of the limited powers at the system's disposal. The intent of the Federal Reserve Act might be to make money available for productive, as opposed to speculative, purposes. But the system lacked the kind of controls that could do this. A member bank in need of money could easily discount commercial paper when in fact its reserves had been depleted by speculative loans. Enforcing a distinction was all but impossible, and bankers such as Strong were keenly aware of that fact.

Since the 1920s a good deal has been written about Federal Reserve policy during the period and about Hoover and Strong. These writings, however, have not explored the Hoover-Strong relationship in detail. Nor have they brought out its role in the policies that helped to produce Federal Reserve decisions and policies and reflected larger struggles over the system's status and powers. This is true both of accounts written in the 1920s and 1930s and those produced a generation later.

Early accounts include Harold Reed's *Federal Reserve Policy 1921-1930* (1930) and W. Randolph Burgess's *Interpretations of Federal Reserve Policy in the Speeches and Writings of Benjamin Strong* (1930), both relying primarily on public testimony and speeches as statements of the policies pursued and the philosophy behind them. Lawrence Clark's *Central Banking Under the Federal Reserve System, with Special Consideration of the Federal Reserve Bank of New York* (1935) also relied heavily on congressional hearings and the Federal Reserve Board's annual reports and in doing so tended to ignore or slight such matters as conflicting domestic and foreign considerations, the criticisms that arose about FRBNY participation in England's return to gold, and the late 1925 controversy generated by the efforts of Hoover and Miller to curb speculation.

Also among early studies were those discussing the "formative period" of the Federal Reserve System. Benjamin Beckhart's *Discount Policy of the Federal Reserve System* (1924), for example, traced Federal Reserve operations up through 1923 and offered a substantial discussion of European Central Banks as a background for understanding Federal Reserve policies. In addition, Beckhart included a retrospective and prospective analysis in which he argued for the administration of the system by disinterested experts. Focused on early operations as well was W.P.G. Harding's *Formative Period of the Federal Reserve System* (1925). Along with a description of developments and functions up through 1924, Harding included a number of useful appendices and an informative discussion of the Joint Commission of Agricultural Inquiry and the movement to place a farmer on the Federal Reserve Board.

In the 1950s and 1960s, works based on new archival openings began to appear, including Sir Henry Clay's *Lord Norman* (1957), Lester Chandler's *Benjamin Strong, Central Banker* (1958), and Andrew Boyle's *Montagu Norman* (1967). Each of these examined various aspects of the relationship between the Bank of England and the FRBNY. But only Chandler seems to have recognized the degree of cooperation between Strong and Montagu Norman, and even Chandler failed to place this special relationship within the larger framework of

contending national and international interests. There were also a number of
other weaknesses in Chandler's treatment. His discussion of England's return to
the gold standard failed to consider the problems involved in maintaining the
exchange ratio at the established figure, and in discussing speculation he
claimed that whatever protests Hoover made came during 1924 and ignored the
controversy of late 1925.

Milton Friedman and Anna Schwartz also offered new insights into policy
formulation in *A Monetary History of the United States, 1867-1960* (1963), a
work in which the discussion relating to Federal Reserve policy during the
1920s was based primarily on the *Charles S. Hamlin Diaries*, and the excerpts
they contained of Federal Reserve Board and Open Market Investment Committee meetings. What they failed to do was to relate monetary to fiscal and
commercial policy, and apparently, they did not consult fully the *Hamlin Diaries*. At least, they completely overlooked the Federal Reserve fight of 1925.

Another major work in the 1960s was Elmus Wicker's *Federal Reserve
Policy, 1921-1933* (1966), which examined monetary policy formulation during
the first twenty years of the Federal Reserve System and laid special emphasis
on the role of Treasury as well as that of Federal Reserve officials. One weakness in Wicker's work was his reliance on Chandler's biography of Strong rather
than on Strong's papers. In addition, like Friedman and Schwartz, Wicker overlooked or found little of significance in Hamlin's account of the division within
the Federal Reserve Board during 1925 and 1926. Indeed, Wicker hailed the
period as the "quiet years" rather than one of struggles for control that were
linked to the failure of economic policy in 1929.

Since the 1960s, several other works have appeared, among them Lester
Chandler *American Monetary Policy 1928-1941* (1971), Benjamin Beckhart's
Federal Reserve System (1972), Melvyn Leffler's *The Elusive Quest* (1979),
and Frank Costigliola's *Awkward Dominion* (1984). Only the first two of these,
however, were focused specifically on Federal Reserve policy, and in neither
was policy making in the 1920s the prime concern. Chandler's survey of the
period 1920 through 1928 was offered as background for what followed, and
Beckhart's focus on crucial periods stressed the World War I period and its immediate aftermath.

Costigliola's primary concern, in so far as he dealt with the Federal Reserve System, was with its role in foreign relations and particularly with the use
of the FRBNY to implement the policies of Charles Evans Hughes and Herbert
Hoover. His tendency throughout was to attribute too much power to Hoover
and Hughes, too much independent policy making to the FRBNY, too much
importance to schemes for Federal Reserve banks specializing in foreign trade,
and too much harmony between the policy makers. He ignored, in particular, the
frequency with which Federal Reserve policy led to brusk confrontations between cabinet officers such as Mellon, Hoover, and Hughes. The former nor-
mally supported Federal Reserve decisions, whereas Hoover increasingly sought
to challenge them. One case in point was the debate over the issue of foreign
loans; another was the argument over interest rates; and Hughes, as well, had
his confrontations with Strong.

Leffler's work is still one of the best dealing with American efforts to aid European stabilization. It is solidly grounded in material from the Hoover Presidential Library, the archives of the FRBNY, the Library of Congress, and other archival repositories. Though, again, the focus is on foreign relations rather than on the domestic issues also affected by policy decisions.

This work, then, differs from preceding works in its focus, scope, and the sources consulted. The focus is on the Hoover-Strong relationship, as seen from a political rather than a purely economic perspective. The scope includes both the domestic and international aspects of Federal Reserve Policy formulation, and the new sources consulted allow it to provide not only fresh details but a broader interpretation.

A number of writers have placed the blame for the depression on the policies that were developed during the autumn of 1927. It is my contention that the foundation for that policy was laid with America's decision to underwrite the Dawes plan, the decision to underwrite England's return to the gold standard, and the involvement in European monetary stabilization. I also argue that the Federal Reserve System's problems stemmed from the fact that it never really had a chance to become established before being called upon to finance World War I, and that in the wake of the war there developed a struggle for dominance over Federal Reserve policy formulation between the FRBNY and the Federal Reserve Board, which itself was plagued by internal divisions on policy matters. These problems militated against the formulation of a coherent policy and the assumption of an effective leadership role by the board.

Briefly, I develop my argument as follows. In chapter 1, I examine the clash of views involved in the establishment of the Federal Reserve System and the emergence of factions espousing differing views of the system's role and power. I argue that the original aims of the Federal Reserve Act were being thwarted by the developments stemming from the unexpected demands put upon the new system, that the New York financial community had become more powerful, and that political considerations encroached upon and undercut the notion of monetary control by a disinterested public body. I turn in chapter 2 to the system's role in foreign loan supervision, the participation by the United States in settling the reparations question, and efforts by the FRBNY to participate in the development of the Dawes plan. I also show how factionalism involved in these developments remained intertwined with persisting farm bloc criticism of Federal Reserve policies.

Chapter 3 examines England's return to the gold standard, focusing particularly on the relationship between the FRBNY and the Bank of England and arguing that the scheme resulting from this collaboration had far reaching consequences and made greater demands on domestic economic policies than could have been foreseen. The story it tells is central to this work, especially as background for the crucial developments examined in chapter 4. In it, I focus on the developing controversy over the effectiveness of using the rediscount rate to control speculation and inflation, arguing that 1925 marked the beginning of an active effort to underwrite international economic stability and that it was this issue that served to widen the gulf between the various factions in the system.

Chapter 5 follows the continuing struggle to define the Federal Reserve System and the accompanying attempts by the Federal Reserve Board to reassert its leadership role. Coming into this story in one way or another are various legislative proposals, clashing regional attitudes, and rival forms of expertise. In Chapter 6 examines the further debates over greater centralization of control in the hands of the Federal Reserve Board, the Chicago rate controversy that sparked some of them, the easy money policy adopted in the autumn of 1927, and the subsequent debate over the use of open market operations to check speculation. I argue that the decision to underwrite England's return to the gold standard called for lower interest rates in the United States than in England, and that this easy money policy gave an impetus to the speculative expansion that eventually culminated in the stock market crash of 1929. Finally, Chapter 7 provides an assessment of the failures to achieve greater policy coherence and of the claims that would later be made in regard to the coming of the Depression.

Chapter 1

The Emergence of Factions: Differing Views on the Roles for the Federal Reserve System

This bill creates a "central bank." This plan is much more centralized, auto-
cratic, and tyrannical than the Aldrich plan. It is true we are to have 12 regional
banks; but these are but the agents of the grand central board, which absolutely
controls them. The power is not with them; they are not in any material matter
given independent action; they must obey orders from Washington.

Rep. M. Towner (R. Iowa)[1]

The Federal Reserve System was officially established on December 23, 1913,
when President Woodrow Wilson signed Public Act No. 43, 63rd Congress, or
the *Federal Reserve Act*. The act was the outcome of a banking reform movement that grew out of the panic of 1893, but its immediate origin lay in the financial havoc wrought by the panic of 1907. The movement recognized that
there were inherent defects in the American banking system, among which were
the lack of an elastic currency, no adequate means of rediscounting commercial
paper, and inadequate supervision of banking. The system, as Mark Sullivan
later noted, was "a tangle of inadequacy and antiquation,"[2] and Congress was

---

1. Congressional Record, 63rd Cong., 1st sess., pt. 5: p. 4896.
2. Mark Sullivan, Unpublished Manuscript, in Mark Sullivan File, PPI, HHPL.

seeking to correct these deficiencies when it established the Federal Reserve System.[3]

This chapter will begin with the clash of views involved in the establishment of the Federal Reserve System and will then examine the emergence of factions espousing differing views of the system's role and power. It will be concerned particularly with its operation during the war, the views of it held by Herbert Hoover, the debate over its role in the slump of 1920, and the growing influence of Benjamin Strong and the FRBNY within the system. All of these are important if one is to understand the clashes and controversies of the post-1922 period.

In the aftermath of the 1907 panic, Congress had established a National Monetary Commission, headed by the Senate Majority Leader Nelson Aldrich of Rhode Island. The Commission had then studied banking reform for the better part of four years, and had eventually submitted a proposal to Congress. By this time, however, the Republicans no longer controlled Congress, and one result was an alternative to the Aldrich Bill submitted by Representative Carter Glass of Virginia. Both measures were seen by their proponents as offering a way to correct the deficiencies that reformers had been pointing out since the 1890s. And in the eyes of some, the Indiana Monetary Convention of 1899[4] was "as much the intellectual godfather of the Federal Reserve Act as the National Monetary Convention."[5] Two of the participants in that Convention, Charles Hamlin, who served on the executive committee, and H.P. Willis, "a guiding light intellectually," would subsequently be involved in shaping and administering the Federal Reserve System.

As introduced, the Glass Bill was opposed by numerous business organizations, economic journalists, and bankers, with the latter favoring instead the Aldrich plan that had been submitted to Congress in 1911. In November of that year the American Bankers Association had unanimously endorsed the plan, and its members continued to favor it over the Glass Bill. Consequently, the Federal Reserve Act would pass only after a bitter fight.[6]

The Aldrich plan had called for a central bank, chartered for a period of fifty years and controlled primarily by the larger banks. As critics saw it, the scheme would lodge control in the hands of Wall Street, especially since a bank's vote was in direct proportion to its capital stock. The plan lost out, Lawrence Clark concluded, because it "was patterned too much after the European central banks," was "not adapted to American conditions, geographical and eco-

---

3. See, for instance, Lawrence E. Clark, *Central Banking Under the Federal Reserve System* (New York: Macmillan, 1935).

4. The Indianapolis Monetary Convention was a private convention of bankers, businessmen, Chambers of Commerce, etc.

5. Arthur Kemp to Mark Sullivan, April 15, 1950, in Mark Sullivan File, PPI, HHPL.

6. Clark, *Central Banking*, pp. 26-29.

nomic, and was contrary to the American tradition of local autonomy and of opposition to centralized financial power in private hands."[7]

The Glass Bill, on the other hand, provided for twelve regional banks under the general supervision of a Federal Board, which, as with other progressive boards, was to be appointed by the president and consist of a group of disinterested "experts." The intent, according to board member Adolph Miller, was to concentrate "authority and national credit policies . . . in a single, independent disinterested public body having a national viewpoint."[8] But in his judgement, the intent was not achieved in implementing the resulting Federal Reserve Act. In practice, the board consisted of bankers, economists, and industrialists, each with special interests to advance.

The version of the Glass Bill that became the Federal Reserve Act also stipulated that each district would be governed by a board of nine directors, six of whom would be elected by member banks and three appointed by the Federal Reserve Board. This meant that the Federal Reserve Banks were in reality owned and controlled by member banks. They were governmental only to the extent that their policies were subject to review and approval by the Federal Reserve Board. The idea was to allow a measure of autonomy yet keep them in line with national policies,[9] and in theory this was how the Federal Reserve System was supposed to operate. In practice, however, the board would have difficulties in exercising its envisioned powers.

During the war, Federal Reserve policy was shaped in accordance with the wishes of the Treasury or sometimes those of war administrators like Herbert Hoover. And in the 1920's, it was dominated and guided by the FRBNY. The latter, according to Owen Young, was "indisputably the dominant force in the Federal Reserve System so long as Benjamin Strong was governor,"[10] which meant that something approaching the central bank envisioned in the Aldrich Plan had actually taken shape. Not everyone, however, agreed with Young's assessment of Strong. Eugene Meyer, for example, would argue that while Strong had turned the position of Governor into the dominant position at the FRBNY, he lacked the financial ability and had actually been maneuvered into

---

7. Clark, *Central Banking*, p. 29.

8. Adolph Miller, "Federal Reserve Policies: 1927-1929," *American Economic Review* 25 (September 1935): 442.

9. Under the 1913 Act the Federal Reserve Board was composed of eight members, including the Comptroller of the Currency and the Secretary of the Treasury, ex officio. The remaining six members were to be appointed by the President. The stipulation under the Federal Reserve Act was that there could be no more than one member from any one district, and that appointments should be made with due regard to fair representation of the financial, commercial, industrial, and agricultural interests, as well as the geographical divisions of the country.

10. Josephine Young Case and Everett Needham Case, *Owen D. Young and American Enterprise* (Boston: David R. Godine, 1982), p. 256.

the governorship of the FRBNY in order to keep him from becoming president of the Bankers Trust Company.[11]

When the Federal Reserve System was established, every effort had been made to limit the geographical size, and thereby the influence, of the New York Federal Reserve district. New York, after all, had dominated financial affairs in the United States since the establishment of the Second Bank of the United States. But it soon became apparent that despite the best intentions and planning, New York had again achieved dominant status. The intent in 1913 may have been to reassign the locus of power within the banking community, but that power, contrary to Representative Towner's prognostication, gradually shifted back to Wall Street. By 1925 the most powerful figures in the arrangement were the central bankers such as Benjamin Strong and the representatives of private institutions such as J.P. Morgan.

From the beginning, the board was also the scene of conflict over leadership and influence, in part perhaps because the achievement of legitimacy within the federal bureaucratic structure was slow in coming and often placed members at odds with the Secretary of the Treasury. According to Charles Hamlin, the "real underlying trouble arose from the failure to give definite status to [the] Reserve Board."[12] Its members, he said, were treated "respectfully personally," but nevertheless felt degraded and humiliated and officially looked down upon by Secretary William McAdoo. This was true, he said, of Adolph Miller, Warburg, Paul, and Frederick Delano, as well as himself. They all resented the challenge to the board's independence, and at one point Hamlin considered resigning in protest but abandoned the idea because it was unlikely to make the slightest impression upon President Wilson, who, to his thinking, had no idea of the importance of the board nor the work that it performed.[13] Like Hamlin, Adolph Miller also fought to maintain the integrity and independence of the Reserve Board, initially as an ally of Benjamin Strong against the influence of the Treasury but later as a champion of the board against domination by the FRBNY.

From the start, Strong viewed the system as operating too modestly and in ways that failed to achieve for it a secure position in the national banking structure. In October 1916 he wrote to Franklin Locke, a director of the New York Reserve Bank, that the "discouraging thing about the Federal Reserve System lies in its inability to find a normal and natural place in the banking structure of the country." It seemed instead "to be a sort of excrescence."[14] And in a subsequent letter letter to Henry Towne, a director of the bank, Strong expressed his

---

11. Mark Sullivan to Herbert Hoover, March 24, 1949, in Mark Sullivan File, PPI, HHPL.

12. Hamlin Diary, August 28, 1918. Hamlin also noted that if the members individually felt humiliated it would in the long run injure the whole system.

13. Hamlin Diary, June 27, 1920. Hamlin further argued that Wilson would view his resignation as "only another office to be filled along political lines."

14. Benjamin Strong to Franklin D. Locke, October 23, 1916, in Strong Papers, FRBNY.

fear that the New York Bank would not "establish itself with its members and with the country generally until it has met the test of a real crisis."[15]

Within less than a year Strong had his crisis. With the entry of the United States into World War I the government was confronted by a financial problem of unprecedented magnitude and complexity. It needed to raise large sums to prosecute the war. Yet federal taxes were few, federal machinery for tax administration was undeveloped, and the Federal Reserve System was scarcely two and one half years old and not at all well established. As Strong remembered the situation, the system involved "a new kind of banking that had never been practiced in the United States since 1836,"[16] and in which no one in the United States had any real experience. The war called for a "complete revolution, not only of banking methods, but of the methods of conducting the business of the Treasury of the United States." And this meant that the fledgling system was called upon "to conduct the business in the field of the Treasury of the United States, which in turn had to finance" not only America's war effort but also "a large part of that of the allied countries."[17] During the war years Federal expenditures increased from approximately $750 million per year to more than $18,500 million per year, and in the words of Lester Chandler "the Federal Reserve System became an integral part of the war financing machinery . . . both as a creator of money and as a fiscal agent,"[18] a development that he found "hardly surprising" given the circumstances.

As passed, the Federal Reserve Act had contained a provision that permitted the Secretary of the Treasury to shift fiscal functions from the Independent Treasury system and commercial banks to Federal Reserve banks. It was left to the discretion of the Secretary, however, to determine when and to what degree those functions would be shifted. And McAdoo, was slow to take action, at least slower than Strong thought proper. In April 1917 Strong began arguing that the time had come to begin the process of shifting fiscal responsibility to the Reserve banks so as to make them the real, active, and effective fiscal agents for the Government and establish their place "in the country's banking system . . . for all time."[19] In this assessment Strong was on the mark, for by the end of the war the Federal Reserve System had achieved a secure position in the banking structure of the country, although not in the way envisioned by the authors of the Federal Reserve Act.

With the addition of fiscal agency duties, the distinction between the various functions of the Federal Reserve System became blurred. Monetary policy was now subordinated to the wishes of the Treasury. As Adolph Miller later

---

15. Benjamin Strong to Henry R. Towne, November 8, 1916, in Strong Papers, FRBNY.

16. Joint Commission on Agricultural Inquiry, Hearings, 67th Cong. 1st sess., Vol. 2 (1922), p. 813.

17. Ibid.

18. Lester Chandler, *Benjamin Strong* Central Banker (Washington, D.C.: Brookings Institution, 1958), p. 101.

19. Benjamin Strong to Pierre Jay, April 22, 1917, FRBNY.

stated, from the time the United States entered the war to the beginning of 1920, Federal Reserve discount policy was shaped not "in accordance with money market conditions [or] with the idea of using reserve bank rates as an instrument of effective control of the money market," but rather "with the primary purpose of assisting the Treasury in the floatation of its great bond issues and its short term certificates."[20]

The majority of these bond issues, which had been apportioned among the Reserve Banks, were floated in the New York money market, the only real money market of significance in the United States. Consequently, the FRBNY not only acted as fiscal agent for the Treasury but for other Reserve banks as well. Similarly, the FRBNY became the Treasury's representative in foreign transactions and the agent of other reserve banks in dealing with foreign parties, an arrangement that continued after the war. If the intent of the Federal Reserve Act was to limit the influence of New York and shift the locus of power within the banking community, the necessities of war time finance undermined efforts to do this. Although Congress might attempt to decentralize the banking structure of the country, it could not relocate the nation's financial center, and the net effect was to centralize the banking business of the Treasury in the hands of the FRBNY. This Strong welcomed. But in seeking fiscal agency responsibility, it is doubtful that even he could have imagined the degree to which New York would be able to dominate the system. Centralization came not because of his efforts but because of his bank's location in the nation's financial center.

Federal Reserve policy, then, was treated "as an element of the Treasury's loan policy, the federal reserve system virtually ceasing to exercise, for the time being, its normal function of regulating credit."[21] Treasury Secretary William McAdoo and Assistant Treasury Secretary Russell Leffingwell dealt directly with the various Reserve Banks, and as Strong remembered, "all of the measures and policies that were adopted as the result of the relationship direct between the Treasury and the Federal Reserve banks."[22] In so far as government loans were concerned, these banks received their instructions directly from the Treasury, not through the Federal Reserve Board, and they formulated their policies accordingly.

In Strong's view there had been no other way. He later insisted that Federal Reserve policies during the war had to conform to the Treasury's policies. The ultimate responsibility for financing the war had rested with Congress and the Secretary of the Treasury. The Reserve System could not act as "a super-government in finance,"[23] since efforts to do so would have been "an invitation

20. Adolph Miller, "Federal Reserve Policy," *The American Economic Review* 11 (June 1921): 185.

21. Ibid.

22. Joint Comission on *Agricultural Inquiry*, Hearings, Vol. 2, p. 672.

23. Benjamin Strong to E.W. Kemmerer, December 18, 1922, in Strong Papers, FRBNY.

to Congress" to modify its powers. And this, he insisted, was "a perfectly unthinkable and most dangerous possibility."[24]

During the same period that the Treasury was using the Federal Reserve System to create and maintain an artificial money market, Herbert Hoover, as head of the United States Food Administration, was attempting to use the system's resources to establish artificial commodity markets. Like other war administrators, he tended to treat it as part of a larger apparatus intended to redirect credit expansion in accordance with war needs.[25] And as early as July 1917, he inquired as to whether member banks could rediscount loans made against warehouse receipts for potatoes. Governor William P.G. Harding replied that such rediscounts would be possible, provided the commodity had been properly stored and insured,[26] which was welcome news to Hoover. He sent an immediate response in which he praised "the fine course of action taken by the Federal Reserve Board."[27] It would, he said, open up "great possibilities in the improvement of the whole marketing conditions in the United States."[28]

Hoover then sought to extend the Reserve Board action to other commodities such as onions, peanuts, peanut cake, and cottonseed cake, which he held were adversely affected from immobility in finance. He also noted that he was assembling experts from across the country to conduct a study of warehouse conditions, which he hoped would yield suggestions that would then be forwarded to the Reserve Board. In his view, the nation needed not only to assure proper preservation but to increase warehouse capacity, and it would help if warehouse receipts for more commodities were eligible for rediscount. In addition, he intended that the study be followed up with active campaigns enlisting the help of chambers of commerce, the banking community, agricultural organizations, and local governmental units in the tasks of ensuring that commodities were properly warehoused rather than retained on farms or turned over to speculative dealers. This, he said, would take some time to develop. But when a definite program had been worked out, he hoped to secure the Federal Reserve Board's assistance in implementing it.[29]

In August 1917, Hoover also became concerned about the banking practice of charging a higher interest rate on cattle loans. This problem had been raised by Ed C. Lassiter, a Texas rancher serving in the Food Administration, who had contacted Reserve Board member Paul Warburg and found him sympathetic to

---

24. Ibid.

25. Adolph Miller, "Federal Reserve Policy," *The American Economic Review* 11 (June 1921): p. 187.

26. W.P.G. Harding to Herbert Hoover, July 28, 1917, in Board of Governors, Federal Reserve Board File, HHPL.

27. Herbert Hoover to W.P.G. Harding, August 1, 1917, in Board of Governors, Federal Reserve Board File, HHPL.

28. Ibid.

29. Ibid.

the idea of applying pressure to hold such rates down.[30] Lassiter was particularly anxious about the tendency of banks in the Dallas Reserve district and western banks in general to charge a higher interest rate (8 percent) on cattle loans than on other types of loans (7 percent). The effect of this disparity resulted in an increase in cattle prices and ultimately an increase in the purchasing price of the consumer.

Hoover then took up the matter himself. He informed the board that he was undertaking a campaign to bring about a larger amount of cattle feeding in the United States, and since the interest paid by ranchers on their cattle loans represented between 35 and 40 percent of the total production cost, a ceiling of no more than seven percent on cattle loans would be helpful. He also believed that the banks could afford to do this, since most Federal Reserve banks offered a five percent rediscount rate on six months' paper based on livestock. And in late August he did get action. Governor Harding sent a letter to the Governors of the Reserve Districts urging that they take Hoover's request into consideration. He did not wish, he said, to apply pressure, but he thought it important to "point out to . . . member banks this opportunity of rendering very effective help in the present food crisis."[31]

James Lynch, the Governor of the San Francisco Federal Reserve Bank, argued that the existing eight percent rate was not a handicap in view of the high price of cattle.[32] But other Districts recognized the need to aid the cattle industry and responded accordingly. The Dallas and Minneapolis districts both issued circulars to member banks in which they repeated Hoover's concerns and noted the shortage of livestock in Europe. The Dallas bank also argued that it was important for the United States to be prepared not only to furnish meat for itself and its allies but also for a good part of the world after the end of the war.[33] Hence, promises were made to view with favor the rediscount of paper used in the "advancement of this great industry,"[34] and member banks were urged to cooperate in making such loans. The Minnesota bank stated that "co-operation will certainly be productive of good results from every point of view."[35]

Such episodes illustrated the Federal Reserve Board's willingness to credit Hoover's views and accommodate him whenever possible, and in the sugar crisis of early 1918 he again turned to the board for assistance. At the time the difficulty in obtaining commodity loans, the curtailment of credits to German

30. Paul M. Warburg to W.P.G. Harding, August 7, 1917, in Federal Reserve Board File, FRB, Washington, D.C.

31. W.P.G. Harding to Federal Reserve District Governors, August 22, 1917, in Federal Reserve Board File, FRB, Washington, D.C.

32. James K. Lynch to W.P.G. Harding, August 28, 1917, in Federal Reserve Board File, FRB, Washington, D.C.

33. R.L. Van Zandt to all banks in the Eleventh Federal Reserve District, Circular, September 8, 1917, in Federal Reserve Board File, FRB, Washington, D.C.

34. Ibid.

35. Theodore Wold, to all banks in Federal Reserve District Number Nine, Circular No. 19, August 31, 1917, in Federal Reserve Board File, FRB, Washington, D.C.

banks in Cuba, the higher price of Cuban sugar, and the slow movement of sugar from Cuba to the world market were threatening to bring the sugar industry to a standstill. The Cuban banks, moreover, had exhausted their resources to aid the industry, and the result, as Hoover saw it, might well be a "sugar famine" in the United States, especially if the efforts of the Committee of American Sugar Refiners to arrange for credits through New York proved unsuccessful. In his appeal to the board, Hoover noted that the resources of these banks were "already taxed," that they were loath to undertake the organization of such a loan and were doing so "only out of the national interest involved," and that the matter was now one "of utmost national interest." [36] He asked the board to support the scheme, since to him, "the matter [had] become one of critical moment and [required] most expeditious handling."[37]

Hoover was also supported by Secretary of State Robert Lansing, who feared that without the credits the sugar crop would not be harvested and the result would be serious economic and political difficulties both in the United States and Cuba. It was necessary, he thought, that credits be extended in order for sugar producers to continue to pay their employees and meet other operating expenses. In the past, he stated, laborers had never had to wait for their money and "as they know that the world needs sugar, the cane must be paid for or it will not be harvested."[38] Part of the problem was that a large number of the cane cutters came from other countries specifically for the harvest. If these workers were not paid, riots would likely take place along with the burning of cane and sugar mills, and there was a probability that enemy agents, eager to embarrass Cuba, the United States and the Allied Powers, would be quick to take advantage of opportunity such as this, to foster political unrest.[39] Lansing urged Secretary of the Treasury McAdoo to take whatever measures were necessary to arrange for the credit, and McAdoo responded by having the Federal Reserve Board "cooperate in facilitating a solution."[40]

Again, too, the board responded positively. In a reply to Hoover, Governor Harding stated that it was "anxious to do anything in its power to assist in the financing of the Cuban sugar crop."[41] He had, he said, spoken with Benjamin Strong about the situation, and the latter had given him assurances that he would do all that he could to convince the New York banks of the importance of providing the needed financing.[42] The board, he continued, did not have all the de-

36. Herbert Hoover to The Federal Reserve Board, February 12, 1918, in Board of Governors, Federal Reserve Board File, HHPL.

37. Ibid.

38. Robert Lansing to William Gibbs McAdoo, February 12, 1918, in Board of Governors, Federal Reserve Board File, HHPL.

39. Ibid.

40. William Gibbs McAdoo to W.P.G. Harding, February 13, 1918, in Board of Governors, Federal Reserve Board File, HHPL.

41. W.P.G. Harding to Herbert Hoover, February 13, 1918, in Board of Governors, Federal Reserve Board File, HHPL.

42. Ibid.

tails of the proposed financial scheme. But he understood that drafts, secured by warehouse receipts or shipping documents, would be drawn either directly on banks or through some corporation controlled by the Food Administration. And he made it clear, both to Hoover and in correspondence with Strong, that due to the emergency of the case and "the vital public interest involved," the board was prepared "to go to the limit of its authority" to modify existing regulations in order to make warehouse receipts or shipping documents for the sugar eligible for rediscount at Federal Reserve banks.[43]

Hoover, then, found the wartime Federal Reserve Board to be friendly and cooperative. Strong, on the other hand, yearned for the time when the system would be "released from this government borrowing bondage and able to deal with money rates on sound lines."[44] And in the immediate postwar period, as the Treasury sought continued domination of the system, he found himself at odds with Secretary Carter Glass, one of the authors of the Federal Reserve Act. In Strong's view the system must be kept free from politics for "political control would be its death blow."[45]

The major issue of contention in the immediate postwar period was Treasury control of the rediscount rate. During the war the sale of bonds had been encouraged by having Reserve Banks establish lower or "preferential" discount rates on loans collateralled by Treasury obligations and by fixing returns so as to insure that banks accepting such collateral made a profit.[46] This was a set of arrangements that meant very little discounting of commercial paper[47] and a significant expansion of bank credit that the Federal Reserve System was unable to check because it could not place a limit on a member bank's total lending power and at the same time ensure "an almost unlimited power to lend to the Treasury or those borrowing to buy Treasury obligations."[48] Banks ended up holding large quantities of government securities against which they could borrow from Federal Reserve banks, though the proceeds could be lent for anything. After the war, the Treasury insisted that the system be continued so as to facilitate the postwar Victory Loan. But by 1919 Strong and Miller were arguing

43. W.P.G. Harding to Benjamin Strong, February 13, 1918, in Board of Governors, Federal Reserve Board File, HHPL; W.P.G. Harding to Herbert Hoover, February 13, 1918, in Board of Governors Federal Reserve Board File, HHPL.

44. Benjamin Strong to R.H. Treman, September 12, 1919, in Strong Papers, FRBNY.

45. Benjamin Strong to James Logan, September 30, 1922, in Strong Papers, FRBNY. This struggle was to burden the System for three more decades. During World War II the Federal Reserve System found itself subordinated to the Treasury once again, and in the aftermath of that war a similar power struggle ensued. This time, though, the Federal Reserve Board fought for, and by 1950, gained its independence. See A. Jerome Clifford, *The Independence of the Federal Reserve System* (Philadelphia: University of Pennsylvania Press, 1965), ch. 8.

46. Chandler, *Benjamin Strong*, p. 117.

47. Ibid., p. 118.

48. Ibid.

against maintaining the artificially low rates. In their view, the rediscount rate had to be raised in order to prevent inflation and speculation.

Miller's attitude had been foreshadowed by his wartime advocacy of using the rediscount rate to help curtail expansion in non-essential industries,[49] a position that Hamlin and others on the board had opposed.[50]

Strong, however, had supported the wartime Treasury policy and was relatively slow to embrace Miller's position. The real need, he told Montagu Norman in February 1919, was for the Reserve Banks "to liquidate about a billion [dollars] of their advances."[51] And writing to Miller at the same time, he suggested that a "natural process of liquidation" starting "after the next loan" might take care of the matter.[52] It was hard to say, he continued, whether the process ought to begin right away or be delayed a while. And it might be sounder finance if the Government issued bonds at a higher interest rate, which in turn would provide the Reserve Banks the opportunity to increase the rediscount rate on all types of paper except international bills.[53] In addition, he saw the issue as being complicated by the international situation. Liquidation had to come if there was to be "a free gold movement throughout the world."[54] But a sharp increase in bank rates could have serious effects world-wide, and he was not certain that the United States could afford a free gold movement until the economic terms of the peace treaty were known.

Miller admitted that the process would be an uncomfortable one for nearly everyone and, "for some, a very costly and ruinous one."[55] He also suspected that the country might be in for some serious financial and political troubles because of the currency and credit disorders, especially since the expansion that had taken place in 1918 and would undoubtedly continue in 1919 was "pretty nearly all pure inflation." But liquidation was essential. Of that, he told Strong, "there [could] be no question."[56]

---

49. Charles S. Hamlin to W.P.G. Harding, June 28, 1918, in Hamlin File, Adolph Miller Papers, Library of Congress, Washington, D.C.

50. Ibid. Hamlin wanted to ration credit in the same way food was rationed. Hamlin thought it best to move cautiously and conservatively in raising interest rates. Moreover, he thought it best to rely on the judgment of the New York and Chicago Reserve Banks when considering rate increases. Hamlin held that they were in the field and that he would "hesitate to disregard their judgement, unless it were shown beyond a reasonable doubt that their judgement [was] in error."

51. Benjamin Strong to Montagu Norman, February 5, 1919, in Strong Papers, FRBNY.

52. Benjamin Strong to Adolph Miller, February 5, 1919, in Strong Papers, FRBNY.

53. Ibid.

54. Ibid.

55. Adolph Miller to Benjamin Strong, February 26, 1919, in Strong Papers, FRBNY.

56. Ibid.

There was, however, to be no rate increase in early 1919. At the January 17 meeting of the Federal Reserve Board, Miller, now supported by Hamlin, wanted to raise the rate immediately from 4 percent to 4 1/2 percent. Secretary Glass, however, sent word that he was opposed. A raise in the rate, he insisted, "would necessitate immediate raising of rates on U.S. Treasury certificates and the rate on the next bond issue,"[57] and already, he noted, the Treasury was experiencing a good deal of difficulty placing 15 day notes at the 4 percent rate and commercial paper secured by Government collateral. Governor Harding and Vice-Governor Albert Strauss agreed with this argument, and Hamlin then changed his position so as to oppose a rate increase until at least after the Victory Loan was floated. The board went along with the view of the Treasury that issuing Victory notes at a higher rate would result in demands to refund Liberty bonds in order to prevent their depreciation.[58]

Keeping rates low was also seen by some as a way to "help readjust business to a peace time basis and . . . aid in absorbing the men discharged from the army and the navy."[59] At the same time, Miller's concerns appeared to be overstated. Some private bankers predicted that interest rates would remain high, that liquidation would follow, and that prices would decline with the cancellation of war contracts. And in early 1919, as production declined, unemployment rose, the price index fell, and speculation on the New York Stock exchange declined, it seemed that the economy was indeed entering a recession and that the natural process of liquidation anticipated by some had begun. As Benjamin Beckhart stated, "the trend was downwards, and businessmen felt sure that it would continue so for some time."[60]

This, though, did not prove to be the case. As Government borrowing was reduced, more purchasing power and credit became available to the private sector, much of which was employed in land, securities, and commodities speculation. In Beckhart's words, the "speculative spirit which had been held in abeyance during the war was released."[61] And by this time, the selective controls and margin requirements that had been imposed in October 1918 had been lifted. They had produced strong complaints from stock brokers and the New York Stock Exchange as represented by its president H.G. Noble.[62] They were responsible, he said, for leaving the market thin and vulnerable and were no longer needed as they had been during the war. Strong would later testify that this had been a mistake and that he would have preferred to retain the controls

---

57. Hamlin Diary, January 17, 1919.

58. Ibid. The four Liberty bonds were issued at 3 1/2, 4, 4 1/4, and 4 1/4 per cent respectively; the Victory notes were issued at two rates, 4 3/4 and 3 3/4 per cent, the latter were exempt from taxes.

59. Benjamin Beckhart, *The Discount Policy of the Federal Reserve System* (New York: Henry Holt, 1924), p. 320.

60. Ibid. p. 315.

61. Ibid. p. 335.

62. H.G. Noble to Benjamin Strong, January 21, 1919, in Strong Papers, FRBNY.

for some time to come. But the ending of other wartime controls had signaled a return to "business as usual."[63]

Driven by the "speculative spirit," the economy during the second quarter of 1919 experienced a rise in prices, an inflation of money and credit, and an increase in speculative loans. By June there had been a number of "million share days," and the Federal Reserve Board was now becoming concerned about the scope of this speculative activity. In a letter to Reserve Banks, Governor Harding pointed out that the situation was in need of careful scrutiny since there was "undoubtedly an element of danger to the financial position of the country." The board, however, was not willing to support a rate increase to correct the situation because this would interfere with government financing. It insisted instead that the Reserve Banks apply direct action and "moral suasion" to bring the situation under control.[64]

By September there was a growing feeling in financial circles that the discount rate should be advanced. Strong now favored such action, but, as he noted to Montagu Norman, a decision on the matter would most likely not be made until immediately following the conference of governors on November 12.[65] In the meantime, he sought to convince the directors of the FRBNY of the need for an increase in the rate. Speculation, he noted, had become widespread, wages and prices were surging upward, and bank credit had continued to expand. The war had required massive credit expansion so as to accommodate the subscribers to governmental loans.[66] But now that government borrowing had been reduced, it was time to impose a check "upon the employment facilities of the Reserve Banks by increases in discount rates."[67]

The Treasury was still opposed, fearing the effects on "important refunding operations" and a further decline in the market price of Liberty bonds. But, the directors of the New York Bank supported Strong's position and on November 3 they voted to increase the discount rate on commercial paper to 4 3/4 percent. The Federal Reserve Board then gave its approval, even though Secretary Glass was still not convinced that it was judicious to raise the rate at this time.

The action did have an impact on the stock market. Prices there fell and the amount of credit employed in stock speculation began to show a downward trend. Speculators also reacted with anger and denunciation, and a number of journalists demanded that the Federal Reserve System be investigated. Inflation, however, was not confined to the stock market; nor was speculation there the fundamental problem. It continued in the commodities market, and bank credit continued to expand. Strong was convinced that an additional rate increase was needed, but on this he was opposed by Secretary Glass and Assistant Secretary Leffingwell, who insisted that a raise in the rate before January 15 would inter-

---

63. Joint Commission on *Agricultural Inquiry*, Hearings, vol. 2, pp. 665-80.

64. Federal Reserve Bulletin, June 1, 1919, p. 524.

65. Benjamin Strong to Montagu Norman, October 20, 1919, in Strong Papers, FRBNY.

66. Benjamin Strong, Memorandum for the Record, November 3, 1919, FRBNY.

67. Ibid.

fere with the marketing of a new Treasury issue after the first of the year. In Glass's view, moreover, credit expansion would not lead to inflation provided it was used to produce and distribute goods. And his view proved decisive. Strong tried to convince the other Governors to push for an immediate rate increase, but most were reluctant to oppose Glass and voted against an increase.[68]

As Glass saw it, the Federal Reserve Banks should not rely too heavily on the discount rate in order to prevent abuses of their facilities. Instead, they should continue to employ direct action and "exercise a firm discrimination in making loans to prevent abuse of the facilities of the Federal Reserve System in support of the reckless speculation in stocks, land, cotton, clothing, foodstuffs and commodities generally."[69] In the New York Reserve District bankers had been "educated" to refrain from relying on Federal Reserve Banks "very extensively" in order to make a profit on the stock exchange rate, and those who gave evidence of doing so were admonished for this practice. Benjamin Strong, however, was not satisfied with such an approach, and in a letter to Montagu Norman argued that in the long run nothing was as effective as imposing a rate that would be unprofitable, and that if this "turn of the screw was not enough" then one would just have to "give it another."[70] The FRBNY, Strong insisted, was determined to put a halt to the mad march of speculation and expansion whether it took place in stocks, commodities, real estate, or whatever. It had to be particularly mindful about speculation since the stock market was located in his district, and "a large part of the stock speculation . . . had been financed with funds borrowed . . . from the Reserve Banks with government securities as collateral."[71]

As noted previously, the Federal Reserve System was never intended to underwrite speculation, whether, on Wall Street, the commodities market, or in real estate.[72] But in practice it had no way to insure that member banks loaned only for productive purposes. A member bank, when it needed money, could easily discount government, commercial, or agriculture related paper when in fact its resources had been depleted by speculative loans. And in practice, the use of direct action, warnings, and moral suasion was not effective. Governor Roy Young of the Minneapolis Reserve Bank noted that speculative loans could be controlled to some extent, but that in the final analysis there was no control. This was because borrowing institutions could "camouflage their reply more or less,"[73] and on this point Richard Van Zandt, Governor of the Dallas Reserve Bank, agreed. His bank, he said, had been employing direct action for a year and

68. Chandler, Benjamin Strong, p. 152.

69. Carter Glass to W.P.G. Harding, November 5, 1919, in Carter Glass Papers, University of Virginia, Charlottsville, VA.

70. Benjamin Strong to Montagu Norman, November 6, 1919, in Strong Papers, FRBNY.

71. Beckhart, *Discount Policy of the Federal Reserve System*, p. 32.

72. Public Act No. 43, 63rd Cong.

73. Roy Young statement to the Governors Conference, November 20, 1919, FRBNY.

a half, admonishing some banks and going so far as to withhold credit if they could not "explain satisfactory use of the funds which they [wanted] to borrow." But this was "not what [one] would call effective in any way."[74]

Strong argued that it was time for the Reserve System to be viewed as a system, rather than a lot of isolated banks. Moreover, he thought it important to arrive at a policy that would prevent what he was "certain would result from the excessive application of this direct action . . . which is simply to drive the infection from one place to another."[75] According to Strong, a portion of the money and credit employed in the New York stock market came from banks in other states, such as Georgia, Florida, Louisiana, Mississippi, North and South Carolina, and Texas, that did not borrow from the Reserve Bank. And in view of these circumstances, it was beyond him what the New York bank could do to control the situation.[76]

He and other FRBNY officials, however, agreed that inflation and speculative tendencies could not be brought under control without a raise in the discount rate. By this time the Boston Reserve Bank had also reached the same conclusion, and on November 24 both banks voted to seek the Reserve Board's permission to advance their rates. Assistant Treasury Secretary Leffingwell was furious and went before the board to argue against the rate hike. It would, he said, make it impossible for the Treasury to market its upcoming issue, and he reminded the board that the Treasury had only agreed to the November 3 increase because Governor Strong had said it was necessary to ensure that stock exchange accounts were adequately covered, that clearing house banks could function properly, and that buying rates on bills were properly adjusted.[77] Leffingwell was convinced that the new request resulted from collusion between Strong and Norman, and that the latter had successfully forced the British Treasury to raise its rates. In his view it was "exceedingly unfortunate . . . that this agitation of rates" was coming at a time when the Treasury had to "raise $500 million every two weeks to keep from defaulting."[78] And in the end, Leffingwell's views prevailed. The board promptly rejected both requests to permit a rate increase.

In Strong's mind neither the Federal Reserve Board nor the Treasury Department really understood the magnitude of the problem. They talked about checking inflationary forces, but their emphasis remained primarily on speculative and stock market loans. The Treasury seemed to have an *ideé fixe* about speculation, even to the point of suggesting that the Money Committee of 1918 be reconstituted to help control the situation, and that the FRBNY undertake, "either directly or indirectly through the New York Clearing House Association,

74. Richard Van Zandt statement to the Governors Conference, November 20, 1919, FRBNY.

75. Benjamin Strong statement to the Governors Conference, November 20, 1919, FRBNY.

76. Ibid.

77. Chandler, *Benjamin Strong*, p. 161.

78. Ibid.

to induce banks in the city to require larger margins upon Stock Exchange loans."[79] Such action, Strong thought, could never reach the real offender, the margin speculator, and in the end it would drive the "Stock Exchange speculative business more largely into the hands of houses of larger capital."[80]

In Strong's view only a small portion of the credit expansion that was taking place could be attributed to Stock Exchange transactions. The bulk of the increase was due to loans growing out of agricultural, industrial, and commercial transactions, and this would continue unless a general control over those business activities that were overextended was effected through changes in the discount rate. In addition, Strong now wanted to do away with preferential rates because many of the loans collateralled by Treasury obligations were being employed in the speculative markets.

Consequently, Strong confronted Secretary Glass about the board's refusal to allow the requested rate increase. He argued heatedly, by Glass' account, that the FRBNY had the legal right to put the rate into effect, regardless of how the board felt in the matter. Glass disagreed, arguing again that rate increases would penalize commerce and that the Reserve Banks should use direct action and warnings to induce the curtailment of loans for speculative purposes. Strong then became indignant, "aggressively refused," and "avowed his purpose to proceed on his way,"[81] whereupon Glass, equally heated, threatened to have President Wilson remove him from his position. It was well within the power of the board, Glass declared, to impose rates on the banks, regardless of the wishes of any bank.

As a result of the scene in Glass's office, the Secretary decided to seek a legal ruling on the board's powers. He requested an opinion from Attorney General Mitchell Palmer, and in a decision rendered on December 9, the latter affirmed the jurisdiction of the board. This was a decision, however, that would come back to haunt Glass in the autumn of 1927 when he questioned the authority of the Federal Reserve Board to order the Chicago Reserve Bank to lower its rate.

From the Treasury's standpoint, the decision turned out to be unneeded. The day after it was rendered, Assistant Secretary Leffingwell informed the board that conditions had improved a great deal and that it was now free to take whatever action it considered appropriate. The board then notified the Reserve Banks that it would now consider any requests for rate advances and the elimination of preferential rates. The FRBNY was the first to take action and raised is rediscount rate on war paper secured by Treasury notes and certificates of indebtedness from 4 1/4 percent to 4 1/2 percent. The rate was raised again on December 30 to 4 3/4 when the FRBNY abolished preferential rates. The latter action, how-

---

79. Benjamin Strong to W.P.G. Harding, November 28, 1919, in Strong Papers, FRBNY.

80. Ibid.

81. Carter Glass to Charles Hamlin, September 12, 1927, in Charles Hamlin Papers, Library of Congress, Manuscript Division, Washington, D.C.

ever, proved premature. On January 23, 1920, the differential was reestablished at the insistence of Leffingwell and remained in effect until June 1921.

In the meantime, Strong had been advised by his doctor to take an extended vacation and in January 1920 began a one-year leave of absence. Prior to his departure, however, he again sought to justify his actions to Glass. Economic conditions since 1914, he argued, had been distorted by the war and war finance, which had precluded any opportunity to learn from experience under normal conditions how the Reserve Bank and the New York Money Market could be made to function together.[82] He regretted, he said, the extent to which wartime exigencies had required his personal domination of the New York situation, and he wondered whether he or his successor might not some day bring discredit on the system because of poor judgment. But at the same time, he was concerned that the exercise of control, such as it had been, "by a governmental body in Washington" could at some point "lead to a political control of the system with the ever present possibility of misuse."[83]

Soon after Strong's departure the FRBNY voted to raise its rate from 4 3/4 percent to 5 1/2 percent. The Treasury, however, objected, insisting that the 4 3/4 percent rate on paper backed by Treasury certificates should be maintained but that the rate on commercial paper ought to be advanced to 6 percent. And again, the Treasury had its way. Strong was in Hot Springs, Arizona at the time, and some, such as Chandler, have argued that had he been in New York he would have put up a fight to stay with the moderate rate increase and to keep rates uniform.[84] Yet it seems likely that his protestations would have mattered little and that the Treasury, armed with Attorney General Palmer's, opinion, would have prevailed anyway.

The outcome, Strong later wrote to Norman, was not at all what he would have recommended, "nor indeed, confidentially, did [it] meet the advice of my associates in the Bank." It amounted to a "compromise between differing views of our own with differing views in the Federal Reserve Board and finally, radically different views held by the officers of the Treasury."[85] It seemed to him that Treasury officials had become advocates of dear money. But he did believe that a moderate rate increase was justified as a way of halting the consumption of resources in "extravagant living and wasteful expenditure" and preserving America's power to render aid to Europe.[86] He also doubted that the high rates now being quoted for stock market loans were a direct result of Reserve Board action. Banks had already been moving to curtail "the advances they were making for the support of a dangerous speculation in industrial stocks, particularly

---

82. Benjamin Strong to Carter Glass, January 14, 1920, in Strong Papers, FRBNY.

83. Ibid.

84. Chandler, *Benjamin Strong*, p. 187.

85. Benjamin Strong to Montagu Norman, February 6, 1920, in Strong Papers, FRBNY.

86. Ibid.

oils and automobiles."[87] What they did not seem to realize was that "loaning money to an industrial concern which is making profits on contracts to deliver goods a year or hence longer" was "dangerous" and could lead to a day of reckoning when unfilled orders could be represented by unliquidated inventories.[88]

The day of reckoning arrived sooner than Strong had anticipated. The first warning signs of the impending crisis came with the collapse of the silk market in Japan in March 1920, a month after Strong's letter to Norman. As a result Japanese exchanges were closed for almost two months, an action that created uncertainty in international investments and was particularly worrisome because of the possibility that the Japanese might withdraw substantial amounts of gold from the United States. Investors feared a contraction of credit and began to sell securities in large amounts, the result being that prices tumbled on the New York Exchange. In May this was followed by a world wide decline in wholesale prices and by November the U.S. economy had plunged into a depression. Interest rates, though, remained high. In June the FRBNY had raised its rate on commercial and agricultural rediscounts to 7 per cent, and there it remained until May of the following year when it was reduced to 6 1/2 percent. The fact that it was not reduced sooner would later be one of the many criticisms aimed at the system for its handling of the crisis.

By mid-January 1921, Strong was back at the New York Bank and was among those firmly opposed to any early reduction in the rediscount rate. On February 5 the FRBNY, following Strong's recommendation, raised the rate on paper secured by Treasury notes and 90-day certificates of indebtedness, putting them on an equal basis with other Government securities. And it was apparently proud of its role during the crisis. On February 21, Strong wrote to Norman that New York had experienced the greatest liquidation of "any single department," that stock market loans were now around two-thirds of what they had been, and that a good portion of these had been transferred to interior banks. He was also convinced, he said, that the existence and successful operation of the Federal Reserve System could be credited with stabilizing effects on the minds of bankers and businessmen and with having made it possible for the United States to "escape commercial and bank failures during this unprecedented liquidation." The worst of the shock, he thought, was over, as the "so called classical 'panic' period [had] passed."[89]

In an article published in June 1921, Adolph Miller agreed with Strong about the steadying and moderating influence of the Federal Reserve System. But at the same time, he asked whether the policy pursued by the system since

---

87. Ibid.

88. Ibid.

89. Benjamin Strong to Montagu Norman, February 21, 1921, in Strong Papers, FRBNY. In March he reiterated his confidence in the system when he noted that "If there had been no Federal Reserve System in this country, bankers would now be insisting that borrowers pay their loans, and, were this to force sacrifice sales of inventories at present quoted prices, we would have a long list of insolvencies, closing mills, unemployment etc." Benjamin Strong to Montagu Norman, March 21, 1921, in Strong Papers, FRBNY.

1918 might not have contributed to the severity of the crisis. He wondered, in particular, about the wisdom of maintaining an artificial money rate "carried to the point that it was by the differential rate upon so-called war loan paper," and in the light of subsequent developments he questioned whether this "was not a costly device to the country."[90]   On this issue, moreover, Professor Benjamin Beckhart, of Columbia University, would later agree with Miller. Had the Victory notes and Treasury certificates of indebtedness been floated at market rates, Beckhart argued, the Reserve Banks would not have had to continue the process of "manufacturing" credit in ways that contributed to the speculative inflation of the postwar period.[91]

Miller also argued that it would have been of far greater advantage to the country if the Federal Reserve System had exercised restraint during 1919. It should have acted in September of that year, thus checking the runaway and speculative markets that developed during the second half of the year. By doing so, he thought, it could "have rendered an inestimable service to the country" and prevented much of the economic hardship experienced in 1920 and 1921.[92] And on this, too, Beckhart agreed with Miller. The adoption of a sound monetary policy in 1919, he argued, would have prevented the "saturnalia of speculation" at home and perhaps have made the Allies more willing to initiate similar measures. The Government, to be sure, might have been forced to refund the Liberty bonds. But in Beckhart's estimation, "the avoidance of the era of inflation would have fully compensated for the increased interest charges."[93]

In 1922 a similar assessment was also made by the Joint Commission of Agricultural Inquiry, created at the insistence of the new farm bloc to investigate the causes of the depression.[94]   The Commission concluded that much of the speculation and inflation might have been retarded or even prevented if the Federal Reserve banks had increased their rates in the spring of 1919, and that if this had been the case the subsequent liquidation would have been less precipitous, the decline in prices less abrupt, and the hardships on the nation diminished.[95] Some members of the Commission, however, including Representative Ogden Mills of New York, refused to accept those portions of the majority report that attributed the price decline of late 1920 to the increase in Federal Reserve inter-

90. Adolph Miller, "Federal Reserve Policy," *The American Economic Review* 11 (June 1921): 186.

91. Beckhart, *The Discount Policy of the Federal Reserve System*, p. 320.

92. Adolph Miller, "Federal Reserve Policy," *The American Economic Review* 11 (June 1921): 186.

93. Beckhart, *The Discount Policy of the Federal Reserve System*, p. 320.

94. About the establishment of the farm bloc, the *New York Times* said that "this changed political condition of a powerful legislative group for the first time in an American Congress—has destroyed old time leadership. At present the Republican leaders in the Senate cannot control. They are controlled by the group which is insisting upon legislation intended to benefit the farmer." *New York Times*, October 3, 1921, p. 8.

95. U.S. Congress, *Report of the Joint Commission of Agricultural Inquiry*, 67th Cong. 1st Sess. (Washington: Government Printing Office, 1922), pp. 44-45.

est rates. Mills argued that such a finding would lead to the conclusion that the "Federal Reserve Board and Federal Reserve Banks constitute an agency by means of which prices may be raised or lowered." And in his view, this opinion was "so contrary to economic facts and to the purpose of the Federal Reserve System, that it should not be permitted to pass unchallenged."[96]

The farm bloc, though, was convinced that Federal Reserve policy had much to do with the economic downturn and the drastic worsening of the farmer's economic position. The banking machinery of the country, it believed, was not adequately adapted to the farmer's needs and did not provide adequate credit facilities for farmers and ranchers whose turnover was only once a year. The problem, as Senator Arthur Capper viewed it, was that banks were not pre-pared to carry credit for any extended period of time,[97] and on this Capper had the support of Herbert Hoover, who was now Secretary of Commerce. Hoover believed that the Federal Reserve System should not be called upon to carry agricultural paper for more than six months because it constituted a "mobiliza-tion of the demand deposits of the country." To do this would jeopardize the entire commercial banking structure upon which the farmer was dependent.[98] But there should be some way of providing agricultural loans ranging from six months to three years, which could not be provided by either the Federal Re-serve System or the Federal Farm Loan Board.

There were also some members of the farm bloc who maintained that the system had deliberately discriminated against the farmer and that farming was not even recognized as a business in the Federal Reserve Act. This was the view, for example, of Senator Smith Brookhart of Iowa.[99] Somewhat oddly, too, the

96. Ibid. p. 159.

97. Arthur Capper to Herbert Hoover, July 9, 1921, in Farm Credits File, Commerce Papers (hereafter referred to as CP), HHPL. Capper proposed to ameliorate the situation by amending the Farm Loan Act to create a new department in each of the twelve Farm Loan Banks which would be capable of making loans for properly warehoused agricul-tural staples for a period ranging from six months up to one year and on breeding cattle for a period of up to two years. He envisioned that the capital for this would come from a $200 million fund to be established by Congress. The money for this fund, he thought, could be obtained by amending Section 7 of the Federal Reserve Act "to authorize the Treasury to pay into the Farm Loan Bank monies received from time to time from the Federal Reserve Banks on account of their franchise taxes until" the total amount of $200 million was reached.

98. Herbert Hoover to Arthur Capper, July 19, 1921, in Farm Credits File, CP, HHPL. Hoover wrote to Senator Capper that "six months is too short to borrow from planting to some months after harvest unless his produce is to be forced into the markets just after harvest instead of over the crop year. This matter has added importance at the present time because of the recent heavy losses of the farmers, because of the large carry overs, because the poverty of foreign buyers tends to delay their buying until their own crops are exhausted, and thus necessitates our farmers holding on longer unless he would depreciate his price."

99. Beckhart, *The Discount Policy of the Federal Reserve System*, p. 475.

Manufacturers Record, a financial weekly published in Baltimore, also took up the cause of rural America. Richard Edmonds, the editor of the *Record,* sent a scathing letter to Secretary Mellon in which he argued that:

> thousands of bankers, especially the small country bankers, chartered by the states, and upon whose work the prosperity of the smaller communities must depend, live in constant terror of the activities of the Federal Reserve Board in trying to compel them, by force, under the threat of destruction, to yield to its demands. Bolshevism is not more contrary to the property rights of the people than this method of the Federal Reserve Board.[100]

Strong believed that the pressure for easier credit conditions "came from no other class than those engaged in agriculture."[101] But he thought it wise "to meet, in part at least, the demand for lower rates," since "bullheaded resistance in this instance is always liable to invite political retaliation."[102] He must have been pleased, too, when the Commission of Agricultural Inquiry concluded that the charges of conspiracy and deliberate discrimination against rural banks were not warranted by the evidence. On the contrary, it said, the expansion of bank loans in rural districts through June 20 was relatively greater than in industrial sections.[103]

Others also spoke up in support of the Federal Reserve System. Senator George McLean, Chairman of the Senate Banking Committee, stated that there were two branches of government "which, above all others, should never be made the subject of politics–the Supreme Court and the Federal Reserve Board."[104] Herbert Hoover, as well, expressed his confidence in the system when he stated that thanks to it, this was "the first time in our history that we have passed . . . a commodity crisis without a panic."[105] If it had not been for the "federal reserve system," he thought, which had been "established with great foresight some years ago," a "terrible financial panic would have resulted."[106]

---

100. Richard Edmonds to Andrew Mellon, June 14, 1921, in Manufacturers Record File, CP, HHPL.

101. Benjamin Strong to Montagu Norman, May 5, 1921, in Strong Papers, FRBNY. A month later Strong noted to Norman that "the whole Federal Reserve System is being blamed for bringing on the deflation, so called, and especially some of our colleagues in the West, where the farmers, cattle men, and wool growers have been rather hard hit." Benjamin Strong to Montagu Norman, June 8, 1921, in Strong Papers, FRBNY.

102. Ibid.

103. U.S. Congress, Report of the *Joint Commission of Agricultural Inquiry*, 67th Cong. 1st Sess., (Washington: Government Printing Office, 1922), p. 117.

104. *New York Times* December 20, 1921, p. 24.

105. Address before the American Manufacturers Export Association at the Waldorf Astoria in New York, October 6, 1921. In Federal Reserve File, CP, HHPL.

106. Address before the Ohio Manufacturers Association, Hotel Ohio, Youngstown, Ohio, June 7, 1922, in Federal Reserve File, CP, HHPL.

Instead the country passed the danger point and hosts of bankruptcies and bank failures were prevented.

By 1922 the system had weathered its first storm and had prevented a financial panic like the one in 1907. But it had yet to operate in normal times. Shortly after its creation, it had been called upon to help finance both the American and Allied war efforts and had done so in ways that contributed to the speculative boom and bust after the war. The depression made it a villain in the rural areas of the country, and to a large extent critics were correct in pointing out that the original aims of the Federal Reserve Act were being thwarted by developments stemming from the unexpected demands put upon the new system. The New York financial community became more rather than less powerful, and political considerations had quickly encroached upon and undercut the idea of monetary control by a disinterested public body. The system's early years had been punctuated by factional differences over the powers it should have, over who should wield them, and over its capabilities for good or evil. And two of the characters involved, Benjamin Strong and Herbert Hoover, would become even more important in the factionalism that was yet to come.

Chapter 2

The Clash of Factions, 1921-1924

The Continent of Europe has made remarkable progress in recuperation from the war in every direction except one. That is the continued fiscal degeneration of practically all of the former combatant states and this degeneration now threatens not only their entire future but affects world commerce as a whole.

Herbert Hoover[1]

American economic activity began to show a marked degree of improvement during the second half of 1921. Yet bankers, economists, and government officials remained concerned about European difficulties and their potential impact on continued recovery. In Herbert Hoover's eyes the United States could not isolate itself and hope to maintain economic stability at home. Such problems as militated against European recovery would "react upon us."[2]

This chapter will examine Federal Reserve policy in the context of American efforts to bring about European economic stabilization. It will focus initially on efforts to gain a role in foreign loan supervision, on Strong's rejection of the scheme as "paternalistic," and on how this affected the relationship between the two men. It will then look at the participation of the United States in settling the reparations question and especially at efforts by the FRBNY to participate in the

---

1. Herbert Hoover to Warren G. Harding, January 4, 1922, in President Harding File, CP, HHPL.

2. Herbert Hoover, Address before the U.S. Chamber of Commerce, Atlantic City, April 28, 1920.

European discussions surrounding the Dawes Plan. And finally, it will note how the factionalism involved in these developments remained intertwined with persisting farm bloc criticism of Federal Reserve policies and accompanying divisions within the Republican Party.

Even as American bankers and officials sought to sustain domestic economic growth, in the years from 1921-1924, they also sought, in the words of Melvyn Leffler, "to put together a matrix of economic policies and decision making instruments that would prove capable of balancing the needs of the domestic economy with the requirements of European stabilization."[3]   They wished, in particular, to find solutions to the questions raised by war debts and reparations, since these were believed to be obstacles to the resumption of normal commercial relations.[4] And leading bankers and businessmen realized that the two were interrelated. As Owen Young put it, "their defacto relationship was . . . almost as visible on Main Street as on Wall [Street]. Only as Germany paid reparations could the United States look with any real confidence to Allied repayment of our ten billion dollars in loans."[5] Some also urged caution and prudence in any negotiations on the matter. As John Foster Dulles saw it, debt repayment was in order, but Americans should carefully choose the "mode and the moment, lest we add venom and not balm to the gaping wound that is draining the vitality of modern civilization."[6]

The situation was also complicated by the refusal of the United States to ratify the Treaty of Versailles. As Hoover had predicted in early 1921, this refusal had put the United States in the awkward position of negotiating with a Germany that had given "first mortgage" to the Allies,[7] and the result was ill will that was having a further adverse effect on an already demoralized trade. "Hate," Hoover thought, was "an even worse blockade than tariffs or discriminating combinations."[8] Nor were matters helped by European resentment over the effects of the war in leaving Europe heavily indebted to the United States. The latter had now replaced Britain as the world's leading financial power, but

---

3. Melvin Leffler, *The Elusive Quest, America's Pursuit of European Stability and French Security, 1919-1933* (Chapel Hill: University of North Carolina Press, 1979), p. 43.

4. See for instance correspondence between Benjamin Strong and Herbert Hoover 1921 to 1922 in Foreign Loans File, CP, HHPL.

5. Josphine Young Case and Everett Needham Case, *Owen Young D. and American Enterprise* (Boston: David R. Godine, 1982), p. 274. It should be noted that Great Britain and France were the principal debtors and expected German reparations to cover their "bill" in the United States. Great Britain, though, expressed the willingness to renounce reparations claims if the United States would cancel her debt in return.

6. John Foster Dulles, address delivered at the 33rd luncheon discussion on foreign affairs under the auspices of the League of Free Nations Association, Hotel Commodore, New York City, March 12, 1921.

7. Herbert Hoover to Charles Evans Hughes, April 6, 1921, in State Department, Hughes File, CP, HHPL.

8. Ibid.

European economies were in a shambles and one could argue that the living standard in many countries had been lowered for a whole generation.

In 1921 it seemed clear to both Herbert Hoover and Secretary of the Treasury Andrew Mellon that European recovery was dependent upon American assistance. And at their urging,   President Harding invited a small group of bankers to a private conference at the White House, the purpose being to discuss ways in which American bankers might help to ease the European situation.

Included in the group was Benjamin Strong, who was anxious to present the views being developed by the FRBNY. These recognized that there were two major problems, the need to stimulate business at home, and the need for a revival of exports. But the first, Strong said, should be sought by methods other than a reduction in Federal Reserve interest rates. These could produce another "period of expansion and inflation with all the accompanying evils of speculation and extravagance."[9]   Instead, the pressure to liquidate should be stopped and credit made available on liberal terms to lending institutions that needed it. In this view, Strong was also supported by former Reserve Board member Paul Warburg, who suggested that Federal Reserve banks form a pool to provide relief to country banks wishing to discount agricultural paper.[10]

As for exports, there was sentiment among some of the conferees for tying any loans to foreign countries to the purchase of goods in the United States. In addition, Hoover argued that such loans ought to be scrutinized to ensure that they would be employed for reproductive purposes and not squandered on military expenditures and unbalanced budgets or used to bolster inflated currencies. With the notion of "constructive" loans Warburg agreed, but he thought that a hard and fast rule to force the borrowing country to apply loan proceeds in this country would have severe repercussions. So did F.I. Kent, Vice-President of the Bankers Trust Company in New York. Kent pointed out that his bank had been carrying on negotiations with the City of Marseilles for a possible loan of $20,000,000, which would be used to make much needed port improvements but would not necessarily be spent in the United States. This was an example of a constructive loan that ought not to be discouraged by requiring "the disposal of the funds in any particular manner."[11]

In Strong's view, the gentlemen who advocated Government supervision of foreign loans did not have a full realization of where the difficulties with foreign trade lay or of the fact that they were not likely to yield to artificial restrictions or stimulations. The export trade, he argued, depended on the capacity of American manufacturers to compete with producing countries, which meant that the United States must be able to produce as cheaply if not cheaper than they did. It must do nothing to hinder the orderly readjustment of production costs, especially those related to wages. And American policy should recognize that

9. Benjamin Strong to Parker Gilbert, May 23, 1921, in Strong Papers, FRBNY.

10. Paul Warburg to Herbert Hoover, May 28, 1921, in Foreign Finance Conference File, CP, HHPL.

11. F.I. Kent to Herbert Hoover, May 26, 1921, in Foreign Finance Conference File, CP, HHPL.

one of the most serious difficulties faced by American exporters was "the erratic and rapid fluctuation in the foreign exchanges," which was likely to continue if new restrictions were placed on "borrowing by foreign governments in this market."[12] The more that foreign governments were able to borrow in the United States, Strong said, the sooner stable exchange conditions could be achieved and the easier it would be for foreign nationals to purchase American exports.

The Treasury was also disturbed by the possibility of bankers having to submit their foreign loans to the Government for approval. In the long run, it thought, this might prove "more harmful than helpful to foreign trade."[13] It would be a good idea, Parker Gilbert argued, to have both the Treasury and the State Department advised about pending loans to foreign governments, thus giving them ample opportunity to offer any objections that they might have. But it would be harmful "to require bankers or foreign Governments, before offering foreign Government issues in this country, to get anything like a formal approval from the Treasury or the State Department, or even a statement that there are no objections to the offering."[14]

There was, however, despite the disagreement about supervising foreign loans, a general consensus that economic conditions in Europe would not improve unless governments, banks, and industrial concerns had ample access to American credit. And bankers in the United States were willing to extend such credit, provided that the loans could be insured against "foreign credit risks, including the dangers of political and social disturbances."[15] To Hoover, this was a legitimate concern, and in June of 1921 he asked Strong for his opinion concerning an insurance scheme being advocated by Congressman Louis McFadden. He also wondered whether American merchants and bankers might take advantage of the ter Meulen plan, which was designed to enable war ravished countries to finance essential imports, provided they possessed approved national securities. Developed by a Dutch banker and adopted by the League of Nations in December 1920, the plan allowed eligible governments to issue bonds against pledged securities approved by an international commission and to use the bonds as collateral for import and export credits to facilitate trade through private channels. The plan was not supposed to "finance Governments except in special, approved cases."[16]

---

12. Benjamin Strong to Parker Gilbert, May 23, 1921, in Strong Papers, FRBNY.

13. Parker Gilbert to Benjamin Strong, June 11, 1921, in Strong Papers, FRBNY.

14. Ibid.

15. Paul Warburg to Herbert Hoover, May 28, 1921, in Foreign Finance Conference File, CP, HHPL.

16, Herbert Hoover to Benjamin Strong, June 4, 1921, in Foreign Finance Conference File, CP, HHPL. Assets pledged as security were required to yield a regular revenue such as customs duties, state monopolies, and the like. A gold value was assigned to them in order to fix the amount of bonds that a borrower might issue. Once the amount had been fixed, the borrowing government would issue bonds maturing in five, ten, or fifteen years, with an agreed rate of interest. Sir Drummond Fraser address delivered before the

In his reply Strong noted that a number of objections had been raised about such insurance schemes, one of the strongest being that they provided an incentive for investors with little experience and modest means to get involved. There was also the problem of defining just what "political risk" was, at least in any way that would "avoid endless controversies and litigation."[17] And beyond this, they constituted a type of insurance that would probably increase the cost of goods and pass these costs on to everyone even though only a small group of reckless risk-takers would be the real beneficiaries. In this respect, they resembled the schemes that had been advanced to guarantee bank deposits and were like them a violation of fundamental insurance principles. Furthermore, Strong argued, if there were a political breakdown in Central Europe, the loss might be "100 percent," and "no contribution of any percentage of the selling price could cover a risk of that character."[18]

Strong noted, however, that the British government was offering credits up to £26 million sterling, with ter Meulen securities as collateral.[19] And American bankers, he thought, might take advantage of the ter Meulen scheme if political risks were minimized to their satisfaction. In his view, this would require "our government taking an active and official part in the plans for European reconstruction,"[20] and he was concerned that any effort to develop exports to Europe would be more likely to succeed if it were carried out by organized methods rather than leaving it to the initiative of individual traders.

Following his exchange with Strong, Hoover also interested himself in further developments concerning the ter Meulen plan. Later on in 1921, British bankers, the World Cotton Conference, the Congress of the International Chamber of Commerce, and the American Bankers Association all endorsed credits based on the bonds. And at the ABA convention, Sir Drummond Fraser, the plan's organizer, provided a detailed description of how it worked. One of its strong points, he thought, was that the bonds would support credits under conditions where ordinary banking transactions were unsuitable. Exporters could and would extend credit for longer periods than the banks, and with ter Meulen bonds as collateral they could conduct financial arrangements through a corporation, such as those authorized under the Edge Act.[21] The advantage of this

---

convention of the American Bankers' Association, Los Angeles, October 1921, in Sir Drummond Fraser file, CP, HHPL.

17. Benjamin Strong to Herbert Hoover, June 9, 1921, in Foreign Finance Conference File, CP, HHPL.

18. Ibid.

19. The British Government assumed 85 percent of the risk of loss and the exporter the remaining 15 percent.

20. Benjamin Strong to Herbert Hoover, June 9, 1921, in Foreign Finance Conference File, CP, HHPL.

21. The Edge Act was passed by Congress in 1919. It provided for the incorporation of private investment trusts under the federal government. They were regulated by the government, and capital to finance their ventures came from both private sources and the

would be "longer advances," since a corporation of this sort could obtain "its funds from its own debentures at 5, 10, 15 years subscribed by investors."[22]

While in the United States, Fraser also discussed the plan with Hoover, hoping to enlist his support in getting it a "fair trial." And following the discussion, Hoover submitted the plan to William E. Lamb, the Commerce Department solicitor, for his assessment of it. The latter concluded that it had potential but was also problematic. The plan, he noted, required that the borrowing country pledge its resources in ways that would mean the suspension of all prior obligations and hence a postponement of any payments on its war debts. In addition, he found it difficult to see how the international commission would be able to assign a value to the bonds of any of the war-torn countries. Actually, there were few European countries that could join together in order to secure a billion dollars' worth of credit, even if they gave an express promise to repay the debt by a specified date. But still, in Lamb's view, the ter Meulen scheme was not unlike that used by creditors in the case of a failed commercial institution. If a creditor had confidence in the ability and integrity of the management, he might be willing to extend further credit, and if he announced this confidence at a meeting of other creditors, they too were inclined to give further assistance. In such a case, the company usually issued demand notes to cover its obligations. And although these notes might not be worth more than the open account, they were nevertheless "in the form of a direct obligation to pay" and the "psychological effect" was "to make the holder believe he [had] a real security."[23] Hence, the success of the plan would rest not upon the security that was offered but on the belief in the honesty and integrity of the borrowing country to put its industries back on a paying basis.

Hoover, in his reply to Fraser, pointed out that economic recovery in Europe depended upon each country achieving balanced budgets, currency reorganization and stabilization, wise control of imports and exports, and credits for reproductive purposes. It was hopeless, he thought, to expect that any credit from private sources would be made available to these countries until the first three requirements had been met. But, he warned, any effort to achieve these reforms must be initiated by the European governments themselves. Reforms brought about through the political action of foreign governments would risk being wrecked "on the rocks of conflicting political objectives."[24] The ter Meulen plan, he concluded, would be helpful once the needed reforms had been

---

War Finance Corporation. They received payment for U.S. exports in foreign securities, and in turn reimbursed exporters with dollars.

22. Sir Drummond Fraser address delivered before the convention of the American Bankers' Association at Los Angeles, October 1921. in Sir Drummond Fraser file, CP, HHPL.

23. William E. Lamb, ter Meulen bond plan for stabilization of International Trade and the Extension of Credit therefore, undated, in Sir Drummond Fraser file, CP, HHPL.

24. Herbert Hoover to Sir Drummond Fraser, October 31, 1921 in Sir Drummond Fraser File, CP, HHPL.

achieved, and it could act as an inducement to secure these reforms.[25] In addition, he thought that some credit assistance would be required to facilitate currency reform and that this would be handled by the banks of issue of the principal countries, thereby avoiding "political action in the economic and financial affairs of each of these states." This, he emphasized, would not replace the ter Meulen plan. On the contrary "the two plans would supplement each other"[26] and help to secure the German financial stabilization that was the key to European reconstruction in general.

Adolph Miller had also discussed the matter with Hoover and agreed that currency restoration and stabilization in Germany was the key to financial reform in Europe. Privately, however, Miller thought that currency reorganization and international credits could not wait for the "reestablishment of complete budgetary equilibrium." It was difficult to see "how a balance in taxation and expenditure [could] be reached until economic recuperation" in central Europe was more complete. And the latter would require international credits, "more exchange stability and a better currency condition."[27]

It seemed clear that international credits would not be forthcoming until signs of fiscal reform had manifested themselves, and this was especially true in Eastern and Southeastern Europe, where fiscal and currency conditions had become progressively worse. Hoover pointed out that the economic revitalization of these areas was essential, not only to American commerce but also to that of other states. But he feared that it would be impossible for these countries to accomplish economic reforms without the assistance of private finance and commerce. In August, Hoover and Strong had discussed these problems at length and had agreed that the public banks in Europe and the United States could do much to aid in the recovery. Strong, though, was not willing to pursue the matter with central banks in other countries without Administration support, and to that end he requested that Hoover provide him with supporting correspondence.

Hoover had then drafted a letter in which he recapitulated his and Strong's concerns. In addition, he stated that it was the hope of the Administration that Strong would be able to pursue the matter with other central banks of issue in order to come up with a plan for financial cooperation of a "purely private character." This should deal with the rehabilitation of currencies and the provision of initial raw material in Eastern Europe, but aid to the countries in the area should be conditional upon their inaugurating and maintaining economic policies that would give promise of economic stability. In the absence of "such helpful action of this kind . . . by private institutions of great responsibility to the public," Hoover thought, recovery of foreign commerce would be prolonged over many years.[28]

---

25. Ibid.

26. Ibid.

27. Adolph Miller to Herbert Hoover, October 31, 1921, in Foreign Finance Conference File, CP, HHPL.

28. Herbert Hoover to Benjamin Strong, August 30, 1921, in Benjamin Strong File, CP, HHPL.

After reading a draft of the letter, Strong had generally concurred, but did suggest that Hoover include "a plan for furnishing adequate securities for credits granted"[29] This, he stated, would be especially desirable in the case of Austria, where potential investors would want some guarantee that their loans would be well secured. Clearly, Strong welcomed Hoover's idea that stabilization efforts be divorced from political action and addressed by financiers instead. This he had already discussed with Montagu Norman and Sir Charles Addis, who on their visit to the United States had stressed the need to prevent a potential calamity in Eastern Europe. And in a letter of September 15, Norman asked to be kept informed about action taken in response to "Hoover's letter." Central Bankers, he thought, were destined "to play their own great part."[30]

The letter that Strong had anticipated, however, never came. When the proposal reached Secretary of State Hughes, he seriously questioned its advisability, arguing that the matters were primarily of a political nature and could be dealt with only by political action. This fact, he said, could not "be escaped by describing" them as economic.[31] He also noted that part of the proposed letter clearly pointed to governmental action "as underlying the plan," which in turn raised questions about "the nature and scope" of such action and required that anything done in this country to promote it must be supervised and directed by the United States Government in an appropriate manner.

In addition, Hughes was concerned that the proposed letter, despite its guarded language, would in reality be an authorization to conduct indirect negotiations with foreign governments on behalf of the President, all without the usual defined limits and supervision and therefore with the potential to produce moral commitments that might prove to be embarrassing. If a plan of private cooperation proved to be feasible, he thought, it should be pursued as a private venture and without any attempt to make it appear as though it had governmental sanction. This would ensure that discussions were kept to their true purpose, and any questions or plans coming out of such negotiations could, if foreign governmental action was involved, be submitted to the government for consideration. Under no circumstances, Hughes said, would the United States assume commitments of any sort until it was known exactly what the plan was. Nor did he see this as hindering the implementation of any plan. It "would simply avoid making it appear" that the United States Government supported such action "when in truth it is not intended that this Government shall now assume any responsibility in the matter."[32]

This was not what Hoover had anticipated, and he had to inform Strong not to expect any "definite statement from the Administration, either affirmative or

---

29. Benjamin Strong to Herbert Hoover, September 1, 1921, in Benjamin Strong File, CP, HHPL.

30. Montagu Norman to Benjamin Strong, September 15, 1921, in Strong Papers, FRBNY.

31. Charles E. Hughes to Herbert Hoover, September 1, 1921, in Benjamin Strong File, CP, HHPL.

32. Ibid.

negative," about FRBNY cooperation with European central banks to ameliorate conditions in Central and Eastern Europe.[33] At the time, Pierre Jay, Chairman of the FRBNY, had already begun a preliminary investigation of conditions in Austria and had planned to meet with Norman and Dr.Gerard Vissering, Governor of the Dutch National Bank, to determine what joint action might be taken. But now the failure of the Administration to give its approval led the FRBNY to consider postponing the Austrian investigation indefinitely. Norman called the development "most disappointing," though he still hoped that Strong would be able to get consent to proceed. An investigation, he said, would "at least arouse hope and so help to maintain exchange rates."[34]

Norman also noted that conditions in Austria had deteriorated to the point that it was uncertain whether the Government would be able to continue. And with this assessment, Jay concurred. The situation, as he saw it, had become progressively worse, with the exchange rate falling much faster than the currency volume had increased. Yet the Austrian Finance Minister, in his travels to London and Paris, had been unsuccessful in securing the much needed aid. Discouragement in Austria, said Jay, was intense, and the longer aid or the promise of it were delayed the greater would be "the difficulty of organizing assistance and amounts required," the magnitude of "the crisis when prices fall," and "the period of depression affecting our direct and indirect trade with Austria."[35]

Strong continued to press the issue with Washington. He forwarded copies of the cables received from Jay and Norman to Hughes and asked to meet with him in order to discuss the matter further. He also sent a copy of the cables to Hoover, along with a letter expressing concern that Austria would collapse if some constructive aid were not forthcoming. He thought that Hoover's familiarity with the situation would undoubtedly "give emphasis to these communications."[36] In addition, he asked Hoover whether "it would be desirable or possible" to indicate to Norman that he might approach the United States Government about the need for assistance.

The State Department, though, remained recalcitrant. Strong's visit with Hughes did not change the latter's mind. Hughes still thought it unwise for the government to make any formal commitments, "even to the extent of expressing no objection to such a program."[37] One could imply that there would be no objections if a private plan, without governmental support or responsibility, were pursued. But Strong feared that any such plan would be left in a perilous posi-

---

33. Benjamin Strong to Charles E. Hughes, September 24, 1921, in Charles Evans Hughes File, CP, HHPL.

34. Montagu Norman to Benjamin Strong, Cable No. 78, September 24, 1921, in Benjamin Strong File, CP, HHPL.

35. Pierre Jay to Benjamin Strong, September 24, 1921, in Benjamin Strong File, CP, HHPL.

36. Benjamin Strong to Herbert Hoover, September 24, 1921, in Benjamin Strong File, CP, HHPL.

37. Benjamin Strong to Montagu Norman, November 1, 1921, in Strong Papers, FRBNY.

tion. "Political or other developments might, without some such preliminary understanding," result in a repudiation and withdrawal of support, and require "complete abandonment of American participation."[38]

In the absence of Administration consensus, Hoover could do little but offer moral support to Strong. Nor could he lend much encouragement to James A. Logan, one of the unofficial American representatives to the Reparations Commission, who wrote him that Louis Locheur, the French Minister of Reconstruction, was saying that "the biggest financial crash of history was bound to arrive" unless aid was extended.[39] Norman, in the meantime, had decided that the "whole Austrian question . . . should be left alone for the present." Hughes's attitude, he feared, would land Strong "in such a position as to necessitate complete abandonment of American participation,"[40] and without American cooperation, he believed, the European countries could not work together.

Consequently, Strong's quest for Central Bank cooperation was not to be achieved in 1921. But the discussion that year did lay the groundwork for its realization in the future. And in Hoover's involvement, one can see both his desire to organize a return to prosperity and his belief that the Commerce Department should learn what business needed by way of service and then "apply such forces as the government could bring to bear to that end."[41]

In addition, the rebuff by Hughes was important for future interdepartmental relations. Prior to the incident, the Commerce Department had received copies of cables and correspondence related to reparations questions from the State Department. But in the fall of 1921, the practice was abruptly discontinued, and in December Hoover requested its resumption on the grounds that the reparations problem was essentially a commercial problem. Commercial policies, he argued, revolved around the reparation question, and unless the Commerce Department had access to all the information that was available to the government it would not be able to "direct the administration of policies in those phases that of necessity lie in this Department."[42]

Hughes responded that he would be glad to provide paraphrases of communications having a bearing on commercial polices, but that he was not comfortable with providing copies that might contain confidential information intended exclusively for the work of the State Department.[43] Hoover was "deeply pained" and argued that "the problems surrounding reparations, the conse-

38. Ibid.

39. James A. Logan to Herbert Hoover, November 3, 1921, Herbert Hoover Archives, Institution on War, Revolution, and Peace, Stanford, CA.

40. Montagu Norman to Benjamin Strong, November 14, 1921, in Strong Papers, FRBNY.

41. Herbert Hoover, Address to the Convention of Office Appliance Manufacturers, November 3, 1921.

42. Herbert Hoover to Charles E. Hughes, December 6, 1921, in Charles Evans Hughes File, CP, HHPL.

43. Charles E. Hughes to Herbert Hoover, December 13, 1921, in Charles Evans Hughes File, CP, HHPL.

quences that flow therefrom, and the policies adopted" were of the utmost importance "in the economic relations of our Government."[44] Hence, it was utterly impossible to separate the political from the commercial phase. And besides, to suggest that a fellow Cabinet officer could not "be trusted with the necessary information on the political phases seemed not only personally intolerable" but likely to lead to governmental actions based upon inadequate information.

In his reply, Hughes expressed regret that Hoover had "apparently misunderstood." So far as Hoover was personally concerned, he said, there was nothing he wished to conceal from him. On the contrary, he would be willing to discuss, in confidence, the factors entering into his conduct of foreign relations.[45] But he was not willing, nor did he have the right, to communicate matters of a highly confidential character to another department. Once transmitted, such information would become a part of the other department's files and therefore accessible to people not entitled to the same confidence that he would extend to a fellow Cabinet member.

Hoover remained unsatisfied but unable to change Hughes's mind. Nor did he like the eventual outcome of the White House meeting with the bankers that he had helped to arrange. There it had been agreed that the bankers should keep the State Department informed of any loan negotiations with foreign governments, but no statement about this had been issued to the press. Not until December 13 did Hughes decide that a statement should be made. It was necessary, he thought, to confirm the understanding for bankers who had attended the conference and would also inform the remainder of the financial community of the State Department's desire to be kept informed with regard to such negotiations. He was concerned, he said, because a number of foreign loans had recently been floated by American bankers without informing the State Department about them.[46]

Accordingly, Hughes asked Mellon and Hoover to review a draft of a proposed press release, which in essence requested only that the State Department be kept appraised about the negotiation and progress of financial arrangements with foreign governments. Mellon raised no objections.[47] But Hoover thought that the State Department was encroaching on his territory and including in its request a "whole gamut of purely economic matters in which the State Department is not interested," but which came "within the purview" of the Commerce Department.[48] Hughes fired back that he could have taken exception to Hoo-

44. Herbert Hoover to Charles Evans Hughes, December 15, 1921, in Charles Evans Hughes File, CP, HHPL.

45. Charles E. Hughes to Herbert Hoover, December 16, 1921, in Charles Evans Hughes File, CP, HHPL.

46. Charles E. Hughes to Herbert Hoover, December 13, 1921, in Charles Evans Hughes File, CP, HHPL.

47. Andrew Mellon to Charles E. Hughes, December 9, 1921, in Charles Evans Hughes File, CP, HHPL.

48. Herbert Hoover to Charles E. Hughes, December 13, 1921, in Charles Evans Hughes File, CP, HHPL.

ver's position that such matters were foreign to the work of the State Department. But he would not do so because he assumed that Hoover was conversant with the work of the State Department and would accordingly not withhold anything pertinent to its work from Hughes. Similarly, he would not withhold any pertinent information from the Commerce Department.[49]

Hoover's position was that the Commerce Department had already established a relationship with the business community through the creation of a cooperating committee of the American Bankers Association. In this way, it was laying a foundation for the better coordination of "American foreign investments with our economic interests" through the development of "certain principles" that bankers would insist upon and through continuing consultation on matters affecting American commerce. Hence, a notice in the form suggested by the State Department would only cause confusion. Moreover, bankers would feel obligated to tell their clients that the State Department at least saw "no objection on political grounds," and this in practice would lead "the more ignorant public" to assume a measure of governmental responsibility for a loan's "intrinsic soundness."[50] In his view, an informal negotiation by the Commerce Department with bankers could effect the desires of the State Department while resulting in fewer responsibilities.

Hughes finally agreed that foreign loans floated in the American market were primarily a commercial transaction and that a suitable understanding between the Commerce and State departments was desirable. But it was necessary, he said, for him to be adequately informed about such loans. He reminded Hoover that at the White House conference, President Harding had suggested that he should inform American bankers about "the program which the State Department would like to have followed concerning these loans."[51] He had no objection, he added, to receiving information from American bankers through the Commerce Department. But he could not take the position that the bankers should not approach the State Department directly nor that the Department should not deal directly with them when the "conduct of the Department's business . . . as in the matter of these foreign loans" made it desirable.[52]

On December 30, Hoover pointed out that the Executive Committee of the American Investment Bankers Association and leading foreign lenders agreed with him that a public announcement from the State Department would have an adverse impact on investors looking to purchase foreign securities. It would demand that underwriters produce some formula that would indicate the attitude of the government about the particular loan being announced, and such a formula could not help but produce a "psychological reaction" and, "in the more ignorant

49. Charles E. Hughes to Herbert Hoover, December 16, 1921, in Charles Evans Hughes File, CP, HHPL.

50. Herbert Hoover to Charles E. Hughes, December 13, 1921, in Charles Evans Hughes File, CP, HHPL.

51. Charles E. Hughes to Herbert Hoover, December 24, 1921, in Charles Evans Hughes File, CP, HHPL.

52. Ibid.

public mind," attach "a certain measure of Governmental responsibility." The war, Hoover said, had provided ample experience with this type of difficulty, and it should now be avoided. He suggested instead that he secure an assurance from the Executive Committee of the Banker's Association and others that the State Department would be consulted in such matters and thereby avoid the difficulty that a notice from the Government to the public would pose.[53]

Hughes, though, was not to be dissuaded, and Hoover may have undermined his position by suggesting to President Harding that the government take a position against loans used to purchase armaments, pay for the cost of wars, or finance non-reproductive governmental expenditures. He was particularly concerned about loans to Greece and Brazil for armaments purposes, and in a memorandum to Hughes, he argued that while he did not think such loans could be absolutely controlled, the current American efforts to achieve disarmament (i.e., the Washington Conference) justified a request that American bankers refrain from making them.[54] Allowing such loans would result in a waste of surplus capital[55] and would do nothing to improve a European financial situation being aggravated by uncontrolled inflation, excessive land armaments, an unsettled reparations issue, and economic disruption in Eastern Europe.[56] Loan policy, in other words, ought to be brought into line with the need to deal with these basic obstacles to commercial stability and should work in conjunction with plans for reduced armaments, feasible reparations, and the restoration of sound currency systems.[57]

As the discussion between Hoover and Hughes continued, Montagu Norman and Benjamin Strong were also continuing their exchanges on the European situation and especially the Austrian case. Writing on February 6, 1922, Norman again expressed hope that the matter could be "taken up by a consortium of Central Banks"[58] and wondered if Strong could still pursue this with Hoover and other members of the Harding administration.[59] If not, he would have to consult with Vissering to see what arrangements could be concluded in Europe. Strong, though, was not optimistic. The Federal Reserve System, he noted, was having

53. Herbert Hoover to Charles E. Hughes, December 30, 1921, in Charles Evans Hughes File, CP, HHPL.

54. Herbert Hoover to Warren G. Harding, December 31, 1921 in Miscellaneous Loan File, CP, HHPL; Warren G. Harding to Charles E. Hughes, January 12, 1922, in Miscellaneous Loan File, CP, HHPL.

55. Herbert Hoover to Warren G. Harding, December 31, 1921, in Miscellaneous Loan File, CP, HHPL.

56. Herbert Hoover Statement for the Press, January 23, 1922, in Public Statements File, CP, HHPL.

57. Herbert Hoover to Warren G. Harding, January 4, 1921, in President Harding File, CP, HHPL.

58. Montagu Norman to Benjamin Strong, February 6, 1922, in Strong File, FRBNY.

59. Ibid.

difficulties, partly because this was an election year with a good deal of political posturing[60] and repeated accusations that the system was the archenemy of agriculture. The agriculture bloc, he added, had been aggressive in defeating legislation, and it posed an obstacle to the administration's legislative agenda as well as a threat to split the Republican Party.[61] This was apparent in the bloc's active effort to have a farmer appointed to the Federal Reserve Board whenever the next vacancy should occur,[62] and Strong was against doing anything that would embarrass an administration upon which the Federal Reserve System had to rely for protection against political attacks and interference. The administration, he said, had supported the system "in a satisfactory and definite fashion,"[63] and for that reason it was important to avoid taking any independent action that could have negative political effects on the system's best friends.

In Strong's view, it was impossible to confront this "determined hostility" in Congress because of "ignorance" and because of the incapacity of Senators and Congressmen to speak in defence of the system," regardless of how they felt.[64] But from the standpoint of the farm bloc leaders and their Western supporters, there was as little reason for a farmer to produce his crops at a loss as there was for New England mills to operate if their products could not be sold. The bloc's spokesmen strongly resented criticism from such Easterners as Secretary of War John W. Weeks, and they saw as their greatest foes the financial power of Wall Street and "the formerly powerful protectionists of the Eastern country" whom they would no longer allow "to run amuck as in other days."[65] Strong had no doubt about their political clout, and in still another letter to Norman he again expressed the view that actions should be avoided that might leave the Federal Reserve System vulnerable to Congressional efforts to modify its underlying principles. The system, he explained, was simply a creature of Congress, which meant that its powers and responsibilities could be modified or

---

60. Benjamin Strong to Montagu Norman, February 2, 1922, in Strong Papers, FRBNY.

61. Strong was not alone in this. See, for instance, *New York Times* beginning September 1921 through March 1924. The coverage of this topic was particularly heavy during December 1921 and January 1922.

62. *New York Times*, December 20, 1921. According to the *Times*, "The putting forward of the bill to put a farmer on the Federal Reserve may be the 'bloc's' answer to the President as well as . . . Secretary Weeks. . . . The bill . . . is to all intents and purposes a 'mandate' to the President to name a farmer as one of the five members of the Reserve Board." Members of the farm bloc were well aware that the next vacancy would occur in August, when Governor Harding, who had earned their enmity, would be up for reappointment. As it turned out, the bloc was unwilling to wait. In June 1922 it secured an act raising the number of Reserve Board members from five to six, and Milo D. Campbell of Michigan was then appointed as the new farmer member of the Board.

63. Benjamin Strong to Montagu Norman, February 18, 1922, in Strong Papers, FRBNY.

64. Ibid.

65. *New York Times*, February 12, 1922, sec. 7, p. 2.

eliminated almost overnight. Hence, one had to exercise one's best judgement in order to determine "at what point it [was] possible to stand firmly for principles" without risking the "consequences of having those principles overruled."[66] Until the atmosphere cleared in Washington, he thought, there was nothing that the FRBNY could do in the Austrian matter other than to keep itself and government officials informed as to conditions. Norman was concerned about the propaganda directed against the FRBNY. He was also disappointed that nothing was to come from his having brought the FRBNY into a closer relationship with various Central Banks in Europe.[67] But he would have to await the outcome of developments in the United States.

Also in the picture by early 1922 were several congressional proposals for some kind of American assistance to those seeking to improve the situation in Europe. Senator William Borah recognized the need for such assistance, and Senator Robert Owen introduced a bill to create a Federal Reserve foreign bank, to be located in New York and to be supervised by the Federal Reserve Board. As envisioned, the bank would conduct business like any other reserve bank but would differ in that it could establish branches and agencies overseas in order to facilitate international commerce. Herbert Hoover considered the plan, but thought that the European countries had not yet attained the level of stability required for extension of this type of assistance. Until inflation had been arrested, he told Senator Charles Curtis, extending American capital to Europe would amount to "pouring money down an infinite sink."[68]

In addition, there was a resolution sponsored by Senator Henry Cabot Lodge. Introduced early in February of 1922 it authorized the Treasury to extend the debt incurred by Austria for purchases made from the United States Grain Corporation and for other purposes for a period of up to twenty-five years and to release Austrian assets pledged as collateral for these debts, provided that substantially all the other creditor nations took similar action.[69] To Strong this was evidence that the administration continued to have an interest in the Austrian situation. It showed, he thought, that administration leaders did not wish to in-

---

66. Benjamin Strong to Montagu Norman, March 4, 1922, in Strong Papers, FRBNY.

67. Montagu Norman to Benjamin Strong, March 30, 1922, in Strong Papers, FRBNY.

68. Herbert Hoover to Sen. Charles Curtis, January 26, 1922, in Federal Reserve Board and Banks File, CP, HHPL; see also SF 2915, 67th Cong., 2nd sess; Borah, Congressional Record, 67th Cong., 2nd sess., 1922, 62, pt. 2: pp. 1684-85.

69. U.S. Congress, Senate, *Joint Resolution authorizing the extension, for a period of not to exceed, twenty-five years, of the time for the payment of the principal and interest of the debt incurred by Austria for the purchase of flour from the United States Grain Corporation, and for other purposes.* Pub. Res., No. 46, 67 Cong., 2d sess., 1922, S. J. Res. 160.

terpose any obstacles in the way of dealing with it and that they might be willing to assist in resolving the matter.[70]

While Strong continued to hope for appropriate American action, the State Department had decided to go ahead with the statement detailing its policy on foreign loans. This was released on March 3 and elicited relatively favorable comments. James Logan, for example, still acting as America's unofficial reparations commissioner, was pleased to see it and seemed to think that it was in line with his warnings against efforts to "peg" exchange rates through "the medium of private loans."[71] Such arrangements, he told Hoover, should not be countenanced since doing so would make it impossible for Europeans to get down to "straight business" and "talk sense."[72]

Following the State Department release, the Commerce Department also discovered an "urgent need" to develop a "definite, consistent and constructive policy" of its own. Such a policy, argued Grosvenor Jones of the Bureau of Finance and Domestic Commerce, should be based on general political and economic aspects and should be "reasonably conservative and far sighted."[73] In his view, the government had a three-fold responsibility in the matter. It had a responsibility to the investor who looked to his government to protect his foreign loans, regardless of whether or not it approved of the loan; to bankers who should be able to rely on the government for guidance and advice; and to foreign governments that might be led to borrow unwisely if American bank credits were used too frequently.

American investors, Jones went on to explain, had been led to believe that foreign loans were required to help restore financial stability abroad and as a result had taken up more foreign securities than anyone had anticipated. They needed protection if this desirable level of interest was to be maintained, and the protection Jones had in mind was a determination of whether the fiscal policy of the borrowing government was sound before a loan was extended. If the policy was unsound, the government's borrowing in the American market should be restricted until it changed its ways. A little "paternalism" of this sort, Jones thought, would do more good than harm. In addition he suggested that if any loan proceeds were used for public improvements, American companies ought to be given an opportunity to bid for portions of it. However, he would not go as far as the National Foreign Trade Council was advocating and require that a certain percentage of the proceeds must be spent in the United States. This would be a "galling condition to impose," and would lend credence to the asser-

---

70. Benjamin Strong to Montagu Norman, February 18, 1922, in Strong Papers, FRBNY.

71. James Logan to Herbert Hoover, March 9, 1922, in Herbert Hoover Archives, Institution on War, Revolution, and Peace, Stanford, CA.

72. Ibid.

73. Grosvenor Jones to Herbert Hoover, April 1, 1922, in Foreign Loans File, CP, HHPL.

tion that the United States wanted to "impose its financial domination upon the world."[74]

Jones and other Commerce Department officials thought that limits should be placed on foreign loans by American banks in the same way that credit lines were fixed for their domestic clients. The reason, according to Jones, was two-fold. First, there was a definite limit of credit that could be extended in the American market. And second, not all foreign governments were equally cred-itworthy. Hence, the Investment Bankers Association, working together with the Commerce and State Departments, ought to establish limits on borrowings a year in advance, and it was the bankers who ought to take the lead in the matter, If they did so, they would be more committed to keep foreign loans within ac-ceptable limits.[75]

Hoover agreed with Jones' analysis but wanted written documentation, the extension of loans to be in American dollars, and a requirement of sufficient collateral from borrowers whose financial records for the preceding 25 years were not adequate. To Jones the first two stipulations seemed reasonable, but the effect of the third, he thought, would be that "practically all risky loans would be excluded."[76] Moreover, it would have to be modified in the case of the newly created countries, which had to assume part of the debts of their former govern-ments and therefore had not had sufficient opportunity to get their financial af-fairs in order. In addition, Jones was particularly insistent that the criteria adopted by the government be acceptable to the bankers. Once the Commerce and State Departments had settled upon the fundamental requirements for for-eign loans, he argued, they should then seek to have them accepted by invest-ment bankers so that the latter might co-operate with the government in rejecting loan applications that did not meet the requirements. If undesirable loans were denied at the source, that is by the bankers themselves, the government would be spared a good deal of inconvenience and embarrassment. Yet its objective of "a more conservative attitude toward foreign loans" would be achieved.[77]

Such views, however, again brought the Commerce Department into con-flict with Benjamin Strong. The latter took issue with the claims that restrictions on foreign loans would prevent the export of American capital and denied as well that exports would be stimulated by requiring borrowers to purchase goods in the United States. He pointed out that when a foreign loan was placed in the United States, the proceeds would be credited to an account in the borrower's name in an American bank. This credit could be used either to withdraw gold from the United States, to pay current debts in this country, or to pay for goods, services, and investments bought in the American market. And under current conditions, he continued, there would be no withdrawal of gold since its export would have to be at a loss. The proceeds would go to pay debts "owing to our merchants and bankers" or to purchase needed goods; and if dollars were ex-

---

74. Grosvenor Jones to Herbert Hoover, undated, in Foreign Loans File, CP, HHPL.
75. Ibid.
76. Ibid.
77. Ibid.

changed for other currencies to be spent abroad, these dollars would then be available to purchase goods or services in the United States. Hence, the restrictions being proposed would do more harm than good. They would "reduce the amount of dollars otherwise placed at the disposal of foreign borrowers," and this would postpone the liquidation of indebtedness and hinder rather than stimulate exports.[78]

Strong also found fault with the proposal to place restrictions on the total amount that governments could borrow and to force them to demonstrate that they had begun serious efforts to balance their budgets. It was in the general interest of the United States, Strong argued, and "entirely apart from the consideration of the relative effects on foreign countries needing credit," not to set a ceiling on the total amount that could be borrowed.[79] This would only hamper the nation's ability to make use of its immense power to extend credit. Nor did Strong think it wise to force foreign governments to cut expenditures for military or other non-productive purposes. This, he insisted, was a political question, upon which American businessmen would and should be reluctant to express their opinion, and if enforced it would mean exclusion of a wide range of governments and a decline in American exports.[80]

In his response to Strong's arguments, Hoover accepted the premise that foreign loans must ultimately lead to the export of goods or gold and that they were vital to reviving American and world commerce. He was not prepared, however, to accept Strong's "implied conclusion that no standards should be set up,"[81] and unless the banking community itself developed such standards, Congress would sooner or later "impose control." There were "other and larger considerations than those enumerated by Governor Strong," and these meant both that the government had "certain unavoidable political and moral responsibilities toward these operations" and that American bankers had certain "internal responsibilities" to American commerce.[82]

Hoover also noted that international credit operations differed from domestic credit transactions in that there was no method for recouping failed foreign loans other than by diplomatic intervention. Hence, there was an implication, "whether desired or not," that the federal government would assist American investors "in relation to such transactions," and this meant that from the outset the "security and form" of foreign loans should "involve a fair hope" that government intervention would not be required. In addition, he noted, there was the need to get Europe away from a war atmosphere, and restrictions limiting the use of loan proceeds to reproductive purposes would at least "give the tendency"

---

78. Benjamin Strong to Charles E. Hughes, April 20, 1922, in Foreign Loan File, CP, HHPL.

79. Ibid.

80. Ibid.

81. Herbert Hoover to Charles E. Hughes, April 29, 1922, in Foreign Loan File, CP, HHPL.

82. Ibid.

to do this.[83] Admittedly, Hoover continued, the argument about responsibility could be carried to extremes. But there was a practical middle ground. There was information that the government had no "moral right" to withhold from its citizens, and the government should at a minimum observe the same standards as "would be expected of a reasonable businessman dealing with his customers."[84]

Finally, Hoover argued that American bankers had a responsibility to domestic commerce. He pointed out that complaints had been received from the West that the flood of foreign loans was leading to an increase in interest rates, and he was sympathetic with these. He noted that foreign loans were being negotiated on terms that yielded from two to three percent above the amount that many American customers could afford to pay, that these loans were being floated in a market where capital was limited, and that this was decreasing the ability of domestic borrowers to secure credits and was therefore detrimental to domestic industry.

In his response to Hoover's criticisms, Strong stated that his memorandum had been purposely confined to a narrow economic point of view. It had not attempted, as Hoover had, to open the "door wide to the consideration of the political and moral responsibility of officers of our government in this important matter." He had not considered that to be within his sphere of expertise. But granting that the United States could not afford to encourage or give moral support and comfort to nations that contributed to the continuance of the unsatisfactory political, social, and economic conditions confronting the world, he still doubted whether influence should be exercised by placing restrictions on loans to the nations concerned. There were more effective methods, and the key to finding them lay in the policy of the government "towards the whole subject of inter-governmental debts."[85] He was convinced, moreover, that when a "government assumes any responsibility whatever for assent or dissent in a given transaction," it may well turn out "that its greatest responsibility arises through failure to act rather than through affirmative action." In the final analysis, if the Federal Government passed on the soundness of a loan, even to a small degree, this seemed likely to "inaugurate a system of responsibility" to which there might be no end "except by the assumption of full responsibility."[86] It might, he told Hughes, seem ungracious to dissent from the position of so conscientious an official as Hoover. But once regulation, supervision, or control were employed, there would be no limit to which such controls might develop and "no limit to the responsibility which government may ultimately be called upon to assume."[87] It could involve the United States in the very disputes that Hoover was so eager to have it escape.

---

83. Ibid.

84. Ibid.

85. Benjamin Strong to Charles E. Hughes, June 9, 1922, in Foreign Loans File, CP, HHPL.

86. Ibid.

87. Ibid.

In the past Hoover and Strong had corresponded about such matters directly. But in this case, Strong's initial memorandum, challenging the Commerce Department's position, had been addressed to Hughes, and the latter had then forwarded copies of it to Hoover and Mellon for their comments. Neither Mellon nor Hughes entered the fray or commented on either position. But the "indirect" nature of the Hoover-Strong exchange appears to have left its mark on their relationship. Prior to this exchange they had consulted one another frequently about matters relating to commerce and banking, but afterward   the contacts between the two were few and relations kept deteriorating. Hoover's desk calendar shows that over the next four years he had only one more official appointment with Strong.[88]

As the debate over loan restrictions continued, both Hoover and Strong also continued to be involved in efforts to develop a plan for exchange stabilization. In early 1922, Hoover had hoped that this might be achieved through U.S. participation in the Genoa Conference.[89]   But political considerations had led the Administration to reject this idea, primarily so Strong thought, because it did not want to sit at the same table with the Russians, consider inter-allied debts, or take on economic commitments until military expenditures by European nations could be discussed as well.[90]

Strong, moreover, was not disappointed by the decision. He agreed with Norman that not "much good" could come from a purely political affair, especially since the French would not consider reparations readjustments until they knew how "their indebtedness to the United States was to be settled."[91]   Hence the only positive outcome to the conference that he could see was that it would bring the restoration of the gold standard, which had been abandoned during the war, closer. And in the long run, he thought, the conference would yield better results if the United States did not participate. It might in that case recognize the role that Central Banks could play and pave the way for progress once the trea-

---

88. Herbert Hoover, Appointment Calendar, 1901-1964, Special Collections, HHPL. Hoover also continued his efforts to achieve government supervision of foreign loans. By 1925 this had become a reality as the State Department now regularly consulted the Secretaries of Commerce and Treasury, as well as the President, about loans to foreign governments or municipalities. State Department, Leland Harrison, Foreign Loans, Memoranda, May 28, 1925, Library of Congress, Washington, D.C. This is also set forth in a memorandum from Harold Phelps Stokes to Grosvenor Jones, which noted the arrangement with the State Department to advise the Commerce Department in every case. Harold Stokes to Grosvenor Stokes, June 18, 1925, State Department General file, HHPL.

89. The matter had been dropped in September at Secretary Hughes' request because of the pending Washington Arms Conference. Hoover, though, continued to hold out hope that the United States would participate in an international conference that would deal with the European economic, and in particular the Austrian, situation.

90. Benjamin Strong to Montagu Norman, February 18, 1922, in Strong Papers, FRBNY.

91. Montagu Norman to Benjamin Strong, February 6, 1922, in Strong Papers, FRBNY.

ties were ratified and the American Funding Commission was functioning. It would then become clearer as to what help the United States could provide in solving European problems.[92]

Despite Hoover's hopes, then, there were no official American delegates at the Genoa Conference. William B. Causey and Alvin B. Barber, however, serving respectively as American Relief Administration technical advisors to Austria and Poland, attended as members of the Austrian and Polish delegations, and it seems probable that they served also as Hoover's representatives.[93]

In April, Hoover again raised the issue of Central Bank co-operation with Hughes. Reports in the press, he said, indicated that the Genoa Conference planned to invite the Federal Reserve Board to send a delegate to the kind of conference that he had proposed the previous summer, and this invitation, he thought, should be accepted provided it did not involve the assumption of any obligation on the part of the United States. "The delicate situation in Europe," he thought," might be ameliorated" if the United States demonstrated that it was prepared to cooperate "in manifestly mutual matters."[94] Hughes, though, replied that he was not aware that any such invitation had been issued, either by the Geneva Conference or the Bank of England, by whom he thought such a meeting would be called.[95]

In the meantime, Strong had learned from Norman that such a meeting would indeed be called. On April 20 the Financial Commission of the Genoa Conference had recommended that Central Banks "in the several countries," not necessarily confined to Europe, "should develop measures of currency co-operation."[96] And as a step toward this, it had urged that the Bank of England sponsor a conference of these banks as soon as possible. It would be necessary, Norman told Strong, for him to take immediate steps to convene this meeting, and it was essential that Strong be present.[97]

Initially, Norman had hoped to convene the bankers' conference in June, but by the middle of May he thought it should be deferred until September or early October because of political considerations in the United States. He also

92. Benjamin Strong to Montagu Norman, March 9, 1922, in Strong Papers, FRBNY; Benjamin Strong to Montagu Norman, March 22, 1922, in Strong Papers, FRBNY.

93. For their activities in this regard, see Donald R. Van Petten, "The European Technical Advisor and Post-War Austria 1919-1923," (Ph.D. dissertation, Stanford University, 1943), pp. 358-365, 583-590.

94 Herbert Hoover to Charles E. Hughes, April 22, 1922, in Federal Reserve Board File, CP, HHPL.

95. Charles E. Hughes to Herbert Hoover, April 26, 1922, in Genoa Conference File, CP, HHPL.

96. Resolution adopted by the Financial Commission of the International Economic Conference, Genoa, on April 20, 1922, as found in Herbert Hoover File, Hoover Institution on War, Revolution, and Peace, Stanford, CA.

97. Montagu Norman to Benjamin Strong, April 27, 1922, Incoming Cable No. 69, FRBNY.

continued to consult Strong about a proposed agenda, and Strong, for his part, was soon expressing fear that not much would be accomplished aside from a repetition of the "pious declarations" that Norman had prepared. He did agree, however, that the meeting had to be held and that at some point he would have to ask his friends in Washington whether it was agreeable to them that he attend. He doubted it would have much point unless he had a clear understanding of what statements he could safely make on the subject of debts.[98]

Still, in a letter to James Logan on July 17, Strong seemed more optimistic. He noted that he and Norman had discussed the proposed agenda with others at the FRBNY, with members of the Federal Reserve Board, and with the Secretary of the Treasury. In addition, he had discussed it with President Harding and Secretary Hoover, and in these talks with administration officials he had found them sympathetic towards private efforts to help repair economic conditions in Europe. Above all, they had a "deep interest" in and could not "stand aloof" from efforts "looking towards restoration of the gold standard," for the United States was the one gold standard country and had the bulk of the world's gold. To withhold assistance on this matter, Strong argued, would seem to be totally unjustified, and if there was to be a return to gold economic stabilization and debt settlement were prerequisites.[99]

As of mid-summer, Strong favored an October meeting. But he was still ambivalent about what the congressional reaction to FRBNY participation might be. Strong was also concerned about Governor Harding's chances for reappointment to the Federal Reserve Board. Writing to Norman, he pointed to the bitter political attacks on Harding and argued that "politics must be kept out of the system" because "political control would be its death blow."[100] However independent the system considered itself to be, he said, it was crucial not to "be so foolish as to invite further troubles."[101] The time for the bankers' conference, he seemed to be saying, had not yet arrived. Norman also thought that the meeting should be postponed. His reason, however, was that he did not think that a London meeting could be arranged at a time when the Funding Commission would be meeting in Washington.

Following the elections in 1922, Strong continued to be concerned about the threat that Congress posed to the Federal Reserve System. The problem was that a combination of the radicals, independents, progressives, agrarians, and labor representatives in both houses had the numbers to hold up legislation, and in Strong's view the specter of sectionalism continued to loom large on the horizon. Evidence of this could be seen in speeches such as those given by Senator elect Henrik Shipstead of Minnesota, who held that New York, by which he meant the "controlling interests there," sat back and looked upon the rest of the

98. Benjamin Strong to Montagu Norman, July 6, 1922, in Strong Papers, FRBNY.

99. Benjamin Strong to James Logan, July 17, 1922, in Strong Papers, FRBNY.

100. Benjamin Strong to James Logan, September 30, 1922, in Strong Papers, FRBNY.

101. Benjamin Strong to Montagu Norman, October 18, 1922, in Strong Papers, FRBNY.

country in the same way that Great Britain looked at India. "They imagine," Shipstead had declared, "that when they need a Senator they can come out here and get one,"[102] but they would learn that Minnesota was not a feudal state, peopled by serfs. Moreover, Wall Street was not the "chosen people to lay down the law."[103] The prospects for the Reserve System, and especially for Governor Harding's reappointment, Strong thought, were not good, and unless the situation was skillfully handled, it might "ultimately involve the system in a real contest of hard versus soft money."[104]

In the end Harding, not wanting to cause the Administration further embarrassment, withdrew his name from consideration for reappointment and was replaced by Daniel Crissinger, a farmer from Ohio, as Governor. Yet this did not end rural-based criticism of the system. Writing in 1923, William Jennings Bryan expressed regret that a system that "should have been the farmer's greatest protection" was now his greatest foe. Controlled by Wall Street speculators, it was engaged in draining the agricultural districts to "keep up a fictitious prosperity among members of the plunderbund." And in his view, it would be better to repeal the Federal Reserve Act and "go back to the old conditions" than to turn the system "over to Wall Street and allow its tremendous power to be used for the carrying out of the plans of the money trust.[105]

The political situation, though, did not keep Hoover and Strong from continuing with their efforts to find an avenue for solving the European financial dilemma. They were no longer exchanging ideas as to how this could best be achieved, but Logan was keeping both informally apprised of any developments and was regularly sending letters to each, most of them identical but some giving Strong somewhat more detail about banking matters.[106]

Hoover continued to offer advice to Hughes and was especially hopeful that the reparations question could be settled now that the settlement of the British debt was being funded. Noting that he had previously protested "publicly and privately that the scheme of settlements, particularly reparations, was entirely unworkable,"[107] he now argued that the Allies had come to recognize that the claims imposed on Germany could never be realized. Even the French, he said, who were not yet willing to reduce the assessed sum as much as others, would

---

102. *New York Times*, November 26, 1922, sec. 9, p. 1.

103. Ibid.

104. Benjamin Strong to Montagu Norman, November 15, 1922, in Benjamin Strong File, CP, HHPL.

105. William Jennings Bryan, "My Forecast on Next Year's Election," *Hearst's International Magazine* (November 1923): p. 23.

106. Copies of the Hoover-Logan correspondence and Logan-Strong correspondence are at the Hoover Presidential Library in West Branch. The originals are located at the Hoover Institute at Stanford University.

107. Herbert Hoover, Memorandum to Charles E. Hughes, February 4, 1923, in Charles E. Hughes File, CP, HHPL.

"probably secure further realization from their experiences in the Ruhr."[108] There was, in other words, a growing appreciation of the "economic trouble" that the allies were making for themselves by "having predicated their fiscal policies upon the collection of impossible sums, with its train of increased domestic debt and inflation."[109] And the time had now come to take constructive steps to secure continental stability, both in the broad economic and humanitarian sense as well as "in the narrow interest of ultimate recovery upon our debts."[110]

On this matter, Hoover's thinking proved to be in line with that of Secretary of State Hughes, and the eventual result, in November 1923, was that the Reparations Commission established two committees, the first to determine a means to balance the German budget and the second to find a way to repatriate German capital from abroad. As a first step toward completing these tasks, the committees were to study Germany's capacity to pay reparations, and the French now agreed to this provided their occupation of the Ruhr would not become the subject of legal scrutiny.

The American members of the First Committee of Experts were Charles G. Dawes and Owen D. Young, both of whom came to Washington to receive their instructions from Hughes and while there also met with Hoover, who furnished them with data, statistics, and his views on the matter. They found Hoover optimistic. But he was also distressed because Hughes had not yet consulted him about any aspect of the study. As he saw it, he could no longer rely on his fellow cabinet officer to "keep him appraised of developments," and he therefore asked Logan to "drop him a note from time to time" with an insider's perspective of the situation. Christian Herter, Hoover's assistant, wrote that the Commerce Department had been practically "told to keep [its] hands off the reparation situation,"[111] even though as "Secretary of Commerce, charged with the duty of determining the economic policies of the Government," Hoover needed to stay informed about what was transpiring.[112] The department's views did not coincide with those of its "friends across the street," and as a result it was receiving only formal documents that appeared to be duplicates of Logan's regular reports to the State Department. Logan, of course, honored Hoover's request as best as he could.

While Hoover may not have been accorded any official role regarding the reparation question, he did continue his efforts to make his influence felt. In January he ordered Charles E. Herring and Walter E. Tower, the Commercial Attaches at Berlin and London respectively, along with Allen G. Goldsmith, the Chief of the Commerce Department's Western European Division, to Paris in order to be available to the American experts in case their assistance was re-

108. Ibid.

109. Ibid.

110. Ibid.

111. Christian Herter to James Logan, December 27, 1923, in Herbert Hoover Archives, Institution on War, Revolution, and Peace, Stanford, CA.

112. Ibid.

quired. Hughes was somewhat taken aback by Hoover's actions. But he conceded that the expertise and information of these gentlemen should be "available to the American members of the Reparation Commission,"[113] and he intimated that if it appeared desirable they could be attached to Logan's staff. The reason this had not been done, he said, was that Herring and Tower already had the designation of Commercial Attaches and did not require any other standing, and that Goldsmith's expectations in the matter had only recently become clear. The State Department, Hughes said, would send a telegram attaching Goldsmith to Logan's staff.[114]

Hughes, however, never followed through on this commitment. Instead, his telegram to Logan stated that Hoover's people would be in Paris for the purpose of information and assistance and that they would "not be attached to the American experts or associated with James Logan."[115] Moreover, they were not to serve on or participate in the work of the committees or sub-committees. Owen Young, who was with Logan in Paris, immediately wired Hoover, "I assume that you have made this arrangement with . . . Hughes and that it is satisfactory to you." He wanted to "make quite sure," he said, since Hughes's cable was not in accordance with what had been expected.[116] In essence, Hughes had reaffirmed his "hands off" policy as far as Commerce Department involvement in the reparation issue was concerned.

Strong fared no better in his attempt to participate in the proceedings. Prior to Young's departure for Europe, he and Strong had discussed the work to be undertaken, and at that time Young had stated that he would like the opportunity to discuss the conclusions of the commission with Strong after the investigation had been completed. Strong had also pointed out that Norman had been urging him to come to London, and in February 1924 Young cabled him that it "would be exceedingly helpful" if he could "visit Norman by March first."[117] On that date, he said, he and Robert Kindersley would be in London to brief him and Norman on Central Bank plans and would like their combined judgement. After receiving the cable, Strong called the State Department to inform Leland Harrison about the cable and to say that he was not willing to go unless Hughes was aware of the trip. But from Harrison he got only a response that there would be no objections provided the consultations would be informal and that he expressed no "opinion as a banker" and made no claim to represent the Federal Reserve Bank, system, or the government."[118] Harrison, moreover, did not wish it to be known that Strong had contacted the State Department. It was to be un-

---

113. Charles E. Hughes to Herbert Hoover, January 10, 1924, in Charles E. Hughes File, CP, HHPL.

114. Ibid.

115. Owen Young telegram to Herbert Hoover, January 10, 1924, in Foreign Finance Conference File, CP, HHPL.

116. Ibid.

117. Benjamin Strong Memorandum for the Record, February 15, 1924, FRBNY.

118. Ibid.

derstood that other business had taken him to London and that any meeting with Young was purely co-incidental.

Pierre Jay then contacted Governor Crissinger of the Federal Reserve Board and advised him about Strong's wish to visit London in response to Norman's request. In doing so, he also mentioned Young's cable and that the matter was strictly confidential but did not refer to Strong's conversation with Harrison. Crissinger responded by saying that the Federal Reserve Board was divided about the wisdom of his going. Some members feared that if it became known that Strong had met Young, the State Department might object and some might conclude that the system was considering or "becoming considered in the whole situation."[119] As a result, Strong felt obliged to tell Harrison about his contacts with the Federal Reserve Board, and upon doing so he found that Harrison was not pleased that the Reserve Board now knew about the proposed meeting with Young. The disclosure, Harrison said, was contrary to the understanding that had been reached about how to handle the matter. But in reply, Strong argued that he had only agreed to two things. One was that he would not disclose that he had consulted the State Department, and the other was the capacity in which he would consult with Young. In his view, the State Department had no right to control what he should tell others about the receipt of Young's cable. If he were to go to Europe, he said, and keep that information from his colleagues "upon the plea that [he] had been pledged to secrecy" by the State Department, he would be guilty of deception.[120] The only question to consider, he thought, was whether the meeting with Young could result in any possible embarrassment to the government.

On February 16 Harrison called Strong to say that the State Department had withdrawn its approval of the proposed meeting with Young, and despite a number of efforts by Strong to effect a change of this ruling the situation remained unchanged. The crux of the matter was confidentiality. Hughes thought that Strong had violated it whereas Strong did not think that he had done so. In England, Norman was not pleased with this turn of events since he had hoped that Strong would be able to come to Europe to aid the "cause of Central banking with the expert committee in Paris."[121] Later, on March 22, Strong did sail for Europe under the guise of getting the "best possible understanding of [Norman's] situation,"[122] but Norman feared that Strong would not arrive in time to accomplish the goal he had in mind.

As it turned out, though, Strong was able to discuss the matter with Young and Logan. In late April, he wrote Pierre Jay from Paris, saying that the great question now before the world was the "Dawes" plan and admitting that his previous prejudices against the plan had been due to a lack of information. Since

---

119. Ibid.

120. Ibid.

121. Montagu Norman to Benjamin Strong, March 14, 1924, Incoming Cable No.60, FRBNY.

122. Benjamin Strong to Montagu Norman, March 14, 1924, Outgoing Cable No. 16, FRBNY.

his arrival, he said, he had been able to study and discuss the report with the authors and found it to be "a most ingenious and in some ways masterful handling of a situation which has always appeared to be 'an irresistible force moving an immovable object.'"[123]   The plan in his opinion afforded France and England the opportunity to join hands, and Germany the opportunity to make a sincere effort to work towards good will and tranquility.

By this time Strong had distanced himself considerably from Hoover while becoming increasingly dependent on Norman, Thomas W. Lamont, James Logan, Parker Gilbert, Owen Young, and Jack Morgan. Through them his views were accurately represented at the London Conference where the financial arrangement for the Dawes Plan were being negotiated. In late August, moreover, Pierre Jay of the FRBNY went to Europe where he remained for several weeks to assist Owen Young. Hughes may have prevented Strong's direct participation in the work of the Commission, but he was not able to stop his influence from being felt.

Nor was Hughes successful in preventing Hoover's ideas from becoming part of the proceedings. They were represented by Goldsmith, Herring, and Tower, who were able to make important contributions. And throughout, Hoover was kept informed by Logan's dispatches. Indeed, the latter's dispatch of September 5 provided a critical and at the same time crucial summary that would have an important bearing on Hoover's subsequent attitude toward Strong and especially toward Norman and the British in coming months.

In his letter, Logan stated that the London Conference had been "one of the most grueling affairs [he had] ever passed through."[124]   There were three Prime Ministers present, earnestly seeking to reach an agreement, yet each had his own difficulties. J. Ramsay MacDonald, in particular, was hampered by Philip Snowden, "who was suspicious and in fact hardly loyal to his chief,"[125]   and who, according to Logan, was dominated by Norman and the City crowd and under their influence constantly threatened to "blow up" the conference. Moreover, Logan said, there was:

> a continual by-play of the bankers with Lamont eating out of Montagu Norman's hand—not knowing exactly what he was doing, but Norman knowing all the time what Lamont was doing. Incidentally, Norman and Snowden were constantly taking the general position "that the American bankers will not agree to this or that," and making a general "sucker" out of Lamont.[126]

As far as the attitude of American bankers was concerned, Logan reported, Clarence Dillon and the City Bank people thought that the proposed loan to Germany was a good one, and in the negotiations they kept challenging Lamont,

---

123. Benjamin Strong to Pierre Jay, April 23-28, 1924, in Strong Papers, FRBNY.

124. James A. Logan to Herbert Hoover, September 5, 1924, in Reparations File, CP, HHPL.

125. Ibid.

126. Ibid.

who was supported by Jack Morgan, concerning his position as the "mouthpiece of American banking opinion."[127] The master mind at the bankers' conference, according to Logan, was Montagu Norman, who had Lamont in his pocket and Hjalmar Schacht, the Governor to be of the new Reichsbank, at his mercy. The whole affair, he thought "was ridiculous and petty in the extreme."[128]

Still, by September the major difficulties had been resolved, and the actions to implement the Dawes Plan were proceeding rapidly. According to Hoover, the plan was the first to attempt to deal with the reparation issue "purely on a commercial and economic basis,"[129] and in his 1924 report on business conditions he pointed out that technical experts from the Department of Commerce, had assisted members of the First Committee of Experts in Paris. He was now optimistic that European stabilization would be achieved and that this would "bring about a revival in world trade and increased consumption of commodities, in which the United States [was bound] to have its share."[130]

European stabilization had been the goal of Hoover, Strong, and a good many others, and for a number of years Hoover and Strong had cooperated in order to make it a reality. In the process, however, their relations had become strained because of differing views of how the American government ought to be involved. Hoover wanted the government to accept some responsibility for regulating foreign loans, while Strong did not. This debate had also affected Hoover's relations with the State Department, which like Strong wanted to avoid any paternalistic actions on the part of the government and thought that Hoover's interference was out of bounds. In addition, it appears that much of Strong's behavior as well as that of Hughes was guided by a keen awareness of the political currents in Washington. They were particularly careful not to give any hint of foreign entanglements or financial commitments, lest they rouse the ire of the isolationists, irreconcilables, and the farm bloc in Congress. In the end, the whole process drove Strong further from Hoover and brought him closer to other central bankers, especially Montagu Norman. It would remain to be seen whether stabilization could be maintained without direct participation by the United States, either directly or through some agent such as the FRBNY.

---

127. Ibid.

128. Ibid.

129. Herbert Hoover, November 17, 1924, Review of Business Conditions during the Year Ending June 30, 1924, CP, HHPL.

130. Ibid.

Chapter 3

Foreign Developments: The Move to Stabilize

> Economic conditions in America give promise of a period of financial stability, thus reducing the risk of dangerous reactions during the initial months of a free gold market, and prevailing sentiment there would be likely to be helpful. We therefore recommend that the early return to the gold basis should forthwith be declared to be the irrevocable policy of His Majesty's Government.
>
> Committee on the Currency [1]

German economic stabilization was the great achievement of 1924, and this, it was hoped, would lead to a general stabilization of exchange rates and ultimately to a period of peace and prosperity in Europe. Some, however, placed greater emphasis on the importance of stabilizing the English economy. This, according to a number of bankers, economists, and leading officials in the United States and Europe, was the key to financial stabilization in Europe as a whole,[2] and in order to achieve stabilization, it was argued, England should return to the gold standard as soon as possible.[3] Ever since 1920 this had been seen by most economists, financiers, and politicians as essential to "any permanent rehabilitation of credit and currency systems." [4]

---

1. Report of the Committee on the Currency and Bank of England Note Issues, February 5, 1925 (hereafter referred to as the "Committee on Currency").

2. Josephine Young Case and Everett Needham Case, Owen Young and American Enterprise (Boston: David R. Godine, 1982), pp. 274-281; see also Melvin Leffler, *The Elusive Quest: America's Pursuit of European Stability and French Security, 1919–1933* (Chapel Hill: University of North Carolina Press, 1979).

3. Benjamin Strong to Pierre Jay, July 10, 1924, FRBNY.

4. At the meeting of the International Financial Conference held at Brussels in 1920, in which 39 nations participated, it was resolved that it was desirable that the countries

John Maynard Keynes, to be sure, was opposed, arguing instead for rigorous control over credit and currency. However, most expert opinion saw no practical alternative to the gold standard, and it was understood by those who counted that the return to gold would be on the same basis that England had left it. Most of those testifying before England's Committee on the Currency favored this, and most considered the nation's honor and prestige at stake in any suggestion that the return should involve a devalued sovereign.[5] The pound, in other words, should again be equal to 123 grains of gold, 11/12 fine, making it equal in value to $4.86 U.S.[6]

In addition to arguments of honor and prestige, advocates of a return to gold on the 1914 basis stressed the need for such a standard in order to bring about desirable price readjustments, provide a defense "against pressure to bring about expansion of credit," and provide a "nexus between the price levels of various countries."[7] An international gold standard, it was said, would be the surest guarantee for both stability in world prices and economic confidence, and both of these were essential to good trade. Currency devaluation could in theory encourage exports. But Britain had to pay "debts abroad, and purchase raw materials from abroad," and it was imperative to invest capital abroad, all things that it could do better if British currency were at a fixed value rather than at a "fluctuating discount."[8] Nor were these arguments persuasive only to British leaders. Visiting the United States in late 1924, Montagu Norman of the Bank of

---

which had left the gold standard return to it. See Edwin W. Kemmerer, *Gold and the Gold Standard: The Story of Gold Money, Past, Present and Future* (New York: McGraw Hill Book Co., 1944) for a discussion of this. See also *Federal Reserve Bulletin*, February 1922, p. 5; Benjamin Strong to Montagu Norman, February 21, 1922, in Strong Papers, FRBNY; and *Reports of the Sub-Commissions on Currency and on Exchange of the Financial Commission of the International Economic Conference, Genoa*, April 20, 1922, pp. 1-4. In the Genoa Conference report it was held that gold was "the only common standard which all European countries could [at that time] adopt," and that it was in the "general interest that European Governments should declare . . . the establishment of a gold standard [as] their ultimate object, and should agree on the programme by way of which they intended to achieve it." A copy is in the Hoover Papers, Logan File, Hoover Institution.

5. Committee on Currency, February 5, 1925. Lord John Bradbury, Chairman of the Committee on Currency, argued that the return to gold "would save Britain from living in a fool's paradise of false prosperity and would force the export industries to become more competitive." See Sir James Grigg, *Prejudice and Judgement* (London: Jonathan Cape Ltd. 1948), pp. 182-184, for the discussion by Bradbury.

6. The legal definition of the gold coin standard was set by Lord Liverpool's Act of 1816. In terms of pure gold 123 grains, 11/12 fine was equal to 113 grains. The pure gold content of the dollar was 23.22 grains.

7. Federal Reserve Bulletin, February 1922, p. 6.

8. Frederick Goodenough, in *Economic World*, February 21, 1925, p. 283.

England reported that "our return to gold is desired by responsible people here and opposed only by certain politicians and cranks" [9]

This chapter examines the effort to bring England back onto the gold standard. Central to the discourse is the impact of the relationship between Benjamin Strong and Montagu Norman to that end. The discussion will also include Hoover's attitude on the gold issue, as well as those of Treasury Secretary Andrew Mellon, economists such as Adolph Miller, bankers, and economic journalists.

In the period immediately preceding the events of late 1924 and early 1925, both Herbert Hoover and Benjamin Strong were firm advocates of getting Britain back on the gold standard. In 1922 Hoover, after a lengthy discussion with Strong, had stated that next to domestic economic problems the matter of greatest concern was European economic stabilization, and part of the solution, he argued, was to be found in the "ultimate establishment of the gold standard"[10] with assistance from the United States either through credits or gold loans.

In March of 1923 Hoover was confident that Britain would soon return to the gold standard. At the time he prepared a statement for Warren Mason of the *London Daily Express* expressing the view that the "restoration of sterling to gold parity will be a great event in world commerce," signalling "the success of indomitable determination to restore their commercial position by the British people," and bringing "mutual benefit to every trading nation."[11] The convertibility of gold into sterling, Hoover argued, would mean that the majority of international trade transactions would be reestablished upon a gold basis, and hence the end of a system under which "constant fluctuation" compelled every merchant "to introduce some extra charge into his trading margins to cover the speculation in exchange,"[12] thereby increasing the cost of distribution and ultimately the cost of living.

Restoration of an international gold standard would also mean the cessation of the flood of gold imports into the United States. Indeed, Hoover had become greatly concerned about the large increase in America's gold reserve. He feared that this contained an element of insecurity, since it could lead to credit and currency expansion, and ultimately an era of unprecedented inflation and speculation. As he put it in a speech to the United States Chamber of Commerce in 1923, the situation could produce an "adverse trade balance" that would "cause this gold to flow abroad with a rush from under our castle of credit and we shall have an unparalleled financial crash."[13] The United States, he thought, would be much better served if its efforts were directed at helping to make foreign currencies convertible into gold, thereby aiding the stabilization of foreign ex-

9. Montagu Norman to Bank of England, January 6, 1925, in Bank of England Revolving Credit File, FRBNY.

10. Hoover, Address Before the United States Chamber of Commerce, May 17, 1922, in Foreign Economic Situation File, CP, HHPL.

11. Hoover to Warren Mason, March 8, 1923, in Gold File, CP, HHPL.

12. Ibid.

13. Address before the 11th meeting of the U.S. Chamber of Commerce, May 8, 1923, New York City, in Public Statements File, CP, HHPL.

change and improvement of foreign commerce. The following month Hoover again expressed his concern about "preventing inflation on the one hand and, for the next few years, preventing too rapid deflation on the other—the preventing of booms and slumps."[14] The gold situation, he argued, had a bearing on this. In the meantime, Hoover thought, this excess gold should not be employed to expand the credit structure, but that it should be "earmarked" for ultimate return to European countries once they were back on a gold basis.[15]

This concern with the inflow of gold was also shared by Andrew Mellon and Adolph Miller. Mellon argued that it "offered a constant temptation to the unsound and inflationary policies," and that if some corrective measures were not taken "it might lead the country into another period of inflation and speculation."[16] And Miller wanted either to require a higher gold reserve against Federal Reserve notes, which would require amending the Federal Reserve Act, or to include a note in all Federal Reserve financial statements that a portion of the gold reserves were being held in trust for other countries. When Strong later briefed Norman on Miller's proposal, Norman "threw up his hands" and remarked "that would mean disaster to you and me."[17]

Miller's remedies were anathema to Strong,[18] but he too was concerned about the dangers of inflation posed by a continued inflow of gold. Given the "excessive gold stock," he told Montagu Norman, "we must entirely ignore any statutory or traditional *percentage* of reserve, and give greater weight to what is taking place in prices, business activity, employment, and credit volume and turnover." Moreover, it was important to recognize the negative impact that this situation could have on Europe, for the effects there could be serious if Americans dissipated their resources in speculation and price boosting.[19] The real answer, he thought, was "to put sterling, yen, guilders, and possibly a few other currencies firmly at gold parity with [the] dollar,—and keep them there,—then with resumption of free gold payment our mutual problems of rates, reserves, credit and prices would largely solve themselves." Inflation, he added, had "no charms which have not been analyzed by Reserve Bank men and rejected as spurious."[20]

---

14. Hoover to J.H. Puelicher, June 13, 1923, in Gold File, CP, HHPL.

15. Irving Fisher in his testimony before the House Committee on Banking and Currency during the Stabilization hearings in 1926 stated that this "was one of the cleaverest suggestions that [had] been made for helping the popular mind reconcile itself to keeping gold apparently idle." House Committee on Banking and Currency, Stabilization, 69th Cong. 1st Sess. (Washington: Government Printing Office, 1926) p. 82.

16. Andrew Mellon to William P.G. Harding, March 6, 1922, FRB, Washington, D.C.

17. Benjamin Strong to Pierre Jay, April 11, 1924, in Strong Papers, FRBNY.

18. Ibid.

19. Benjamin Strong to Montagu Norman, February 2, 1923, in Strong Papers, FRBNY.

20. Ibid.

Like Hoover, Strong had been an active proponent of European economic stabilization as early as 1921 and had continued since then to involve himself in efforts aimed at securing balanced budgets and stable currencies. Also, like Hoover, he was concerned about the possibility of losses by excessive exchange fluctuation. Strong and Hoover had discussed the matter at length in 1922. Following their conversation Strong wrote a lengthy letter to Hoover in which he stated that the task facing them was how to deal with "the causes of the fluctuation in such a way" that it would become safe for those countries which were in the process of or would be shortly returning to the gold standard.[21]

Like Hoover, Strong held that "all trade" had become subject to the possibility of heavy exchange losses, and in a letter to Secretary Mellon he expressed the concern that it was not possible to estimate "how greatly this deterr[ed] the making of contracts involving future payments in foreign currencies . . . but it is considerable." Accordingly, he maintained, "stable exchange rates [would] facilitate foreign trade just as greatly as stable credit facilitates domestic trade."[22] In 1924 he began in earnest to seek a solution to the problem of exchange rates. Where a year ago he had stated that the future was more in England's hands, he now decided that England was to a large extent dependent upon the United States for a constructive plan aimed at achieving monetary recovery and stability.[23] But he was confident that such a plan could be devised, especially in light of the probability of a Republican controlled Congress after the 1924 elections. This, he thought, would usher in a period "of little, if any interference of any serious consequence with the policies and affairs of the Federal Reserve System, except such as may be of a constructive and helpful character."[24]

In late April of 1924 Strong advised Pierre Jay, Chairman of the Board of the FRBNY, that American interests lay "in the earliest possible return to the gold standard, by all nations, especially Great Britain."[25] The latter's interest would also be served, since the action would both benefit its trade and facilitate the repayment of its debt to the United States. Strong then went on to maintain that a mutually beneficial policy could be devised to this end, one that would hold interest rates on the London market higher than those in New York and keep prices in Britain somewhat lower than those in the United States. In addition, he envisioned a credit operation that would be "secret" in the beginning and would be made public only when the pound sterling and the dollar were close to par.[26] These ideas concerning a "purchasing power parity" had been advanced by a number of British bankers, although typically they had been more specific, arguing that price levels in the United States would have to increase by

21. Benjamin Strong to Herbert Hoover, April 22, 1922, in Federal Reserve File, CP, HHPL.

22. Benjamin Strong to Andrew Mellon, May 27, 1924, in Strong Papers, FRBNY.

23. Benjamin Strong to Pierre Jay. April 23-28, 1924, in Strong Papers, FRBNY.

24. Benjamin Strong to Montagu Norman, November 6, 1924, in Strong Papers, FRBNY.

25. Benjamin Strong to Pierre Jay. April 23-28, 1924, in Strong Papers, FRBNY.

26. Ibid.

12 percent in order to produce the outflow of gold that would solve both American and British problems.[27] Strong was hopeful that a way "that could do the job" could be found once the Dawes Plan for German stabilization had been adopted.

In Strong's mind, German stabilization was synonymous with the establishment there of a gold based currency, which, as he saw it, could only be achieved with American credits.[28] Norman was not entirely in agreement. He thought that the stabilization of European currencies on sterling rather than gold might work better, although, since the Dawes Plan stipulated gold he was ready to concede the point and begin improving the dollar-pound exchange ratio as a "definite step towards . . . attaining gold parity."[29] In his reply, Strong seemed somewhat taken aback but tried to be conciliatory. He conceded that the London money market had a better knowledge of German conditions and that it was therefore natural to expect that London would be able to do more for Germany in the way of credit assistance. But, he said, it was more advantageous for the Germans to borrow from New York because it was a gold market and because they should borrow in a "market where the currency is not at a discount with gold so as to escape the loss which might arise through an enhancement of the value of sterling vis-a-vis a German currency at par with gold."[30] In addition, he was concerned that the credit burden would adversely affect the return of sterling to par.

Strong also reminded Norman of his conviction that the Dawes plan represented a first step in European monetary reconstruction. The next step, according to Strong, was debt readjustment on a basis of certainty as well as within the capacity to pay. There might be no great hurry in returning to gold, he said, but there was a need "for taking advantage of the opportunity which now seems to exist for pursuing a policy of progressive stages" that would "facilitate that object, whether it be at the end of months or a year or years."[31]

While Norman wielded a good deal of influence in Britain, he, like all other bankers and economists there, had to await governmental action on the gold question. The Committee on Currency had been studying the question for some time. But in early October 1924, just about the time a committee decision was expected, Britain experienced a unexpected political upheaval in which the Conservatives gained a sweeping majority. One could only wait and see, noted Norman, what the next government would decide. Ideally, a decision on gold should have been reached "along with the coming into effect of the Dawes Report,"[32] but political conditions had postponed any official discussion.

---

27. Benjamin Strong to Piere Jay, April 11, 1924, in Strong Papers, FRBNY.
28. Benjamin Strong to Montagu Norman, June 3, 1924, in Strong Papers, FRBNY.
29. Montagu Norman to Benjamin Strong, June 16, 1924, in Strong Papers, FRBNY.
30. Benjamin Strong to Montagu Norman, July 9, 1924, in Strong Papers, FRBNY.
31. Ibid.
32. Montagu Norman to Benjamin Strong, October 16, 1924, in Strong Papers, FRBNY.

If Norman appeared apprehensive about political conditions in Britain, Strong displayed a good deal of optimism. He maintained that this political "upheaval" actually facilitated a return to the gold standard, especially since the conservatives had garnered a substantial majority in Parliament and this was likely to mean political stability for some time to come.[33] At the same time, Strong pointed out that domestic developments in the United States had resulted in a situation rather favorable to Britain's return to the gold standard. This was due, in part, to a lowering of interest rates in New York, which helped to arrest gold imports into the United States while at the same time facilitating the transfer of foreign loans from London to New York. Strong, however, was quick to add that he could not predict how long this would last. He could not tell "what influences [might] develop which would cause higher rates in this country and wipe out the disparity between the two markets" upon which Britain depended for a successful return to gold.[34]

Others at the FRBNY also desired to see Britain return to gold payment at the earliest possible moment. This was especially true of those who were directly involved with the reparations question and who held that English stabilization had a direct bearing on the success of the Dawes plan. Parker Gilbert, for one, pointed out to Strong that under the Dawes plan Germany was required to meet her obligations in gold marks and that the method of figuring gold marks was on the basis of the fine gold rate on the London market. This, according to Gilbert, meant that in all transactions relating to the Dawes plan, and to some extent other international exchanges, the Reichsmark had to be reduced to gold marks at what amounted to a nearly 1 percent discount. The reason for this, according to Gilbert, was "the fact that gold marks by the London agreement [were] related to an inactive and restricted gold market" in London, which adjusted "itself only tardily to sterling rates on New York."[35] These problems, he said, would be reduced if England were to return to the gold standard.

J.E. Crane at the FRBNY noted to Strong that the discount on the Reichsmark was due to the premium on the London gold quotation, the basis of which was the statutory price of gold in New York at the New York-London cross rate.[36] The value of the gold mark, he suggested, ought to be figured at New

33. Benjamin Strong to Montagu Norman, November 4, 1924, in Strong Papers, FRBNY.

34. Ibid.

35. S. Parker Gilbert to Benjamin Strong, December 24, 1924, in Dawes File, FRBNY.

36. The reduction of the Reichsmark to the gold mark was influenced by the position of sterling on any given day. On December 29 London gold was quoted at 88s 1d. The Reichsmark on that day, according to J.E. Crane of the FRBNY would have been reduced to the gold mark equivalent as follows:

? Reichsmarks = gold mark
1 gold mark = .3842 grams fine
1 gram = .03215074 ozs. fine

York's statutory price at the New York-Berlin cross rate. Moreover, he argued, if England were to return to the gold standard the open market price for gold on the London market would be close to the statutory price, "in which case there would be little difference between the Reichsmark and the gold mark when making calculations according to the terms of the London agreement." Crane added that this would be possible only if the exchange value of the Reichsmark remained as it stood in late December 1924 and noted also that there would still be some fluctuations between the Reichsmark and the gold mark even after England returned to a gold basis because of the cost of shipment of gold from New York to London and Berlin.[37]

The British Government and the Bank of England were equally anxious to solve the exchange problem. Although the British Government had not spoken publicly on the matter, its leaders agreed that failure to resume gold payments would usher in a period of hardship too serious to consider. It would, according to Norman, result in violent currency fluctuations, which would most likely be accompanied by a "progressive deterioration of the values of foreign currencies vis-a-vis the dollar." In addition, he argued, this "would prove an incentive to all of those who were advancing novel ideas for nostrums and expedients other than the gold standard to sell their wares."[38] This, Norman maintained, would be an inducement to Governments to turn to the printing presses and foster yet another round of inflation. In addition there was the danger that the United States might also drain the world of gold, which would result in a period of hardship and privation and possibly lead to social and political unrest.

The acquisition of a substantial portion of the world's gold by the United States was not regarded as a welcome event by American leaders either. Indeed, there was a general apprehension, shared by bankers, economists, members of the Federal Reserve System, and the Finance and Investment Division of the Department of Commerce that there was an excess of gold in the reserves of the Federal Reserve System. Some were fearful that continued acquisition of gold would usher in a period of inflation. Most hoped that an export of gold would begin to take place instead, and Britain's return to gold, it was held, would be beneficial not only from the standpoint of providing a regulatory mechanism for credit and prices but also because it would result in an outflow of gold from the United States that would lessen the dangers of inflation.[39]

---

1 oz. Fine = 1057d. (88s 1d.)
240d. = 19.85 Reichsmarks.

$$\frac{.35842 \times .03215074 \times 1057 \times 19.85}{240} = 1.0074$$

37. J.E. Crane to Benjamin Strong, December 30, 1924, in Dawes File, FRBNY.

38. Benjamin Strong, January 11, 1925, Memorandum for the Record, in Bank of England Revolving Credit File, FRBNY.

39. See, for instance, Federal Reserve Board Report for February 1922; George Seay to Herbert Hoover, May 29, 1923, in Gold File, CP, HHPL; Finance and Investment

The British recognized that they depended to a large degree on American help to solve their financial dilemma, and in December of 1924 Montagu Norman, Governor of the Bank of England, and Sir Alan G. Anderson traveled to the United States for a round of talks with bankers and Treasury officials. In these, they made it clear that they had not been commissioned, either by the British Government or the Bank of England, to conduct official negotiations. But Norman pointed out that there had been a marked improvement in financial and monetary conditions in most of the European countries and that more settled political conditions, coupled with the adoption of the Dawes, plan now justified a more optimistic outlook. He held that "these, together with the definite funding of the British debt to the United States, made the time appropriate for considering what should be done about the gold standard."[40]

The primary reason for the visit was to ascertain whether conditions in the United States in the ensuing two to three years would be favorable to Britain's return to gold, and this meant that Norman and Anderson were especially anxious to consult with Strong and J.P. Morgan about likely American monetary and credit policy in the immediate future. Norman wanted to be assured in particular that the Federal Reserve System would not pursue a deliberate policy of either inflation or deflation.[41] And beyond this he was interested in determining what kind of support would be available to underwrite the return to gold. He pointed out that this could only be accomplished with financial backing by the United States, and to that end he requested a revolving credit in the amount of $500 million.[42]

Strong seemed amenable, and the result was a plan which, as Strong saw it, "met the needs of the situation and requirements of the Federal Reserve Act." Under it there would be an exchange of letters between the FRBNY and the Bank of England, by which the former would agree to provide the Bank of England a gold credit in the amount of $200 million. During the consultations between Norman, Strong, and J.P. Morgan, arrangements were also made for an additional credit to the British Government by J.P. Morgan and Company, a credit that eventually amounted to $100 million.[43] The Federal Reserve Bank would not be involved in this transaction, other than to be consulted from time to time as to the amount of the credit to be used.[44]

Subsequently, Norman made it a point in all discussions at his bank "that before it is decided which credit should from time to time be used, the Federal

---

Division to Christian Herter, June 7, 1923, Gold File, CP, HHPL; Benjamin Strong to Andrew Mellon, May 7, 1924, in Strong Papers, FRBNY.

40. Benjamin Strong, January 11, 1925, Memorandum for the Record, in Bank of England Revolving Credit File, FRBNY.

41. Ibid.

42. Montagu Norman to Bank of England, January 6, 1925, in Bank of England Revolving Credit File, FRBNY.

43. Montagu Norman to Benjamin Strong, April 8, 1925, in Strong Papers, FRBNY.

44. Benjamin Strong, January 11, 1925, Memorandum for the Record, in Bank of England Revolving Credit File File, FRBNY.

Reserve Bank of New York should be consulted."[45] He was also certain that the Bank of England's decisions in that regard would be guided by Strong's advice. In effect, Strong and Norman, with Morgan's help, had hatched the entire scheme, and at Strong's behest three members of the New York Federal Reserve Bank Board, Gates McGarrah, Clarence Woolley, and Owen Young, drafted the correspondence that the Bank of England would later submit to the Federal Reserve Bank in order to formally request the revolving credit arrangement. The final version, though, was prepared by Strong, Norman, and George L. Harrison.[46]

One should also note that D.R. Crissinger, Governor of the Federal Reserve Board, and Dr. Walter Stewart, a member of the Federal Reserve Board, were present during some of the discussions with Norman. According to Strong, they were thoroughly acquainted with all aspects of the proposal and had expressed themselves as being in favor of it.[47] Charles Hamlin, who represented a consensus on the board, noted that the United States ought to favor England's return to the gold standard if for no other reason than from a purely selfish perspective.[48]

In addition, the proposed scheme was discussed at the January meeting of the Open Market Investment Committee, which was attended by all members of the committee as well as Governor Crissinger, Vice-Governor Edmund Platt, and Walter Stewart. The consensus among committee members was that England's return to the gold standard was necessary and inevitable. Moreover, they believed that such a move would be greatly to the advantage of the United States and, according to Strong, were unanimous in their approval of the proposed plan, and in saying that the Federal Reserve System ought to provide assistance in accordance with the guidelines established by the FRBNY. Any arrangement with the Bank of England, the committee said, ought to be made by the FRBNY "and not with the Federal Reserve System, either through the Committee or the individual banks, or through the Federal Reserve Board."[49] It was the committee's view that the matter could be officially brought to the attention of the other Reserve Banks later, at which time they could participate in the venture, if they so desired.[50] Later, after the plan became publicly known, Strong did extend such an offer, and all chose to participate, the Boston Federal Reserve Bank go-

---

45. Montagu Norman to Benjamin Strong, February 10, 1925, in Strong Papers, FRBNY.

46. Benjamin Strong, January 11, 1925, Memorandum for the Record, in Bank of England Revolving Credit File, FRBNY.

47. Benjamin Strong, January 13, 1925, Memorandum for the Record, in Bank of England Revolving Credit File, FRBNY.

48. Hamlin Diary, January 8, 1925.

49. Open Market Investment Policy Excerpts, 1923-1928, in Adolph Miller Personal file, CP, HHPL.

50. Ibid.

ing so far as to request a larger share of participation should another bank fail to take advantage of the opportunity.[51]

On January 12, 1925, Strong and Montagu Norman met with Secretary of the Treasury Andrew Mellon to discuss the plan they had developed. According to Strong, Mellon was in favor of the proposal and stated that:

> he could assure Governor Norman that so far as the Federal Reserve Board and the Administration was concerned they would interpose no objection, and favored the program, and that this applied not only to the transaction contemplated with the Federal Reserve Bank of New York, but, generally, to such credits as might be required of American Bankers.[52]

There was no indication, though, that Mellon would discuss the arrangement with the Secretaries of Commerce or State, both of whom were by this time routinely consulted on arrangements of this type. This disturbed Hamlin, who insisted that it was "a political as well as a banking matter," and that the State Department should be fully informed and its approval secured. There is no indication that the matter was ever brought to the attention of the State Department.[53]

Strong also discussed his proposal with the Federal Reserve Board at its regular meetings on January 10 and April 10 in Washington D.C., meetings, he subsequently maintained, where all members were present and where no one raised any objection to the scheme. Adolph Miller had endorsed the arrangement during an earlier discussion with Hamlin.[54] He was one of those present at both meetings, and at neither did he offer any opposition. Yet within a short time after the April meeting, he began to question both the legality and the wisdom of the action.[55] Perhaps his failure to respond at the April meeting can be ex-

---

51. L. Bleeker to Benjamin Strong, May 27, 1925, Office Correspondence, in Bank of England Revolving Credit File, FRBNY.

52. Benjamin Strong, January 13, 1925, Memorandum for the Record, in Bank of England Revolving Credit File, FRBNY. Charles Hamlin also noted Mellon's approval of the scheme and that Miller, to whom he had spoken, expressed himself in favor of the arrangement as well. Hamlin Diary, January 8, 1925.

53. Hamlin Diary, January 8, 1925. There were a number of discussions between the Commerce and State Department on loans of this type beginning in the latter part of 1924. In May 1925 a number of loans to foreign governments came up for consideration, and a number of these were turned down by the State Department after consulting Mellon and Hoover. The arrangement with the Bank of England was not mentioned in the State Department memorandum which listed all the arrangements under consideration. It appears that Britain was able to secure financial assistance more readily than other governments, something that was not lost on the Italian finance minister, Count Volpi. see Garrard Winston to Benjamin Strong, February 12, 1926, in Strong Papers, FRBNY.

54. Ibid.

55. Benjamin Strong, May 7, 1925, Memorandum for the Record of conversation with Andrew Mellon, in Bank of England Revolving Credit File, FRBNY File; George L.

plained by the fact that there was very little discussion on the details of the arrangement, and very "little participation by the board members in such discussion as was had."[56]

At the January 10 meeting, the proposed arrangement with the Bank of England had been discussed and authorization for it given, but it had deliberately not been made a matter of official record. This was corrected at the May meeting where the Federal Reserve Board passed a resolution noting that approval had been granted on January 10 and directing that it now be made a matter of record. All members were present, and all voted affirmatively with the exception of Adolph Miller, who requested to be recorded as not voting. In a subsequent memorandum for the record, he stated that while he approved of the purpose of the agreement, he "found such grave objection from the standpoint of legality, policy and precedent" that he could not vote for it.[57] This abrupt change appeared extraordinary to Charles Hamlin because Miller had never uttered a word of dissent at any meeting where the subject was discussed. To the contrary, Hamlin believed that Miller had strongly supported the scheme.[58]

Further action would have to await Norman's return to England and the transmittal of the official request from the Bank of England to the New York Federal Reserve Bank. The request was only a formality, but one that had to await the outcome of British Parliamentary action. And it was by no means certain that the British Government would accept the plan as hatched by the charismatic leaders of Lombard and Wall Streets. Norman pointed up that at his bank there was "a general approval in principle but a strange opposition in detail." This would have to be "worn down," and then would "begin the real tug of war . . . parliamentary and political."[59]

In the meantime, secrecy was foremost on the minds of Norman and those working closely on Britain's successful return to gold. Indeed, every effort was made to avoid any public discussion or controversy on the matter. Norman pointed out that consideration of the issue was deliberately postponed until March so that no details of the plan could become public until the United States Congress had adjourned. The British hoped thereby to avert any politically inspired debate, and the attending coverage of it in the press, about the specific details of the arrangement arrived at between London and New York. This was perhaps not so much out of fear of what Americans might think about the matter, but more so of its effect on British public opinion, and therefore Parliament's receptivity to the scheme.

Harrison to Benjamin Strong, May 21, 1925, in Bank of England Revolving Credit File, FRBNY.

56. Walter L. Eddy to Benjamin Strong, May 26, 1925, in Bank of England Revolving Credit File, FRBNY.

57. Ibid.

58. Hamlin Diary, May 18, 1925.

59. Montagu Norman to Benjamin Strong, January 24, 1925, in Strong Papers, FRBNY.

Norman was confident that once discussion on the matter began it would not take long to reach a Cabinet decision, at least not in principle. However, Norman thought that it would take from two to three weeks to settle the administrative details. He held that if consideration began by the end of March a final decision would not be likely before early or mid April. In the meantime he hoped to keep the matter secret, and "of course out of Parliament till the end."[60] His main concern was to delay the political and Parliamentary tug of war for as long as possible.

The latter could have important effects on public attitudes, and Strong was ever mindful of public opinion, cautioning that any disclosure on the subject must be made in such a manner as to evoke only a positive response. He thought it especially crucial that any public statement on the subject should make it categorically clear that the arrangement between the two banks of issue, New York and London, was a "purely bank transaction," relating to the monetary problem with which they were confronted. He also wanted it to be clearly understood that any credit extended to the British Government was a distinctly separate transaction, arranged by the British Government through its fiscal agent, J.P. Morgan, with Morgan's consortium in the United States.[61]

There was also some concern that considerable difficulty might arise in regard to the amount of credit extended by the FRBNY and that it might be best to state openly the amount and provide some details about the nature, if not the specifics, of the plan. Yet it was considered prudent to guard against making any statement that could be perceived, by the public, as constituting an agreement or commitment regarding future monetary policy as it related to domestic credit or market conditions. Much, it was thought, depended upon the spirit of cooperation between the principals.[62] This was the key to success, and the British were not too keen on releasing any statements to the public other than what was likely to be said in Parliament.[63]

Still, Strong, was adamant on the point of some type of public statement. Sensitive to public reaction, he recognized that the arrangement between the two banks could not be kept secret beyond a certain point. Once the debates on the subject began in Parliament the proposed scheme would become known to the public, and he feared that silence on the part of the participants would only lead to suppositions and misleading information in the press, which would force some sort of corrective action on the part of the banks. The undertaking was far

---

60. Montagu Norman to Benjamin Strong, March 21, 1925, Outgoing Cable No. 87, Bank of England.

61. Benjamin Strong to Montagu Norman, April 15, 1925, Incoming Cable No. 64, Bank of England.

62. Ibid.; Benjamin Strong to Montagu Norman. April 15, 1925, in Strong Papers, FRBNY; Benjamin Strong to Montagu Norman, March 25, 1925, Incoming Cable No. 48, Bank of England.

63. Montagu Norman to Benjamin Strong, April 17, 1925, Outgoing Cable No. 10, Bank of England; Benjamin Strong to Montagu Norman. March 25, 1925, Incoming Cable No. 48, Bank of England.

too important to conceal, and a failure to address the matter would only be treated with skepticism. As Strong put it:

> it is impossible to keep the fact of our participation from disclosure, and the minute it is disclosed, we will be flooded with inquiries. We cannot deny participation, and if we cannot admit it, we are placed in the uncomfortable position of simply declining to give any information. Once we take that position we will invite adverse criticism by a large segment of the press, and likely some sort of inquiry later in Washington.[64]

Norman was not unsympathetic, but he was concerned about reaction in his country and sought to keep dissemination of information to a minimum. There had, of course, been discussion of a return to the gold standard in British economic journals for some time. In December 1924, for instance, the *Economist* had noted that events pointed to an early return to parity, and therefore the return to the gold standard by Britain. This was judged to be a positive development in that it would be a "contribution to world reconstruction" second only in importance to the adoption of the Dawes Plan.[65] Other discussion had followed, and Norman understood that an interest by the press in the matter was bound to continue. He also recognized that there was a good possibility that some details of the arrangement would come out during the two readings of the bill in Parliament, but at the same time he was fearful that a statement released by New York relative to the arrangements could pose problems, especially if it came prior to the second reading of the bill and if the tenor of the release were such as to arouse criticism and debate. In order to avoid controversy and needless questions, Norman implored his counterpart in New York to prepare a release that would be but a mere outline of the message that the Chancellor of the Exchequer would deliver to Parliament on the 28th of April. This was the spirit of cooperation indeed.[66]

Strong did not disappoint his ally, for on April 29 he released a statement to the press stating that "in connection with the reestablishment of a free gold market in London" the New York Federal Reserve Bank had completed an arrangement, in which other Reserve Banks would participate, "to place $200 million at the disposal of the Bank of England if desired." No mention was made of the arrangement between the British Government and J.P. Morgan.[67]

At a news conference the following day, Secretary of Commerce Herbert Hoover expressed satisfaction at the pending return of England to the gold standard and predicted that the majority of the international trade would now move

---

64. Benjamin Strong to Montagu Norman. April 24, 1925, in Strong Papers, FRBNY.

65. *Economist*, December 6, 1924.

66. Montagu Norman to Benjamin Strong, April 24, 1925, in Strong Papers, FRBNY.

67. Press Release, April 29, 1925, in Bank of England Revolving Credit File, FRBNY.

on a gold basis. He was hopeful that this action would result in stable prices, which "should redound to the benefit of commerce and industry throughout the world." "The most certain effect," he thought, would be "to reduce the volume of speculative hazard in international trade" and eliminate the "risks that must be taken with currency fluctuating value."[68] Hoover's remarks, though, did not mention the part played by the American banking community in the undertaking, an omission that is puzzling since he probably knew about it and had earlier expressed himself to be in favor of assisting the British in their return to gold parity. One possible explanation is that the omission was deliberate and that it resulted from Miller's stand on the matter and Hoover's desire not to undermine Miller's position on the legality of Federal Reserve participation in providing credit guarantees. It is also possible that Hoover shared Miller's concerns but did not feel it appropriate, as a member of the Administration, to criticize publicly the policy being pursued.[69]

The announcement did elicit a critical inquiry from Charles E. Mitchell, President of the National City Bank of New York. The whole arrangement, he thought, was an unusual step in the development of the Federal Reserve System, and he wondered if it was justified by the Federal Reserve Act. He would appreciate, he said, a memorandum outlining the nature of the agreement and the section of the Act pursuant to which it was carried out.[70] Strong, however, while expressing regret that the announcement should have led to confusion on the part of Mitchell, would not provide the requested information. He would say only that the agreement was carried out in accordance with the provisions contained in Article 14 of the law.[71] Mitchell was not satisfied with such a curt dismissal, but he had no intention of criticizing Strong publicly. Instead, he made it clear that he was sympathetic to the aims of the agreement but questioned whether the same results could not have been established through normal banking channels.

Mitchell also noted that the Federal Reserve Bank had a habit of edging in on members' "fields for profits," a charge that had recently been levied by the

---

68. Herbert Hoover Press Conference, April 30, 1925, Public Statements, HHPL.

69. Relations between the FRBNY and certain Board members, among them Miller and Cunningham, had become strained. Moreover, there was a growing suspicion that Miller was Hoover's man. Charles Hamlin noted that Hoover claimed that Coolidge was disturbed about the relation of the FRBNY and the Reserve Board in regard to open market operations. Additionally, he feared that New York dominated the Reserve Board. Hamlin, though, argued that if there had been any domination, Miller was the one who had been dominated. Hamlin Diary, January 27, 1925, and February 5, 1925.

70. Charles Mitchell to Benjamin Strong, April 30, 1925, in Bank of England Revolving Credit File, FRBNY.

71. Benjamin Strong to Charles Mitchell, May 1, 1952, in Bank of England Revolving Credit File, FRBNY.

American Bankers' Association at their annual meeting in Chicago in 1924.[72] In his reply to Mitchell, Strong attempted to minimize the importance of this point. But privately he noted to Norman that this was one of the reasons, "although possibly a minor one," why he had hoped the bankers' credit would be larger.

The most scathing criticism by Mitchell concerned the nature of the agreement, which, in his estimation, was questionable. About this he raised three points:

> First . . . having made an agreement that goes over a long period, under which it is proposed that you do things contemplated by Section 14 of the Act, for that Act contemplates a short period for any obligation on your part . . . second, I doubt if Section 14 ever contemplated a major operation having to do with stabilization of the currency of another country and involving so large a percentage of the reserve of member banks with you; and third . . . it might be difficult for you to explain . . . legally how you justify the placing of so large a sum at the disposal of the Bank of England if desired.[73]

Strong took issue with this assessment and insisted that the reserve banks were "specifically" provided with broad powers in regard to transactions with foreign correspondents, that the very breadth of these powers indicated that such banks "were expected to function in a broad manner," and that inevitably they "should have to exercise some of these powers" from time to time. Failure to do so, Strong insisted, could well be interpreted as a failure to carry out the provisions of the Federal Reserve Act, which would benefit the member banks whose earnings would thereby be increased.[74] This, though, contradicted his statement to Norman in July 1922, when they were discussing FRBNY participation in a meeting of international bankers called for by the Financial Commission of the Geneva Conference. At the time he pointed out that he had to avoid giving the impression that the Federal Reserve System was "prepared to embark upon a program of extending credit to the various central banks in the world as they might need it for exchange or other purposes."[75] This, he said, would be out of the question because the Federal Reserve Act would not permit it.

In reply to Strong's letter of May 1, Mitchell had also noted that much of the criticism could be eliminated if he could be supplied with a memorandum of the actual transaction. A number of individuals, he said, had an interest in the matter and wished to discuss it. But it was difficult to engage in any realistic

---

72. Charles Mitchell to Benjamin Strong, May 8, 1925, in Bank of England Revolving Credit File, FRBNY; Open Markets Investment Policy Excerpts, 1923-1928, p.10, in Adolph Miller Personal File, CP, HHPL.

73. Ibid.

74. Benjamin Strong to Charles Mitchell, May 28, 1925, in Bank of England Revolving Credit File, FRBNY.

75. Benjamin Strong to Montagu Norman, July 22, 1922, in Strong Papers, FRBNY.

dialogue without knowing any of the facts behind the agreement.[76] Strong did not provide the requested memorandum, but he did outline the basic aspects of the agreement in his reply to Mitchell.

The credit arrangement also drew criticism from Oscar T. Crosby, former Assistant Secretary of the Treasury during the Wilson Administration. In an article published by the *New York Times* on May 5, 1925, Crosby questioned both the legality and the propriety of the plan. The transaction, he thought, was "directly charged with political value," since the credits made available to the Bank of England were to be made available to the British Government.[77]

In this assessment, Crosby was clearly on the mark. While in New York, Norman had sent a cable to his bank in which he assumed that the "Bank of England" would simply act as agent for the British Government. And Strong knew this. A file copy of the transmission bears a disclaimer by Strong saying that it was sent by Norman "without consultation before sending" and that it in no way involved any commitment or representation on Strong's part.[78] Moreover, during the latter part of April Norman wrote to Strong that he was only a go-between and that he had "been trying right along to find a mean between the wishes of the Treasury" and Strong.[79] After reading Crosby's article, Strong also advised the Bank of England of the criticisms, both as to legality and propriety, while at the same time reiterating his admonition of April 15 to Norman that the credit should be understood as having been extended to the Bank of England and not the Government.[80] The fact remained that the money would be available to the British Government, if it so desired.

Crosby was further disturbed by Governor Crissinger's position that the Federal Reserve Board had no right of supervision in the case. Crosby could not see how a transaction of this magnitude and of such international importance could be outside the control of the board "whose members are full fledged government officials." There was also an implication of collusion between Strong and Morgan in Crosby's attack, especially when he noted that Winston Churchill's statement could reasonably lead one to conclude that the two transactions were not at all separate.[81]

Not everyone agreed with Crosby, and the following day the *New York Times* carried an article indicating that bankers and financiers held the New

---

76. Charles Mitchell to Benjamin Strong, May 8, 1925, in Bank of England Revolving Credit File, FRBNY.

77. *New York Times*, May 5, 1925, p. 2.

78. Montagu Norman to Bank of England, January 6, 1925, in Bank of England Revolving Credit File, FRBNY.

79. Montagu Norman to Benjamin Strong, April 24, 1925, in Strong Papers, FRBNY.

80. Benjamin Strong to Montagu Norman, Incoming Cable No. 64, Bank of England; Benjamin Strong to Montagu Norman, May 7, 1925, Incoming Cable No. 80, Bank of England.

81. *New York Times*. May 5, 1925, p. 2.

York Bank's actions to be well within the Federal Reserve Act.[82] Still, Strong was infuriated, and he now proceeded to accuse Adolph Miller of having incited the attack in the press by leaking confidential information to Crosby. He was, of course, aware of and greatly disturbed by Miller's change of attitude in regard to the proposed loan; and the fact that Miller had raised the same concern as Crosby concerning the loan's ultimate beneficiary was to him more than just a coincidence. In a subsequent telephone conversation with Secretary Mellon, Strong stated that "to give a man the material with which to make a public statement involving an attack upon the bank" was " so serious a breach of good faith with us" that charges should be preferred against Miller with the President. He questioned whether Miller understood the serious step he had embarked upon "when he laid the foundation for a public attack."[83]

Mellon, though, urged caution in the matter and suggested that a private talk between himself and Miller might do some good. Accordingly, he did confront Miller about the matter, only to have Miller deny any complicity and argue that Strong himself, through his statements to the press, had provided the information upon which the attack was based. He also pointed to the statement made earlier in the House of Commons. There Churchill was quoted as saying, "I have made arrangements to obtain, if required, credits from the United States of not less than $300 million."[84]

Criticism also came from the *Commercial and Financial Chronicle*, which praised Crosby for his action, but thought that it did not go far enough. The *Chronicle* stated that it could not see where the Federal Reserve Bank obtained the authority to place $200 million at the disposal of the Bank of England, regardless of the motivation. The action appeared to be illegal, and even if by chance it should be within legal bounds, the *Chronicle* held, it was not in accord with the spirit of the law, and "certainly alien to the purpose of the Reserve Act."[85]

In addition, the *Chronicle* took exception to the notion that the loan should be viewed as an ordinary transaction between two banks of issue, as Strong was insisting. On the contrary, it was distinctive and exceptional and "in fact sui generis," and the authority to engage in such an "unusual" and "extraordinary"

82. *New York Times*. May 6, 1925, pp. 22, 37.

83. Benjamin Strong, May 7, 1925, Memorandum for the Record of Conversation with Andrew Mellon, in Bank of England Revolving Credit File, FRBNY. Strong later told Hamlin that Mellon knew that Miller must have given Crosby the information on which the letter was based because one day Oscar Crosby asked over the phone for an interview. Mellon responded that he could not see him that day but would see him "tomorrow," and that Crosby replied, "Why, you are going with me to Warrenton, VA. tomorrow!" Mellon then asked Crosby with whom he thought he was speaking and that he replied "to Dr. Miller," and that Crosby was surprised to find that he had been speaking with Mellon. Hamlin Diary, May 4, 1927.

84. Benjamin Strong, May 8, 1925, Memorandum for the Record of Conversation with Andrew Mellon, in Bank of England Revolving Credit File, FRBNY.

85. *Commercial and Financial Chronicle*, May 23, 1925, pp. 2595-2597.

transaction could never be implied or even inferred. There had to be a specific grant of power, and none was in evidence. Nor had Congress intended to make one. If it had done so inadvertently, then such authority "ought to be speedily taken away."[86] For neither the Federal Reserve banks, nor the Federal Reserve Board, nor even the President and the Administration should be "vested with such huge and prodigious attributes and authority." They should not be allowed to "exercise unchecked control in the putting out of 'obligations of the United States'" with such control "to be used willy or nilly at blind discretion."[87]

"Rumors" were soon circulating that the Bank's actions would be challenged when Congress reconvened,[88] and eventually in 1926, the House Banking and Currency Committee would convene a hearing on the credit arrangement between the FRBNY and the Bank of England. In the meantime, Strong was not without support. Business interests were said to be generally supportive of the agreement, but to believe that Strong ought to provide an explanation of the policy so as to avoid suspicion and trouble later on.[89] And in London the *Economist* reported that the majority of those businessmen and bankers who understood the significance of the event were convinced of the value of Federal Reserve involvement and applauded the agreement. According to it, popular sentiment in the United States held that the one great deterrent to international trade and prosperity, that of unstable currencies, had been removed, and that this had "done as much to create solid confidence in the future as anything since the Armistice."[90]

The *Economist* went on to say that the decision by Great Britain to return to the gold standard validated the belief in its financial greatness, and to praise Strong and Norman for their active efforts and years of patient planning. It also commended the Federal Reserve authorities for their part in the process. The latter, it noted, had been subjected to criticism, both in the United States and abroad, because of their credit policies. But these criticisms had been dismissed by "competent judges" and were rendered insignificant "now that the project for which such steady efforts have been made has come to fruition."[91]

The *Economic World*, an American financial weekly, was also supportive of Strong and the involvement by the FRBNY. It argued that involvement by the Federal Reserve Banks "was not only a proper and praiseworthy assistance" from the United States aimed at ensuring the "success of an all-important measure of world economic stabilization, but also an action amply justified on grounds of our own national self-interest pure and simple."[92] It noted no irregu-

---

86. Ibid.

87. Ibid.

88. J.F. Fowler to W. Randolph Burgess, June 1, 1925, in Bank of England Revolving Credit File, FRBNY.

89. Ibid.

90. *Economist*, May 9, 1925, p. 912.

91. Ibid.

92. *Economic World*, May 30, 1925.

larities in the transaction and dismissed the position taken by the *Chronicle* as one not to be taken seriously. Furthermore, it argued that the tenor of the criticisms was not new and that similar attacks had been levied by "sundry advocates of fundamental changes in the Federal Reserve Act."[93] The *Economic World* then praised the arrangement as being advantageous to the entire world.

Amid the various criticisms that were voiced, there was one issue that was not raised, at least not publicly, and that was the question of parity or the definition of the pound in terms of gold, which would necessarily have a direct impact on the pound's relationship to the currencies of other countries on the gold standard. There was broad agreement that Britain's return to gold standard would be of great advantage to the international community and was an essential factor in making it possible for countries such as Germany to remain on the gold standard. Though, absent from the discourse was the view that this would be beneficial only if the return was at a rate that Britain could support, a rate, in other words that reflected the disparity in price levels between Britain and the United States. The assumption was that Britain would stabilize at the pre-war parity, and most pundits considered this to be desirable. The *Economic World*, for one, stated that financial conditions favored Britain's return to gold at the old parity. There had, it said, been no depreciation of the intrinsic value of sterling through currency inflation, and the "favorable balance on her total interchanges with the rest of the world" brought the "exchange value of the pound almost, if not quite back to mint parity."[94] Moreover, expert advice had evidently come to the conclusion that Britain's gold reserve was sufficient to support the exchange value of sterling at the pre-war parity.

The only critical discussion of note that was had on the subject of parity was that by John Maynard Keynes, Reginald McKenna, and several others during their appearance before the Committee on Currency. They did point out the difficulties.[95] But by the Committee and by people like Norman and Strong, they were considered to be monetary heretics. Strong argued that the restoration of sterling to parity with the dollar on a gold basis would have a "distinctly beneficent effect" on a large portion of the trading world,[96] and the Committee accorded little significance to their views.

Privately, there had also been some discussion on the matter of disparity between Strong and Norman, first in 1922 and then again in November of 1924.

---

93. Ibid. On advocating changes in the system, see, for instance, D.R. Crissinger to Louis McFadden, May 27, 1925, in Federal Reserve File, CP, HHPL.

94. *Economic World*, May 2, 1925, p. 616.

95. Keynes and McKenna argued that a return to pre-war parity would seriously overvalue the Sterling in terms of the dollar and "that the achievement of external equilibrium would consequently entail a deflation of British wages and prices, and that such a deflation would bring prolonged strikes and a permanent contraction in some of the country's heavy industries." Stephen V.O. Clark, *Central Bank Cooperation 1924-1931* (Federal Reserve Bank New York, 1967) p. 73.

96. Benjamin Strong to Montagu Norman, February 21, 1922, in Strong Papers, FRBNY.

But in these exchanges, Strong had taken the position that the differential in prices was sure to adjust itself. Most of the discussion concerning it, he told Norman, was nonsense. For in reality, if Britain could force sterling back to par, it would be in a better position to develop its export trade. Admittedly, he said, there would be some problems. Manufacturing costs would take time to adjust; some manufacturers would be at a disadvantage "against those who suddenly got the benefit of lower prices for raw materials caused by the higher purchasing power of the sterling;"[97] and overseas suppliers would be favored. But this would only be a short term inconvenience. The situation would soon correct itself, and to help it to do so Strong suggested that British manufacturers should mark down the prices of their goods and take a loss in order to be competitive in international markets. In any case, Strong told Norman, the "shock to [British] business establishments would [most likely not] be any greater as a result of an advance in sterling from [$]4.50 to [$]4.87, than that already experienced in recent months" when sterling advanced from $4.30 to $4.50, "or the greater shock resulting from the fluctuations which occurred when sterling advanced to above [$]4.70 and then declined to below [$]4.30."[98]

Given the position of the Committee on Currency and Norman's attitude on the issue, one can safely say that Strong was preaching to the converted. One can also argue, based on the Committee's Report, that it was a foregone conclusion that Britain would return to the gold standard at pre-war parity or a pound-dollar exchange rate of $4.86. There were some who later argued that this rate was too high, as British prices were far above their 1914 levels and the pound-dollar exchange rate from 1920 to 1925 had been a fluctuating one, at one time falling below $3.20 and never reaching $4.86. The latter rate was sustainable only if British domestic prices were deflated or prices in the United States inflated. And there were some critics who later claimed that Norman's real objective was to achieve price inflation in the United States in order to better Britain's competitive position. Apparently, the Committee on Currency also expected rising prices in the United States. Its report rejected a "credit policy calculated to bring down domestic prices" and argued that the same practical result could be expected through "a policy designed merely to prevent them from rising concurrently with a rise elsewhere."[99]

In any event, Strong's discussion of the price differential in November of 1924 was the last time that he brought it up. Nor did any other members of the Federal Reserve System, or for that matter members of the banking community,

---

97. Benjamin Strong to Montagu Norman, November 4, 1924, in Strong Papers, FRBNY.

98. Ibid.

99. Committee on the Currency, February 5, 1925. Not all of the criticism was voiced after the fact. According to an entry made by Hamlin in his diary on May 5, 1924, Governor Harding stated that he was "certain that the movement for lower rates at N.Y. was inspired by Governor Strong, now sick in Gov. Norman's home in London; that Norman wanted inflation in the United States to put us more nearly on parity w. Gt. Britain."

appear fearful that the overvaluation of the pound placed the British in a precarious position internationally. Of primary concern to Strong, Hoover, and those concerned about international exchange fluctuations was the restoration of the gold standard.

Nor did Miller, who had earlier challenged the legality of Federal Reserve involvement in Great Britain's return to the gold standard, appear to be concerned about the parity level. Publicly, moreover, he was now ready to credit America and American financiers with playing a significant role in the restoration of the British gold standard. In cooperating with Great Britain, he said, the United States had "supplied a constructive factor of the greatest consequence in helping to place the economic and financial affairs of the world on a safe and solid basis."[100] The action represented one of the most significant steps in the direction of international economic stabilization since the cessation of hostilities in 1919 and was "an illuminating and gratifying sign of how far toward completion the whole process of post-war readjustment had run its course."[101] France, Italy, and Russia, he noted, had not yet returned to the gold standard. But the self-governing commonwealths of the British Empire and a number of European countries had followed Britain's lead, and the time was approaching when the standard could be restored "to the primary position it occupied before the war as an international regulator of money and exchange."[102]

The active efforts by the Federal Reserve System, in particular the FRBNY, to aid in Britain's return to the gold standard had an impact on the continuing evolution of the System. England's return to the gold standard was not only sought by monetarists and bankers there, but also by a number of leading bankers, economists, and public figures such as Hoover, Mellon, and Strong in the United States. None, though, appeared to be as determined as Strong to bring about this achievement. In the process he increased the influence of the FRBNY within the Federal Reserve System and the international financial community. At the same time he continued to strengthen his hold on the Open Market Investment Committee. Moreover, in the process Strong's influence and prestige were greatly enhanced.

What appeared to be a victory for Benjamin Strong, however, would have far reaching consequences. The scheme developed by him and Norman would require continued support by New York, which would make greater demands on domestic economic policies than he could have foreseen. For the time being, though, and despite the objections to Federal Reserve participation by some, such as Crosby, Miller, and Roberts, England's return to gold and the FRBNY arrangement with London to make it possible were heralded as a great achievement. Following the debate, such as was had, the public controversy abated. The exchange of pejorative epithets over FRBNY involvement was reduced to a few murmurs of hostility and suspicion, and attention now shifted to yet another

100. *New York Times*, May 14, 1925, p. 21.
101. Ibid.
102. Ibid.

facet of the debate over Federal Reserve policy, that of easy money and speculation.

Chapter 4

The Elusive Demon: Speculation

> As a nation our businessmen, bankers, and public officials have gained enormously during the past four years in understanding of the basic factors which create healthy prosperity as distinguished from overexpansion, as well as in understanding of their responsibility in the matter.
>
> Herbert Hoover, January 1, 1925[1]

Little did Herbert Hoover realize when he uttered these words that within less than a year he would be greatly concerned about what he considered to be the questionable policies implemented by some of the very people he praised. By November 1925 Hoover was clearly disenchanted with several bankers and public officials involved in fiscal policy formulation and whom he held responsible for the orgy of speculation then underway. He was concerned especially with the policies of the Federal Reserve Board which, he thought, were not directed, as they should have been, at stemming the tide of speculation. Hoover believed in the Federal Reserve System and its potential to provide responsible fiscal governance, but he was clearly disappointed by its failure to respond to what he considered to be a potential crisis of epic proportions.

This chapter examines the impact of England's return to the gold standard on Federal Reserve policy. Central to the discussion will be the developing controversy over the rediscount rate, especially the arguments concerning its effectiveness as a tool in controlling speculation and inflation. Benjamin Strong, who had earlier advocated employing the rediscount rate in order to curb speculation and inflation, began, instead, to question the effectiveness of the practice. Increasingly, his efforts were directed at supporting England's return to gold, and

---

1. *Economic World*, January 3, 1925. pp.4-6.

he did so, it has been argued, at the expense of domestic requirements. The Federal Reserve System, which had been hampered from the beginning by contending interests, found the rift between the factions deepening during the controversy.

The economy had declined sharply in late 1923 and early 1924, and the effects of this on the business community were not ignored by Reserve Board members in Washington or the Governors of the various Reserve Banks. Remedial action, they believed, would have to be taken, and one method open to the system was to make more credit available to the business community through a lowering of rediscount rates at the various Reserve Banks.

The FRBNY, located in the financial center of the United States, was particularly concerned about the downturn in business and during April 1924 sought to reduce its rediscount rate from 4 1/2 percent to 4 percent. D.R. Crissinger, Chairman of the Federal Reserve Board, had attended the New York Federal Reserve District meeting and upon his return to Washington on April 26 notified the other members of the Federal Reserve Board of the New York Bank's desire to lower its rate. The request was considered, and after two days of discussion it was decided to allow the reduction if, at their next meeting, the New York Directors still desired to do so.[2] On April 30 at 3 p.m. the new rate went into effect.

During the ensuing months the board continued its policy of reducing rediscount rates. By June 12, the FRBNY had further reduced its rate to 3 1/2 percent, and on August 8 it made yet another reduction to 3 percent. At the same time the board opted to increase its purchases of securities through its open market operations. The result was cheap and abundant credit, which aided in the recovery of business and in increasing industrial production.[3] The board had been successful in stimulating business, and it now faced the task of restraining the credit once expansion was under way.

By late 1924 the Reserve Board was confronted by a dilemma. On the one hand, there was an increasing awareness of the need to restrict the amount of available credit. Yet this decision, once undertaken, was likely to lead to criticism on the part of businessmen who had benefited from the abundance and low cost of credit. They clearly would be opposed to any increase in the interest rates. Moreover, there was a potential risk that the business recovery that had just begun might be stalled or, in the worst case scenario, reversed by the restriction and increased cost of credit. The way the board would handle this situation in 1925 was, by some accounts, the acid test of its ability to regulate credit, and in a larger sense the business cycle.

The lowering of interest rates resulted in the availability of large amounts of credit, both actual and potential. But as the condition of business and industry improved, their demand for credit decreased. This created the possibility for idle funds to flow to other sectors of the economy, such as speculative markets.

---

2. Hamlin Diary, April 28, 1924.

3. See, for instance, Benjamin Beckhart, ed., *The New York Money Market* (New York: Columbia University Press, 1932) for a good discussion on this.

There was a considerable boom underway on the New York Stock Exchange, and this was accompanied by a startling increase in the use of credit in the sale of securities. A number of interior banks who had an abundance of credit sent funds to New York for use in "call loans" to stock purchasers. At the same time, there was also speculation in some forms of real estate, especially along the Atlantic seaboard and in the "Florida land boom." Some, such as Adolph Miller and Herbert Hoover, feared that, unless checked, the speculative fever would have catastrophic consequences.

The situation was further complicated by the international economic situation, including England's return to the gold standard and its continuing struggle to shore up the pound. The Federal Reserve System had committed its resources to that end, and the *Chronicle*, which had been critical of this involvement, now argued that the arrangement between New York and London was giving rise to "another rampant stock speculation" that could have disastrous results. "At such a time" it declared, "the prospect of a further saturation of note issues through the entry of the Reserve Banks into the foreign field cannot be viewed with unconcern."[4] In effect, the successful return by Britain to the gold standard would call for a joint Anglo-American monetary policy even though the two nations' domestic requirements were not the same. There would have to be lower interest rates in New York than in London regardless of American conditions. As Norman noted to Strong:

> I agree that we shall need some sort of an understanding between us as to the future gold policy. I think you are helping to this end if you keep your rates as low as possible and lend freely to the rest of the world as your market is now doing. . . . So, for the moment, you must continue with easy money and foreign loans and we must hold tight until we know . . . what the [future gold] policy of this country is to be.[5]

It was also evident by early 1925 that two factions had developed. The first, guided by Herbert Hoover and Adolph Miller, sought to increase interest rates in order to put a halt to speculation and thereby safeguard the domestic economy. The second, led by Benjamin Strong, called for the continuation of low rates and was sympathetic to England and the larger international economy. It also included some who feared that increased interest rates would be detrimental to business and industrial interests. Among the latter was Charles Hamlin, who had stated that he was sympathetic to aiding Britain in her recovery, but had also sought to separate the international aspects of the problem from the domestic ones. "The question" he said, "seems to be whether it is necessary or desirable to increase rates on agriculture, commerce and industry, possibly penalizing them by making credit more expensive, for the sole purpose of checking stock ex-

---

4. *Commercial and Financial Chronicle*, May 23, 1925, p. 2597.

5. Montagu Norman to Benjamin Strong, October 16, 1924, in Strong Papers, FRBNY.

change and real estate speculation."[6] The choice facing the Federal Reserve Board, especially during the second half of 1925, was whether to increase the rate or stay with easy money.

At the October 24, 1925 meeting of the Open Market Committee, Strong had noted that the "easy money" policy begun in 1923 had facilitated the transfer of funds from the United States to London, played an important part in the recovery of the pound to date, and been instrumental in creating the "favorable market for the floatation of foreign loans."[7] In essence, the disparity in rates made it possible to "substantially close the London market to foreign borrowing."[8] In Strong's view, the "easy money" policy had also benefited the United States by lessening the severity of the business recession in 1924.[9] But on this he had been challenged by critics who held that the policy had led to the recession and also to the speculative boom in the commodities market in late 1924 and early 1925.

The *Chronicle*, for one, sought to determine the role played by the Federal Reserve System in permitting or provoking the "gigantic speculation in both grain and stocks," which it noted "was in progress for so many months [and] has signally and utterly collapsed." The *Chronicle* held that it was made plain that not only was speculation of the "most aggravated kind" allowed to flourish, but that Federal Reserve banks stimulated the speculation by making extra credit facilities available. It was argued that the easy money policy of the Federal Reserve System during 1924 and early 1925 had without a doubt served as "the most potent influence" in fostering speculation. Moreover,

> no more reckless speculation has ever been carried on in stocks on the Stock Exchange than which has been spread before our eyes during the last three or four months and as for the speculation in grain . . . so wholly uncontrolled, that we doubt that any occasion in the past can be found that even closely approaches it for sheer recklessness and abandon.[10]

Not surprisingly, the monetary policy initiated by Strong was welcomed by Norman, who in October of 1924 had urged his New York counterpart to continue with "easy money and foreign loans." He noted that domestic conditions dictated that the Bank of England continue with higher rates until the future

6. Hamlin Diary, October 16, 1925.

7. Open Market Investment Policy Excerpts, 1923-1928, pp. 26-29, in Adolph Miller Personal File, CP, HHPL.

8. Benjamin Strong, January 11, 1925, Memorandum for the Record, in Bank of England Revolving Credit File, FRBNY.

9. Open Market Investment Policy Excerpts, 1923-1928, pp. 26-29, in Adolph Miller Personal File, CP, HHPL

10. "The Federal Reserve System and the Speculative Excesses in Grain and Stocks,"*Commercial and Financial Chronicle*, April 11, 1925, pp. 1797-1798.

monetary policy of Great Britain could be determined.[11]   By 1925, moreover, such exchanges between Norman and Strong had become typical. They consulted each other almost daily, especially on the matter of interest rates.[12]

In 1925 Strong sought to maintain the disparity in rates between the London and New York money markets as long as it was feasible to do so. If he could maintain the status quo, he believed, the pound had a good chance of recovery, and at the same time the lower rate would keep the flow of gold into the United States to a minimum, thereby averting the danger of inflation. However, the policy of low interest rates was not without its problems and by some accounts led to an increase in speculation, which proved to be the proverbial thorn in Strong's side. Back in 1919 he had recognized that the Federal Reserve System had some responsibilities in this area.[13] At the time he noted that member banks had been "educated" not to borrow funds from the Reserve System in order to pursue speculative activities. Strong stated that those who did were admonished. He pointed out, however, that nothing "will be so effective as . . . a rate which is unprofitable" and that the bank was prepared to keep the rediscount rate at a level that would "stop this mad march of speculation and expansion, whether it be in securities, real estate, and commodities, or what not."[14]

This position he reaffirmed at the meeting of the Open Market Committee in November of 1924, where he stated that it was generally agreed by economists that the "swings of the business cycle may be lessened by making credit readily available" during recessions and "less easily available when business is booming and speculation is becoming rife."[15]   He continued by saying that the program of the Open Market Committee which contributed toward easier money during 1924 was in keeping with this principle. Yet a year later, in a letter to Senator Irvine Lenroot, he argued that attempting to curb speculation through higher interest rates could "penalize" the entire country and that it might be better to allow speculators to suffer the consequences of their excesses.[16]   Apparently, he failed to appreciate that overindulgence in the market might well "penalize" the entire country as well as the speculators.

In February 1925, after consulting with London, Strong had raised the New York rate in order to diminish the tendency toward speculative optimism. The advance from 3 percent to 3 1/2 percent, he hoped, would obviate the need for a

---

11. Montagu Norman to Benjamin Strong, October 16, 1924, in Strong Papers, FRBNY.

12. See, for instance, the Benjamin Strong File, FRBNY.

13. Benjamin Strong to Montagu Norman, November 6, 1919, in Strong Papers, FRBNY.

14. Ibid.

15. Open Market Investment Policy Excerpts, 1923-1928, p. 26, in Adolph Miller Personal File, CP, HHPL.

16. Benjamin Strong to Irvine Lenroot, December 30, 1925, in Adolph Miller Personal File, CP, HHPL.

larger increase later on.[17] In the *Financial World* the action was hailed as the "most interesting thing this week" and as "another evidence of the conservative and steady improvement in business." The fact that the rate had not been raised before, the paper speculated, was in all likelihood due to the desire to keep funds in London to aid in the recovery of the pound.[18] The decision, according to D.R. Crissinger, was not an easy one, since some of those involved in it felt that the increase might "throw a chill through the entire business of the United States."[19]

The increase was the only one during 1925, even though a number of individuals, including Norman, thought that further raises might be appropriate during the latter part of the year.[20] In the minds of some, speculation remained a threat to the domestic economy. Strong was not oblivious to this possibility, and during May he pointed out to Montagu Norman that the country was still "under the menace of a rather buoyant stock market."[21] Strong attributed the increased stock market activities and the rising prices of stocks to the easier money market conditions. He did not appear to be concerned about the rising prices on the stock exchange, though he was quick to argue that the New York Bank could not reduce its rate any lower since this would almost certainly "be followed by Stock speculation."[22]

By August 1 Strong's view of the situation was modified somewhat. He noted that another rate advance could only be justified "by our fear of a dangerous stock speculation," and he argued that "uneasiness on that score is not now justified to a point where we should advance our rate. . . . We can afford to await further developments."[23] But by the end of the month he was wondering whether the domestic situation was not rendering it "perilous" to continue his accommodation of the Bank of England. He now questioned "whether we can afford to stay at our present level as best we can do."[24] He later mentioned to Norman that his accommodation of the Bank of England had created some difficulties, though he believed that these had been overcome. Strong also pointed out that "there will be an investigation of this business by the Senate, but it causes us no uneasiness."[25]

---

17. Benjamin Strong to Montagu Norman, February 18, 1925, in Strong Papers, FRBNY.

18. *Financial World*, February 28, 1925, p. 1.

19. D.R. Crissinger to Adolph Miller, February 20, 1925, in Adolph Miller Personal File, CP, HHPL.

20. Montagu Norman to Benjamin Strong, September 22, 1925, Outgoing Cable No. 18, Bank of England.

21. Benjamin Strong to Montagu Norman, May 21, 1923, in Strong Papers, FRBNY.

22. Benjamin Strong to Montagu Norman, May 21, 1925, Incoming Cable No. 90, Bank of England.

23. Benjamin Strong to J.H. Case, August 1, 1925, in Strong Papers, FRBNY.

24. Benjamin Strong to J.H. Case, August 25, 1925, in Strong Papers, FRBNY.

25. Benjamin Strong to Montagu Norman, December 3, 1925, in Strong Papers, FRBNY.

These developments were also noted by the *Economist*, which questioned whether the authorities would countenance the misuse of credit for speculative purposes. It was recognized that the Federal Reserve System was sensitive to the legitimate needs of commerce and that this coupled with its concern for the pound sterling and gold standard would keep money rates as low as practicable. This meant that the Federal Reserve Banks were inclined to keep an easy money market, a view that was shared by "stock market enthusiasts" who maintained "that good business and cheap money are assured."[26] Yet, the paper expressed its confidence in the Federal Reserve System and its ability to control market conditions. It was argued that "they would hardly view the prospects for an inflationary boom with equanimity."[27]

In September, Norman noted the changed economic situation and in a cable to Strong urged an "advance to 4 percent." This, he said, "seems necessary for you and will somewhat help me."[28] Strong had informed Norman that there was now a more active speculation in stocks "at advancing prices." He also noted that there was a rather dangerous "speculation in real estate and buildings in a good many places."[29] Strong preferred to make it through the season without raising the rediscount rate, but he also feared that a delay in the rate advance could result in several advances later on. At the same time, he brought to the attention of the Open Market Investment Committee that member banks in principal cities were largely indebted to Reserve Banks. This, according to Strong, meant that "the situation is such that it will be more largely influenced by the position of the discount rate rather than open market operations."[30] He realized the need for quick action, he said, but saw this as impossible since a decision could not be formalized before the New York District meeting on October 1. Even then it was not certain that an advance to 4 percent would be accomplished.

After weighing such factors, Strong finally decided against such an advance,[31] fearing that it would lead automatically to advances in other districts and that this could potentially interfere with the seasonal movement of crops within the United States and to Europe. In addition, he was concerned that higher rates would disturb the international situation by leading to a reduction of foreign loans in the United States and consequently to a decrease in foreign exchange. Again he hoped to be able to maintain the 4 percent rate as long as possible "even favouring that course if [the] decision to do so were a doubtful

26. *Economist*, August 22, 1925 p. 306.

27. *Economist*, August 8, 1925 p. 231.

28. Montagu Norman to Benjamin Strong, September 22, 1925, Outgoing Cable No. 18, Bank of England.

29. Benjamin Strong to Montagu Norman, September 18, 1925, Incoming Cable No. 51, Bank of England.

30. Open Market Investment Policy Excerpts, 1923-1928, p. 54, in Adolph Miller Personal File, CP, HHPL.

31. Pierre Jay to Montagu Norman, September 22, 1925, FRBNY.

one."[32] Strong also pointed to what he believed to be a considerable expansion taking place in the United States. He stated that this was true of the farming community, which was coming out of a "slough" of despond. Other industries rebounding, according to Strong, were railroads, automobile manufacturers, and the steel industry. And these developments, he said, were not speculative. Traders were not overextending and inventories were not piling up. He did admit that good business was always subject to being discounted by "certain classes of speculators, and the reflection of this development is largely in the stock market,"[33] and he recognized that speculation was liable to reach a point where intervention was necessary. But, it was "wiser," he thought, "to take some risk as to the speculative market and reduce the risk as to this international situation to the very minimum, and that means postponing an advance in our discount rate for some period longer."[34]

Still Strong continued to see speculation as a "problem," since stock markets "have widespread psychological influence" and could produce an unnecessary recession. Indeed, by the middle of October, Strong had once again brought up the possibility of having to advance the rediscount rate in the New York district. On October 14 he cabled Norman that his hand might be forced before too long, although he still hoped to avoid "any action beyond [an] advance to 4 [percent] and to delay that as long as possible."[35] The delay, he suggested, could be achieved by having Boston, Cleveland, Philadelphia, and San Francisco advance their rates from 3 1/2 to 4 percent, with a rate advance by the FRBNY to come three weeks or so later. Without such action, he feared, New York could be forced to advance to 4 percent on October 22. He asked Norman for his views on the matter, though, "in more detail than usual."[36]

In his reply the following day, Norman noted that this turn of events was extremely awkward and unexpected. He stated that "as a choice of evils" he preferred that Boston and the other banks "advance promptly to 4 percent," and that the FRBNY advance "if necessary to 4 percent in say 3 weeks."[37] Within 24 hours, however, Strong once again decided to scuttle any thoughts concerning a rate increase. He cabled Norman that after a review of the situation it was agreed that an advance would be "inadvisable if it can be avoided,"[38] and that, as he

32. Benjamin Strong to Montagu Morgan, September 24, 1925, Incoming Cable No. 56, Bank of England.

33. Benjamin Strong to Montagu Norman, September 26, 1925, in Benjamin Strong File, FRBNY.

34. Ibid.

35. Benjamin Strong to Montagu Norman, October 14, 1925, Incoming Cable No. 78, Bank of England.

36. Ibid.

37. Montagu Norman to Benjamin Strong, October 15, 1925, in Strong Papers, FRBNY.

38. Benjamin Strong to Montagu Norman, October 16, 1925, Outgoing Cable No. 56, Bank of England.

noted in his cable on September 24, the FRBNY desired to maintain its present rate for as long as possible "even favoring that course if [the] decision to do so were a doubtful one."[39] He pointed out that the call rate had increased somewhat, and he considered this to be a much better restraint than an increase in the discount rate.[40] For the time being, he remained adamant in his refusal to advance the discount rate, and in Norman's eyes this was now justified. He praised Strong for his insight and declared that he had been right on the mark, "first in August and then 3 weeks ago. All the rest were wrong, Dr. Stewart, the board in Washington and the professors."[41]

If Walter Stewart, as Norman implied, had earlier expressed himself in favor of raising rediscount rates, he had by mid-October experienced a change of heart on the matter. Stewart, the first Director of Research of the Federal Reserve Board, admitted at the October 11 meeting of the board that he saw some evidence that the stock market was being financed by Federal Reserve discounts. He held, however, that there was no reason whatsoever for raising rates "from the point of view of agriculture, commerce or business,"[42] this in spite of the fact that the rediscount rate was 1 percent below the commercial rate. Stewart suggested that Federal Reserve banks instead apply direct pressure on member banks to limit rediscounts to non-exchange related transactions. He maintained that this would remedy the problem, providing that it could be applied.

Stewart was not alone in this assessment. The Philadelphia Reserve Bank, according to Crissinger, was satisfied that direct pressure had enabled it to control the situation and accordingly did not wish to raise its rate, at least not for the time being. Crissinger noted that the same held true for New York, and that direct pressure could be successfully applied in Boston.[43] Strong was not as confident. While conceding some moderate success in the New York district, he did not believe that direct pressure could be properly applied unless the banks were willing to refuse discounts relating to speculative loans. These, he pointed out, should include both real estate and street loans. In effect, this meant rationing credit, which, in Strong's estimation, would have been disastrous.[44] This marked a reversal of the position Strong had taken back in 1919 when he argued that the Bank was determined to put a halt to the mad march of speculation and expansion, whether it took place in stocks or whatever.[45] In line with this, he had

39. Benjamin Strong to Montagu Norman, September 24, 1925, Incoming Cable No. 56, Bank of England.

40. Benjamin Strong to Montagu Norman, October 16, 1925, Incoming Cable No. 83, Bank of England.

41. Montagu Norman to Benjamin Strong, October 18, 1925, in Strong Papers, FRBNY.

42. Hamlin Diary, October 16, 1925.

43. Hamlin Diary, October 19, 1925.

44. Ibid.

45. Benjamin Strong to Montagu Norman, November 6, 1919, in Strong Papers, FRBNY.

insisted in 1920 that New York bankers curtail the "advances they were making for the support of a dangerous speculation in industrial stocks."[46]

Strong, though, did recognize the need for corrective action, and at the November 2 meeting of the Governors Conference he stated that the changes in business and credit conditions had brought about a situation that was "most unusual and most perplexing for the determination of Federal Reserve Policy."[47] He pointed out that loans on stocks and bonds had increased by $300 million, that this reflected an increase of $600 million in "total bank credit advanced by weakly reporting member banks," and that this had been made possible "by an increase of about $250 million in borrowings from the Federal Reserve Banks."[48]   And since he favored neither the application of direct pressure nor changes in open market operations, he now expressed his willingness to consider a raise in the discount rate.

Indeed, Strong was ready to admit, privately, that the speculative appetite in the United States would not "be satisfied by a fling in the stock market." He feared, as did Hoover and Adolph Miller, that it would spread to commodities, and this would be disastrous, because once started it would be extremely hard to stop.[49]   Moreover, by the latter part of November Strong admitted to Norman that a "dangerous speculation" had developed in the stock market. He noted that the situation was "increased in its difficulty . . . by the need for not putting such pressure" on the Bank of England "as would alter the whole credit situation."[50] At the same time, he pointed out that there was some evidence that the speculation had spread to the commodities market, and that there "has been a rampaging real estate speculation in some spots."[51]

Miller, as well, noted that a large amount of credit was being diverted to land speculation and speculative building operations. "A section of the public," he thought, "is losing its bearings and being drawn into a thoughtless arena of speculation,"[52] and he argued that it was time to put a stop to the speculative frame of mind in order to prevent it from extending into legitimate trade and industry. It was time to raise the cost of money and thereby discourage needless borrowing.

---

46. Benjamin Strong to Montagu Norman, February 6, 1920, in Strong Papers, FRBNY.

47. Open Market Investment Policy Excerpts, 1923-1928, p. 56, in Adolph Miller Personal File, CP, HHPL.

48. Ibid. p. 59.

49. Benjamin Strong to Montagu Norman, November 7, 1925, in Strong Papers, FRBNY.

50. Benjamin Strong to Montagu Norman, November 20, 1925, in Strong Papers, FRBNY.

51. Ibid.

52. *New York Times*, November 18, 1925, p. 36; *Economic World*, December 19, 1925, p. 870.

Strong blamed the ongoing frenzy of speculation on a state of mind that emanated, most likely, "from broker's offices" and was being "most assiduously spread throughout the country."[53] Speculators were enthused, first of all, by the healthy outlook for business, second, by the belief that the new Congress would effect a large reduction in taxes, and thirdly and most important, by the assurance of an ample supply of money and a belief that the New York discount rate would not be advanced in light of London's recent reduction to 4 percent. Yet he was still not ready to effect a rate advance. He would delay such a move, at least for the time being, because "the speculator is more influenced by apprehension of things to happen than he is by the happening." If New York were to advance the discount rate to 4 percent, he explained, the speculator would "say, as he often does, that the worst news is out; and then, after a lull, such as occurred last March and April, he would be back at his old tricks again."

With this in mind, Strong employed a scheme similar to the one he had proposed to Norman on October 14 to prolong the apprehension as long as possible. The scheme called for a concerted effort by a number of the Reserve Banks and could appropriately have been named "Operation Damocles."[54] Under it the discount rate would be advanced by one Reserve Bank at a time, over a period of several weeks, the objective being to "create the apprehension" that the New York Bank would advance its rate. The Boston Bank would begin, and when it was discovered that New York would not follow suit and borrowing began moving up again, Philadelphia would then take similar action and this would be followed after appropriate intervals by Cleveland and then San Francisco.[55]

Strong was clearly annoyed by having to follow this course of action. He suggested to Norman that it might be viewed as an attempt to manipulate the stock market. He also pointed out that he hated to do it, and that it was repugnant to him "in every possible respect." At the same time he was concerned that this would interfere with the continued efforts to stabilize sterling since London would have to open its market to foreign loans. He lamented to Norman that it was a "shame that the best sort of plans" could be impaired "by a speculative orgy," but, he added, "the temperament of the people of this country is such that these situations can not be avoided."[56]

Strong justified his course of action on two accounts. The first was that the Stock Exchange loan account had increased "over 50 percent above the high water mark in an advancing stock market." The second, and perhaps more serious consideration, was that almost two-thirds of the money "employed in this speculation" came from banks outside of New York City.[57] And on these points Adolph Miller concurred. He too was alarmed at the increase of "floating

53. Benjamin Strong to Montagu Norman, November 7, 1925, in Strong Papers, FRBNY.

54. Ibid.

55. Ibid.

56. Ibid.

57. Ibid.; see also Benjamin Strong to Irvine Lenroot, in Adolph Miller Personal File, CP, HHPL.

credit," which he felt to be far in excess of the needs of industry, commerce, and agriculture, and he had been urging the Federal Reserve Banks to carry on their work as it was originally intended, and not to act as "life preservers for speculators."[58]   Miller, according to fellow Reserve Board member Charles Hamlin, made it quite clear that there was too much credit in the country.[59]

Strong took issue with Miller's analysis and insisted that there was not too much credit available. Moreover, he argued, an abundance of credit is beneficial to the country. This, though, contradicted his message to Gerard Winston, the Assistant Secretary of the Treasury, in which he noted that "there is now, in fact, more credit potentially available in this country than can be safely used at home without danger of inflation."[60]   Indeed, Strong considered it important enough to ask that President Coolidge include this caution in his address before the Federation of Farm Bureaus of America in Chicago in December of 1925. Miller had also argued that stock prices were too high, to which Strong replied that "prices of stocks, allowing for the 50 percent increase in general prices, are not much above the 1913 pre-war level."[61]

In operation the plan for staggered rate increases was judged by Strong to be successful, and judging from the coverage of it in the press it appears that it did succeed in putting the brakes on speculation, at least for the time being. He admitted that prices had not declined to any great extent, but, he insisted, the "the volume of trading" had been curtailed and a "wholesome air of caution . . . bred throughout the country."[62]   The *Financial World* reported that rate advances were followed by deflation "in some over-manipulated and over-valued stocks" and accordingly that the advances had served a good purpose.[63]   In December, moreover, London raised its discount rate, which, according to Strong, also served to dampen the market somewhat.[64]   Hence he again chose not to advance the New York rate, arguing that speculators would "still have the feeling that the 'Sword of Damocles' is suspended over their heads."[65]

In any event, New York remained the only Reserve Bank not to advance its discount rate, and one is led to wonder if Strong employed "Damocles" more in

58. *New York Times*, November 18, 1925 p. 36; *Economic World*, December 19, 1925, p. 870.

59. Hamlin Diary, November 8, 1925.

60. Benjamin Strong to Gerard Winston, November 27, 1925, in Strong Papers, FRBNY.

61. Hamlin Diary, December 1, 1925.

62. Benjamin Strong to Montagu Norman, November 20, 1925, in Strong Papers, FRBNY.

63. *Financial World*, November 28, 1925, p. 676.

64. When England returned to the gold standard the rules called for raising the interest rates by the Bank of England. Instead the Bank pursued a cheap money policy and resorted to rate increases only when absolutely necessary to protect its gold reserves.

65. Benjamin Strong to Montagu Norman, December 3, 1925, in Strong Papers, FRBNY.

an effort to delay the inevitable or if he truly sought to create an apprehension in the minds of speculators. After the other Banks had raised their rates, Strong argued that in the absence of a crisis situation he could not justify an advance in his rate for at least two or three weeks or more likely before the New Year because of important Government financing on December 15.[66] Strong, though, knew better. By his own admission, to Norman, he was aware of the "dangerous speculation" in the stock market, real estate, and to an extent commodities. And as he noted to Norman, he had given serious consideration to raising the New York rate prior to the New Year, arguing that there was evidence that it could not be avoided.[67] He knew that a strong case could be made for a rate advance but decided to argue against one, and on this he was supported by the majority of the Federal Reserve Board. Of those that dissented, Adolph Miller held that the rate should be advanced to 4 percent at once, and Edmund Platt thought it should be raised to 4 1/2 percent.[68]

Strong also continued to argue that most of the money employed in speculation came from Banks outside of New York City, and therefore "the advance should take place in the other reserve districts" where these funds originated. According to Strong, this would result in the forced withdrawal of funds from the market, and this would be of sufficient quantity to liquidate local loans and have a positive impact upon the New York money market. Clearly, though, one impact that Strong sought was his ability to remain with the lower rate.[69]

By this time the division over the interest rate question had become clear. Miller held that the paramount need was to check speculation, and this could only be accomplished by raising interest rates. He asserted this view regardless of the effects that the higher rates might have on the British or on domestic groups. This clashed with Strong's perception that Britain's return to the gold standard and the economic recovery of Europe were the primary issue and that Federal Reserve policy ought to be tailored to that end. By this time, moreover, the relationship between Strong and Miller had become strained and consisted primarily of frequent clashes of acerbity. Strong still remembered the trouble Miller had caused over the New York Bank's participation in England's return to the gold standard, and he strongly resented the lack of courtesy and the attacks by Miller. He was frank about his feelings with other members of the board and refused to have any personal contact with Miller. He also had Miller "come into his room and then and there told Miller and Crissinger that henceforth his relationship with the board would be purely official."[70]

---

66. Benjamin Strong to Montagu Norman, December 1, 1925, Incoming Cable No. 39, Bank of England.

67. Benjamin Strong to Montagu Norman, November 20, 1925, in Strong Papers, FRBNY.

68. Open Market Investment Policy Excerpts, pp. 63-64, in Adolph Miller Personal File, CP, HHPL.

69. Benjamin Strong to Irvine Lenroot, December 30, 1925, in Adolph Miller Personal File, CP, HHPL.

70. Hamlin Diary, October 28, 1925.

Miller later remarked that in order to understand Strong it was necessary "to remember that Strong was in a manner of speaking the archetype of the good New York businessman," and that "he had a very forceful personality and a high value of his own ego."[71]   Miller was also well aware and often critical of the close relationship between Montagu Norman and Strong. Noting that Strong regularly traveled to Europe, visiting Norman on both an official and private basis, he viewed Norman as the source of new phrases that Strong would use upon his return. At one Reserve Board meeting, he recalled, Strong kept saying "What troubles me about the situation in Europe is the valuta."[72]   Edward Cunningham, an Iowa farmer who "had all the strong streaks of down to earth common sense and practicality associated with his type," leaned across the table and asked Miller what Strong was talking about. Miller replied that he meant "exchange."

Strong, though, was not the only one annoyed with Miller. According to Charles Hamlin, Miller's stance also irked some of the board members who did not view the problem of interest rates as singly as Miller did. The majority of the board supported low interest rates, and this led to frequent and brusque confrontations. After one particular exchange on the issue, Miller, according to Hamlin, "was ugly, and said this would be directly feeding the stock market and should be refused."[73]   For many, Miller was too insistent that the quantity of credit was more than was required for commerce and agriculture, that it was employed in speculation on the stock exchange, that this speculation resulted in an increase of credit, and that once this process was under way, it would be difficult to check, ultimately resulting in a collapse.

Discussion of the board's handling of the money market was also taking place in the banking community. The National City Bank of New York, which had been critical during the credit arrangements between the FRBNY and the Bank of England, once again made itself heard, although this time in a different manner. The earlier criticisms had been confined to personal correspondence between Charles E. Mitchell, President of the Bank, and Benjamin Strong. Now, the Bank in the person of George Roberts, a Vice-President, took its case before the American Banker's Association in an article published in that organization's journal in December of 1925.

Roberts began his assault by stating that

When the Federal Reserve System was organized one of the common expectations was that it would reduce the amount of banking funds employed in stock market operations. It was said that the reserves would no longer be employed in

---

71. Jameson Parker to Mark Sullivan, April 1947, in Mark Sullivan File, PPI, HHPL.

72. Ibid.

73. Hamlin Diary, December 21, 1925.

that manner, and that the Reserve Banks, through their discount policies, would be able to exercise a considerable degree of control over market activities.[74]

Indeed, Roberts continued, one of the principal reasons for the division of the country into twelve reserve districts had been to avoid the accumulation of funds in New York and their employment in the stock market. Yet in operation there had been no lack of funds to support exchange transactions since the Federal Reserve System began. On the contrary, one of the biggest markets "ever known" had been under way for well over a year, and one explanation for this phenomenon was the availability of cheap money.

Roberts insisted that there was a direct relationship between the Federal Reserve discount rate and stock exchange transactions, and to support this claim he pointed to the recent action of the Boston Reserve bank in increasing its rate from 3 1/2 to 4 percent. This, he stated "threw the stock market quite off its equilibrium."[75] Roberts, as had Benjamin Strong on a number of occasions, noted the psychological effect of the discount rate. But, he also agreed with Adolph Miller in his assessment that credit must be curtailed when speculative enthusiasm was entering a state of "feverish enthusiasm." And quoting Miller, he argued that reserve credit should be employed "to give steadiness, stability and strength to underlying business conditions."[76]

The fact that other banks had raised their rediscount rates and that New York had not had also by this time caught the attention of Herbert Hoover. He became greatly concerned about the continued expansion of speculation on the New York Stock Exchange, which, he argued, stemmed from cheap money caused by low discount rates. But in his public statements, he did not show the same anxiety as he did behind the scenes. Publicly, he said that speculation should be checked but held that economic conditions were the best that they had ever been and that the economy was basically sound.[77] Privately, he feared that the expansion of credit for speculation would have an adverse effect on the credit fund of the country, and that the speculative fever might extend into commodities and result in a collapse that would affect every part of the nation.[78]

Hoover was especially concerned about the commodities market in light of the crash in stock and wheat prices earlier in the year. At the time he attributed the collapse to wild and foolish speculators, who had gambled on a boom after the Coolidge election, but was quick to add that "the normal process of business [had] not been disturbed."[79] Later he warned that measures would have to be taken to guard against a repeat of the "disastrous speculation such as Livermore

74. George E. Roberts, "Federal Reserve Control of the Money Market," *Economic World*, December 19, 1925, p. 868.

75. Ibid.

76. Ibid.

77. *St. Louis Post Dispatch*, October 19, 1925, Public Statements, HHPL.

78 Irvine Lenroot to D.R. Crissinger, November 23, 1925, in Federal Reserve file, CP, HHPL.

79. *Cleveland Plain Dealer*, April 1, 1925 p. 2.

and others have managed to pull off"[80] and in October was saying that the commodities market was a business that required nothing more than a gambling instinct and had "ceased to be remunerative to intelligent men."[81]

Hoover's concern mounted as he examined an internal Commerce Department review of the economic situation from January 1923 through October 1925. At first glance this seemed to offer little cause for alarm. The attached charts showed that business and industry were doing well, and that total stock prices and interest rates were up. However, the narrative accompanying these charts pointed out that the rise in interest rates was deceiving in that the New York Federal Reserve discount rate had failed to advance. In addition, the report noted the existence of an easy money market in New York. Hoover's response was to request that Julius Klein prepare an analysis of the possible effect of the stock market boom on trade and industry.[82]

Klein could not discern that the events on Wall Street were being echoed in industry. Neither did he believe that business "was led astray by the rise in security prices."[83] He also maintained that the financing of the "boom" had not led to any restriction of credit for either trade or industry, although he cautioned that the absorption of credit on Wall Street had contributed to the rise in interest rates. As far as Klein was concerned, the real danger posed to industry and trade by the "boom" was of a psychological nature. He stated that the increase in the price of securities had "undoubtedly produced a spirit of confidence and optimism in the minds of the American public," which, he argued, ought to be properly restrained in order to be helpful to business.[84] He also noted that should the market collapse the spirit of confidence would give way to a deeper pessimism, and that this would be anything but helpful.

In addition, Klein questioned whether the bull market under way at the end of the year was fostered by easy money. He maintained that it may have been fostered by cheap money during its early stages, but that the main factor appeared to be the considerable reduction in surtaxes in addition to the "distribution of large accumulated surpluses in the form of 'melons.'" Klein thought that Wall Street was "discounting the cutting of melons with a little too much enthusiasm," and expressed the view that once this exuberance abated hardening money rates would serve to prevent any further rise in the market.[85]

As for remedies, Klein suggested that the New York Bank ought to consider raising its discount rate to 3 3/4 or 4 percent. The stock market, he said, had been anticipating some such action for several weeks, and it would probably help to hold security prices down even though it might alarm business in general. Klein

80. Edgar Rickard Diary August 19, 1925, p. 125, HHPL.

81. Ibid. October 13, 1925 p. 160.

82. Fiscal Year 1925 Review, in Economic Situation File, CP. HHPL.

83. Julius Klein to Herbert Hoover, November 9, 1925, in Foreign & Domestic, J. Klein File, CP, HHPL.

84. Ibid.

85. Ibid.

also suggested that the Federal Reserve Banks give a word of caution to their member banks and that this should be accompanied by "a few pronouncements from official quarters in Washington."[86]

Hoover was disturbed by Klein's assessment and pursued the issue with Grosvenor Jones, the Chief of the Finance and Investment Division in the Commerce Department. The two met on November 21, a Saturday afternoon, to discuss the matter of reserve credit. At this meeting, Jones stated that the FRBNY had not been restricting the amount of credit, as it was capable of doing, through its open market operations. This did not sit well with Hoover. But two days later Jones corrected himself, stating that he was mistaken in his earlier opinion. He noted that it appeared that the New York Bank had been making its member banks resort to discounting and that it was therefore in a better position "to put the brakes on the money market through a rise in the discount rate."[87]

If Klein's memo failed to quiet Hoover's fears, his conversation with Jones unsettled him even more. The day after his meeting with Jones, at a time when he did not have the benefit of the corrective memo, Hoover went to see Adolph Miller, who lived two houses down from him on S Street. As Miller later recalled, Hoover dropped in on a Sunday afternoon,[88] coming as was his custom, unannounced. He rang the doorbell and "before the butler could move" had "bounded up the stairs, taking them two at a time,"[89] and made his way to the study where Miller happened to be engrossed in the latest board report. Hoover, as was also his wont, wasted no time on formalities but began with "Are you as worried about this speculation as I am?"[90] Miller replied that he was and that he had just been going over some of the latest figures about it. Hoover then asked Miller to go over the situation in detail with him and stated that if Miller needed any help in dealing with this situation he could get someone, whom the board would hear out, to address the subject. Before Hoover left he had also asked Miller for any books on the subject, which, according to Miller, happened every time they visited. Then armed with books, data, and a draft of Miller's views, Hoover left, apparently determined to take on the board.

Characteristically, Hoover decided to work behind the scenes and through the efforts of others, turning in this case to Senator Irvine Lenroot of Wisconsin.[91] Lenroot was a member of the Banking and Currency Committee and was

86. Ibid.

87. Grosvenor M. Jones to Herbert Hoover, November 23, 1925, Federal Reserve Board and Banks, CP, HHPL.

88. Hoover's visit with Miller would have taken place the day following his conversation with Jones. The correspondence that resulted from the discussion with Miller was dated November 23, 1925.

89. Jameson Parker, Oral History, November 21, 1969, Lorton, VA., conducted by Raymond Henle, HHPL.

90. Jameson Parker to Mark Sullivan, undated correspondence, in Mark Sullivan File, PPI, HHPL.

91. This approach was especially important in this case, and as Arthur Kemp later stated, Hoover "was after all, Secretary of Commerce, not the President nor the Secretary

highly regarded by his colleagues in the Senate. His position also brought him into close contact with Reserve Board members, which would give him some leverage of power. And Hoover respected Lenroot for his ability, whereas the latter had a deep appreciation for Hoover's grasp on public affairs. Convinced that Lenroot would not be ignored by the board, Hoover suggested that the Senator pursue the matter of credit and speculation, and   evidently Lenroot did not need much persuasion. He had also begun to feel some apprehensions about the board's policy and held views similar to those of Hoover.[92]

Lenroot decided to voice his concerns in a letter addressed to Governor Crissinger, which Hoover helped to draft and for which he furnished data and ideas based on his conversation with Miller.[93] The letter raised the concern that increased speculation in the New York Stock Market would penetrate the commodity and production activities of the country and that this would result in inflation and the collapse of the economy. In the words of the letter, the process could bring "the greatest calamities upon our farmers, our workers, and legitimate business."[94]

Lenroot also noted that to him it appeared that the current situation was a repeat of the one in 1919-1920, when a severe inflation in stocks and commodities took place and the Federal Reserve Board did not take action until the situation was beyond control. He pointed out that reserve banks throughout the country apparently felt some alarm and had raised their rediscount rates accordingly, but that New York, which he felt to be the real center of speculation, had taken no action. And again, he expressed fear that cheap money caused by low discount rates was indirectly stimulating speculation on the New York Stock Exchange.

Lenroot was particularly concerned about the activities of New York banks and inquired whether there had been any indications that they had borrowed from the FRBNY for the sole purpose of financing stock exchange transactions. He also wanted to know whether discounts had increased at the FRBNY since its present rate went into effect and whether the bank had made any attempt to check the situation, either by attempting to reduce its rediscounts or reducing its holdings of government securities. In addition to this information, Lenroot requested data concerning the movement of commercial and collateral loans for the period beginning July 1924 and ending July 1925; the amounts of federal

---

of the Treasury. Pressure to influence Federal Reserve policy, by the very nature of the case, had to be exerted indirectly." Arthur Kemp to Mark Sullivan, March 11, 1950, in Mark Sullivan File, PPI, HHPL.

92. Lenroot later commented that Hoover had asked him "not to use his name for the reason that, being a member of the Administration, he did not feel that he should publicly criticize the policy being pursued." Irvine Lenroot, Memoirs, pp. 188-89, Box 13, Lenroot Papers, Library of Congress, Manuscript Division, Washington, D.C.

93. Irvine Lenroot to Lawrence Richey, May 3, 1933, in Federal Reserve File, CP, HHPL.

94. Irvine Lenroot to D.R. Crissinger, November 23, 1925, in Federal Reserve file, CP, HHPL.

reserve investments, to include open market investments and rediscounts secured by government obligations; the rates charged customers in competitive banking centers; and, if possible, the volume of time call money provided to the New York stock market at various times since the beginning of the year.

Still another question in the letter concerned the relationship between the Bank of England and the FRBNY. He was asking, Lenroot said, because a November 21 article in the *New York Times* implied that there was an understanding between officials of the FRBNY and officials of the Bank of England. But the question was clearly related to the debate of late April and early May. Miller's feelings on the subject were well known, and Hoover, as well, had manifested signs of antipathy towards the British. He was particularly concerned about the British monopoly on rubber and about claims that Britain would repay her war debts with "rubber," that is, by placing an export tax on this commodity. Hoover sought to avoid any connection between himself and such claims, but he did state his belief that rubber producers operated under the guidance of the British Government and that this resulted "in a very heavy drain on our people." He seemed convinced that Britain had entered upon a trade war with the United States, and that Norman, whose close relationship to Strong was no secret, deftly manipulated the latter, just as he had Lamont at the London Conference, to the detriment of American commerce and industry and to the benefit of the British economy.[95] Such views had created tension between Hoover and fellow cabinet members and leading businessmen in the United States. Paul Warburg viewed Hoover as a great danger because of his meddling in monetary affairs and saw his interference as an attempt to dominate the State Department.[96] Harvey Firestone of Firestone Rubber had a profound distrust for Hoover and insisted that he was not helping matters with his meddlesome attitude.[97] American attitudes on foreign loans were being ridiculed in Europe, and Hoover, who was seen as the dominant force behind the policy, was deeply mistrusted there.[98]

To some it also appeared that Hoover had been responsible for a rumor that had been circulating which held that Mellon would resign as Treasury Secetary. Parker Gilbert thought it was started by Hoover, who if he could not be Secretary of State, would gladly step into the Treasury Department post.[99]

---

95. Hoover to Clarence MacGregor, August 5, 1925, in Foreign Combinations Rubber File, CP, HHPl; *Economist*, December 26, 1925, p. 1090. The closeness of their relationship can be demonstrated by a statement made to Strong by Norman in January 1924 where he stated that if Strong gave "way to the temptation to take to traveling or lecturing or writing, then, as it looks to me, intimacy between our two banks goes overboard for the present; without yourself it cannot be maintained because the sole understanding presence will be missing." Montagu Norman to Benjamin Strong, January 30, 1924, in Strong Papers, FRBNY.

96. William R. Castle Diaries, Dec 15, 1925, Microfilm, HHPL.

97. Ibid. December 23, 1925.

98. Ibid. Jan 4, 1926.

99. Ibid.

Secretary of State Frank Kellog was furious with Hoover over his meddling in foreign loans. At the State Department Hoover's attempts to control foreign loans were viewed as an attempt to impress American voters. William Castle believed that Hoover had "gone mad on the subject of personal publicity," viewed himself as the only cabinet officer who was 100 percent American, and apparently did not care that his interference created difficulties for the State Department.[100]

Still Hoover exercised care in making his pronouncements and satisfied himself with working behind the scenes. Miller was less cautious in airing his views. He ran into Norman in Crissinger's office where he severely criticized Britain's rubber export duties. Norman was both amazed and disturbed by the attack. To Hamlin it appeared that Miller was only quoting Hoover.[101]

Lenroot's letter, the focused force of which was in the opening paragraph, was presented by Crissinger to the board at its December meeting. Miller recalled that he felt somewhat hypocritical, though "he was concerned to look interested and surprised as language with which he had some familiarity was read to the board."[102] The letter was received with mixed feelings on the part of the board members. It was apparent from its contents that the author was well informed and sought to use this occasion to present an informed and comprehensive opposition to the board's policies. But it was also quite clear that the technical data contained in the Lenroot letter came from within the board, and to some of the members this meant Adolph Miller. Some also surmised that the tenor of the letter was close to the views expressed on different occasions by Herbert Hoover, and adding weight to the suspicion was the knowledge that Lenroot had close ties to both Hoover and Miller.[103]

Miller's feigned surprise was therefore to no avail. Governor Crissinger, for one, noted to Charles Hamlin that he suspected Miller of acting in concert with Hoover to embarrass the board and Secretary Mellon, who had come to the same conclusion, was indignant with Miller, and wanted to know when his term on the Federal Reserve Board expired. Crissinger had to tell him that it had just begun. In addition, Mellon was also annoyed with Hoover, who had approached him about, and was severely critical of, the board's Open Market policy.[104] When Hamlin later expressed the fear that there was a pipeline running from the Federal Reserve Board, Mellon replied that he knew it and felt sure that they had the same person in mind at either end of the line, "meaning Miller and Hoover."[105]

---

100. Ibid. January 7, 1926.

101. Hamlin Diary, January 4, 1923.

102. Jameson Parker to Mark Sullivan, undated, in Mark Sullivan File, PPI, HHPL.

103. In his memoirs Lenroot points out that the Lenroots and Hoovers had become very intimate from the time that Hoover became Secretary of Commerce and that they dined at his home almost every Sunday evening. Irvine Lenroot Memoirs, pp. 188-89, Box 13, Lenroot Papers, Library of Congress, Manuscript Division, Washington, D.C.

104. Hamlin Diary, December 22, 1925.

105. Hamlin Diary, March 11, 1926.

Lenroot, as Hoover had predicted, was not ignored. Crissinger, in his response for the board, argued that there were no indications that the speculation had found its way to the commodity markets or to trade and industry.[106] There was, he admitted, a possibility that stock market speculation could spread into commodity markets and could influence commodity prices. But he maintained that "the close adjustment between current production and distribution of commodities give no evidence that existing business conditions are affected by inflationary or speculative influences."[107]

Crissinger also argued that the inflation in stocks and commodities of 1919-1920 had stemmed from conditions caused by the war. At that time "there was active competition by manufacturers for raw materials and labor" as well as "a rapidly rising price level in all countries" and a "consequent widespread speculation in commodities based on the expectation of further price advance."[108] The conditions in 1925, both in the United States and in the world, were totally different and bore no comparison to the conditions in 1920, "which favored an almost unprecedented inflation" in the United States and elsewhere.[109]

Further, Crissinger maintained that even though the stock market was located in New York and funded through the New York money market, people from all parts of the country helped to finance the transactions. The New York City banks, he said, supplied only 40 percent of the funds used by "Wall Street." The fact was "that business and credit conditions throughout the country have resulted in a flow of funds to the central money market."[110] This argument, of course, was no great revelation. It amounted to a rehash of the report Benjamin Strong had delivered to the Open Market Committee on September 22 and was already familiar to Miller, if not Hoover and Lenroot.[111]

Lenroot's inquiry concerning the possibility of determining whether member banks were borrowing from reserve banks in order to underwrite stock exchange transactions received a guarded response. Generally speaking, Crissinger insisted that it was not possible to determine how member banks applied the credit they had obtained from reserve banks. Typically they borrowed to make up deficiencies in their reserve balances that were "incurred as the net result of all their operations," which meant that it was "seldom possible to trace the connection between borrowing . . . at the reserve bank and the specific transactions

106. When the replies to the Lenroot correspondence were being voted on by the Board, Adolph Miller was recorded as not voting. Federal Reserve Board, *Excerpts from the Minutes of the Federal Reserve Board*, December 10, 1925.

107. D.R. Crissinger to Irvine Lenroot, December 10, 1925, in Federal Reserve File, CP, HHPL.

108. Ibid.

109. Ibid.

110. Ibid.

111. Open Market Investment Policy Excerpts, 1923-1928, p. 54, in Adolph Miller Personal File, HHPL.

that gave rise to the necessity for borrowing."[112] Crissinger admitted, though, that there had been some isolated instances, which had come to the attention of the board, where member banks did in fact borrow from reserve banks in order to underwrite stock exchange transactions. He insisted that in such cases it was customary for reserve banks to call attention to the particular transaction and that member banks then repaid these loans. He insisted as well that Federal Reserve Banks regarded borrowing by member banks for speculative purposes with disfavor.

This may have been the official point of view, but it was apparent that the Federal Reserve System was powerless to control such transactions, and both Crissinger and Lenroot recognized this fact. Indeed, within two weeks of his response to Lenroot, Crissinger informed the Federal Reserve Board that the First National Bank of New York had borrowed $115 million from the FRBNY, and that this money, which had been collaralled by government securities, had been loaned on the New York stock market at rates ranging from 6 to 7 percent. Only one board member, Charles Hamlin, spoke in favor of remedial action, and there was no furor of the kind that one might expect if Crissinger's statements were taken literally.[113]

Another question to which Crissinger responded concerned the volume of discounts at the FRBNY since the rate was last set. In reality, he noted, reserve bank rediscounts had declined from $250 million in February to about $60 million in May, a level of activity that was maintained through September and was altered only by the "usual seasonal" increase in discounts during the last three months of the year. Obviously seeking to distance Federal Reserve transactions from stock exchange activities, Crissinger insisted that any increased activity was not tied to stock exchange loans, and that the volume of such loans was now lower then it was on January 1. New York, Crissinger continued, was one of the banks that had experienced a reduction in rediscounts. Early in the year, its sale of government securities had accounted for a rise in rediscounts, and the most important factor in bringing the subsequent reduction was the February increase in the rediscount rate from 3 to 3 1/2 percent.

In response to Lenroot's questions concerning loans and investments of member banks and reserve banks and the total amount of credit employed by the New York Stock Exchange, Crissinger provided several tables listing loans and money rates but claimed that the board had no information on the use of credit in the stock market. The only information available was the reported street loans of a number of New York City banks, which, he said, were confidential figures voluntarily provided by and representative only of the banks' own accounts and those of their out of town subscribers. He did, however, provide a copy of this data to Lenroot.

The data showed that there had been a rapid increase in street loans beginning in the fall of 1923, and that this had continued to be the tendency through-

---

112. D.R. Crissinger to Irvine Lenroot, December 10, 1925, in Federal Reserve File, CP, HHPL.

113. Hamlin Diary, January 8, 1926.

out 1925. It also indicated that there had been a slight decrease during 1925 in loans made by New York banks for their own accounts or those of their sub-scribers. The conclusion drawn by Crissinger was that the entire increase had come from outside New York and that these outside loans had almost doubled since the beginning of the year so that outside money constituted approximately 60 percent of the money thus employed. This, he said, had been taken into con-sideration during the recent round of rediscount rate hikes by the various reserve banks. New York was not one of those that had increased its rate, and following Crissinger's logic should not be required to do so since 60 percent of the call loan money originated from banks outside of New York. The fact remained, though, that New York banks were the single largest lender when compared to other districts on a one-to-one basis.

Finally, Crissinger responded to the request for information concerning the relationship between the FRBNY and the Bank of England by insisting that there was no understanding between the two institutions other than the arrange-ment entered into in April when Great Britain returned to the gold standard. At that time the Federal Reserve banks had agreed "to place $200 million in gold at the disposal of the Bank of England if desired,"[114] but to date none of the credit had been used. There was, he repeated, "no understanding, formal, or informal, beyond that expressed in the credit itself."[115]

The board's carefully crafted reply did not assent to the view contained in the Lenroot letter and sought to refute the notion that the speculation then un-derway was in any respect a danger to the country's economy. Further, it com-municated no sense of urgency about implementing a change in credit policies; instead Crissinger took this occasion to give a comprehensive and detailed statement about general conditions in industry and business as they stood in De-cember of 1925. This ebullience, though, contradicted Strong's caution to the Open Market Committee only a month earlier, with which Crissinger was well acquainted. At that time, Strong had said that "the most serious element about the recent stock market movement is the possibility of a later recession which," in Strong's view, "might add impetus toward business reaction."[116] But now the board's views were that business conditions were excellent and that this could to a large extent be credited to its policies of low interest rates and abundant credit. It was conceded that low interest rates had a tendency to stimulate speculation in securities, but conveyed as well was the attitude that Lenroot had no reason to be overly concerned.

Lenroot, however, was alarmed, especially by the admission that the speculative activity was not confined to New York alone. He argued, based on the study of the data which the board had supplied, that the inevitable collapse of this activity was even more dangerous to commerce and industry because of

114. D.R. Crissinger to Irvine Lenroot, December 10, 1925, in Federal Reserve File, CP, HHPL.

115. Ibid.

116. Ibid. p. 58.

its national scope and, after consulting with Hoover, wrote a second letter in which he warned that:

> This large movement in New York stock has not been one of realignment of values under new investment, but one of sheer speculation, because your statement shows that "street" loans have increased nearly one billion dollars since this movement began and now have reached the gigantic total of nearly two billion seven hundred million, or about 40% more than any amount hitherto known in our credit history.[117]

Lenroot, echoing Hoover's sentiments, also feared that the banking data did not give a true picture of conditions, since a considerable amount of credit was carried by individuals and corporations. He cautioned that the absorption of credit by Wall Street could raise the interest rates of money used in commerce and agriculture, which made the question a matter of concern to everyone. And he felt that it was important to keep the Federal Reserve System from contributing to the growth of speculation, either directly or indirectly. In addition, the Lenroot-Hoover critique expressed some uneasiness about the noticeable increase in the growth of bill and security holding by the Federal Reserve System, a growth, that appeared to parallel the growth of speculation on Wall Street. There might, they thought, be a connection between the credit released by the Federal Reserve System and the increase of credit absorbed in street loans, "because advances from the Federal Reserve are capable of great pyramiding."[118] Further, the rejoinder pointed up their astonishment at the increase in street loans and insisted that if the amount and increase of these loans were known to the whole country, it would end the orgy of speculation. This did not prove to be the case when the amount of the holdings on Wall Street became known in early 1926, but there was a good deal of discussion.

Lenroot's critical retort to the board's urbane and frank attempt to pacify him, caused another round of irritated concern within the board's hallowed headquarters. Of particular concern was the fact that this second letter contained, almost verbatim, the discussion by the board regarding brokers' loans "when it was deciding on its reply to his first letter." Crissinger told Hamlin that someone on the board supplied Lenroot with this information and that he was sure that "Miller 'leaked' to Hoover, and that Hoover prompted Lenroot's second letter."[119] Winston and Mellon were also convinced that Hoover and Miller were working together and that they "had egged on" Lenroot to write both letters because "they contained statements and agreements which he could not have made without help."[120]

---

117. Irvine Lenroot to D.R. Crissinger, December 23, 1925, in Federal Reserve File, CP, HHPL.

118. Ibid.

119. Hamlin Diary, January 4, 1926.

120. Hamlin Diary, January 9, 1926.

In addition to unsettling conditions at the Reserve Board, the correspondence also resulted in a personal visit by Strong to Lenroot, during which the subject matter of the board's letter was discussed at length. Shortly after this meeting, Strong received a copy of Lenroot's December 23 reply to the board from Crissinger, and this in turn prompted a ten page letter from Strong to Lenroot.[121] The contents of the letter offered nothing new but were instead a summary of the statements made by Strong at various times during 1925 and in certain instances reflected almost identically the position taken by Crissinger in his reply for the board.

On January 12, 1926, Crissinger also replied to Lenroot's latest volley. In doing so he was hardly able to contain his annoyance with Lenroot's intrusions into Federal Reserve Board affairs and bluntly stated that personally he would "appreciate it if you would come to my office where we could talk over the important problems with which the Reserve System has to deal." Moreover, he suggested, they would be able to "reach a fuller understanding" in this way than they could through repeated correspondence.[122] Crissinger did address some of Lenroot's concerns, though, in toto, the reply was an amalgam of the positions espoused by proponents of easy money at various times during 1925. It reflected the "Mind of the Board," and to some this was synonymous with the mind of Benjamin Strong.[123]

Crissinger, as he had done in his first letter, tried hard to dispel the notion that the rise in speculative activity posed any danger to the commodities market. He agreed that the unhealthy speculation was responsible for the rise in security prices and went on to say that these prices would rise to a level that could not be maintained and would then fall. He also suggested that this would affect general business confidence as it might be interpreted as the forerunner of slackened business activity and would in that case lead businessmen to curtail their operations or at the very least exercise greater care in making forward commitments. But any real losses resulting from such a recession, Crissinger argued, would fall upon investors and especially speculators who might be forced to sell at a loss. And there was, he said, no evidence that the speculative activity on Wall Street had spread to the commodities market. On the contrary, commodity prices had exhibited a downward trend even though there was continuing growth in construction and other industries.

Again, though, this contradicted Strong's earlier statement to Norman that there was evidence showing that speculation was extending into the commodities market. And if this earlier assessment was correct, there are three possible

121. Benjamin Strong to Irvine Lenroot, December 30, 1925, in Adolph Miller Papers, Library of Congress, Manuscript Division. This letter bears a P.S., dated January 9, 1926, on p. 10. Strong had held this correspondence to allow Crissinger to reply to the December 23 letter. In the P.S. Strong also notes the changed conditions, i.e. the increase by New York to 4 percent.

122. D.R. Crissinger to Irvine Lenroot, January 12, 1926, Reserve Board.

123. Mark Sullivan noted years later that the Board really had two minds: that of Strong and that of Miller.

reasons for the failure of the board to acknowledge its existence. First, and very likely, is the possibility that Strong withheld information and concerns from the Open Market Committee and the Federal Reserve Board. Second, the board may have been aware of the situation and decided not to acknowledge the existence of speculation in commodities or any concerns it may have had about such activities. This seems unlikely since Miller would have fought any attempts to conceal such knowledge. Third, it may be that the board members, with the exception of Adolph Miller and possibly Edmund Platt, simply could not recognize the speculative trend. If this was the case, it is a sorry testimony to the collective ability of the Federal Reserve Board during the 1920s.

In commenting on the rapid growth of security loans, the board conceded that this was not "an altogether desirable movement in the banking situation."[124] But it had not resulted in a lack of credit for productive enterprises. Since the middle of 1925, there had been a "considerable growth in loans for commercial purposes, as well as a further increase in loans on securities at member banks in leading cities."[125] Nor could the board be persuaded that the growth of speculative loans in itself supported the claim that the rise in security prices could be attributed to speculation. It argued that the increase in prices was due to the judgment of a large number of investors and that "securities, in view of the general business outlook, have been worth purchasing at a rising level of prices."[126] There was no call for intervention since the board did not consider its functions to include passing upon the soundness of the investor's judgment.

Lenroot, in his correspondence of December 25, had also suggested that the board establish a procedure to secure street loan information on an official basis and to publish these figures on a regular basis. And in its reply, the board noted that such a plan had been under careful consideration for some time and that a similar recommendation had been made by its Division of Research and Statistics. The Division, it was claimed, had worked out a plan for securing the desired information, which it would present in a form that would "most adequately serve the public interest and will at the same time enlist the largest measure of voluntary cooperation by the reporting banks." The board noted that it had approved the recommendation by the Division of Research and Statistics and that the figures would be published on a regular basis as soon as the reporting system could be put into operation. This was a far cry from the official action Lenroot had suggested.

The warnings sounded by the Hoover-Lenroot correspondence to the board fell on deaf ears. Nor was Hoover successful when he tried, on a number of occasions, to pursue his agenda of raising interest rates. When he approached Crissinger about his concerns, the latter appeared cool and to a degree reproachful. At the same time Crissinger reminded Hoover that the Federal Reserve Board was created as an independent agency and that this meant it should be free from interference from any Administration. The gist of their relationship

---

124. D.R. Crissinger to Irvine Lenroot, January 12, 1926, Reserve Board.

125. Ibid.

126. Ibid.

was that Crissinger felt Hoover to be out of bounds and that he should concern himself with the functions of the Commerce Department.[127]

Hoover, who had been satisfied to work behind the scenes and through the efforts of others, had in the meantime taken his case directly to the people. In a release for the morning papers of December 31, he stated, matter of factly and with the optimism he had displayed in January somewhat tempered, that there were a number of areas in the economy which required caution. Among these was the continuation of widespread real estate and stock speculation. Although he tried to sound optimistic about the economy in general, he pointed out that unless this fever of speculation was tempered by courage and wisdom it would likely extend into commodity markets. He cautioned that "over-optimism can only land us on the shores of over-depression. . . . What we need is an even keel in our financial controls."[128]

The year 1925 proved to be a significant year in the life of the Federal Reserve System. It marked the beginning of an active effort to underwrite international economic stability. At the same time, it witnessed the widening of the gulf between the various factions in the system and its growing dominance by New York. And despite Hoover's maneuvering, it marked the waning of his influence in Federal Reserve policy formulation. During the war period and in the early 1920s, he had never hesitated in approaching the board directly to solicit its help or to voice his opinion. But with a shift in the makeup of the board that began in 1922, the increasing influence of the FRBNY, and the rift between Miller and other members, the receptivity that Hoover had once enjoyed, especially on the part of the board's Governor, had substantially declined. In 1925 he not only hesitated to approach the board directly but found that his efforts to bring indirect pressures to bear were highly resented.

---

127. Mark Sullivan Manuscript, p. 41, in Mark Sullivan File, PPI, HHPL.

128. Secretary of Commerce Press Release, "Economic Prospects for 1926" for morning papers of December 31, 1925.

Chapter 5

Stabilization:
From Wall Street to Congress

In sounding the future, one should leave statistics and charts behind, and seek
the broad valleys and rolling prairies, view the stuffed barns, the black plowed
soil, harbinger of a crop to come. . . . As we inventory our glory, take in the ur-
ban as well . . . billion dollar corporations sending out their streams of profit-
able employed labor, living in a comfort not remotely approached by an industrial class elsewhere on the globe. . . . This land that is proof against disaster . . .
presages a tomorrow far mightier and rosier than is really logical to predict.

John G. Lonsdale[1]

Herbert Hoover's Commerce Department report for 1925 contained a combination of congratulation and warning. It divided the economy into two areas, the
first of which, the production of goods, was held to be stable and sound and, in
Hoover's view, using a normal portion of the country's credit. It was the second,
speculation in the securities market, that he considered to be violent and dangerous, for it was there that speculators were absorbing an "excess" quantity of
credit, while at the same time creating more.[2] This division existed throughout

---

1. *Commercial and Financial Chronicle*, February 13, 1926, p. 809. John G. Lonsdale was the president of the National Bank of Commerce in St. Louis.

2. U.S. Department of Commerce, Annual Report of the Secretary of Commerce,
1925, U.S. Government Printing Office, Washington, D.C. The problem with Hoover's
use of the term "excess credit" is that there is no objective way to determine what excessive is. The mistake was in employing Federal Reserve credit for speculative purposes.

the period from 1925 to 1928, and Hoover would later argue that it was one of the primary causes of inflation in the United States and abroad, the "crazy boom" in stocks, the collapse of the securities market, and the ensuing depression.[3]

This chapter examines the continuing struggle in 1926 to define the purposes of the Federal Reserve System, focusing particularly on legislative proposals, the attempts to reassert the leadership role of the Federal Reserve Board, the notions of economists versus bankers, Midwestern attitudes, and the ongoing Miller-Strong clash. Hoover was not out front during these episodes, but, as was his style, he worked behind the scenes through the efforts of others, especially Adolph Miller. It was he and Miller who worked closely together on matters of reserve policy, while face-to-face relationships with Strong were virtually nonexistent. An examination of Hoover's desk calendar shows that he had not had an official appointment with Strong since November 14, 1923, and since he did not see him socially it is doubtful that they had any sort of meaningful dialogue on any topic of importance during this time.

In his report for 1925, Hoover wanted to alert the public to the dangers of real estate and securities speculation and of the overextension of installment buying. This was the warning side of the report, and some commentators did take it seriously. The *Commercial and Financial Chronicle*, for example, stated that the country could not "afford to disregard such a carefully and moderately worded warning against overdoing things."[4] And the *New York Times* carried Hoover's warnings along with a statement that it would not do for "Americans to live in a fool's paradise." Business cycles, it said, would not alter their course "just to oblige" America. Nor could economic laws and forces be suspended "at the behest of the richest nation on earth."[5]

Optimism, however, refused to be daunted and Hoover's warnings tended to be more resented than heeded. Americans were evidently satisfied with conditions as they were and appeared optimistic that the future would be even brighter. Even the *New York Times* mixed its praise of Hoover's report with rhetoric that hailed 1925 as an "annus mirabilis both historically and prophetically."[6] The first quarter of the century, it maintained, held the promise of an even better second quarter, with the United States "entering on an era in which old statistics no longer counted."[7]

As justification for such optimism, year end reports, including those issued by the Commerce Department, boasted of more automobiles made, more steel produced, more electricity generated, and more students in schools and colleges.

Whether or not it was excessive was irrelevant. A point that seemed to elude the policy makers of the day.

3. See, for instance, Herbert Hoover to Adolph Miller, October 17, 1934, in Adolph Miller File, PPI, HHPL.

4. *Commercial and Financial Chronicle*, January 2, 1926, p. 1.

5. *New York Times*, January 1, 1926, p. 24.

6. *New York Times*, January 10, 1926, sec. II, p. 10.

7. Ibid.

Many of the reports, journalist Mark Sullivan later wrote, "made exulting comparisons . . . with the year before, [or] with the quarter century just ended," and some, he said, extended "comparison to all time, concluding with the words of superlative climax 'more than ever before.'"[8] Included in the latter were reports of an all-time high on the New York Stock Exchange. It reached a new level on December 31, with "new prices all through the list, some for the year and some for all time."[9]

In the eyes of some, however, there was no justification for greeting the activities in the stock market with satisfaction. Speculative enthusiasm continued unabated, despite Strong's efforts during October and November of 1925 to dampen it through "Operation Damocles." Charles Hamlin believed the situation to be serious, and he listened with dismay as Crissinger reported to the board that the First National Bank of New York had borrowed $115 million from the FRBNY, on a direct note collateralled by government securities, which it then loaned on the New York Stock Exchange at from 6 to 7 percent. This, Hamlin insisted, "called for direct pressure, or perhaps for a higher rate on member banks collateral notes."[10] And the FRBNY now seemed to agree that a check was needed. On January 8, it raised its rediscount rate from 3 1/2 to 4 percent.

Still, Adolph Miller continued to fulminate about the FRBNY's failure to advance the rate in November, when speculation was on the rise. He claimed that Montagu Norman had told him in December that the New York call loan rate made the rediscount rate negligible and that it was beyond him why the FRBNY had not increased its rate some time ago.[11] According to Hamlin, Miller also denounced the draft of the board's annual report prepared by Walter Stewart, especially for its support of the FRBNY decision to remain with the lower rate when other banks had advanced theirs. Stewart argued that higher rates could have resulted in additional gold imports, could have put a higher base under the call loan rate, and could have led to an increase in customer rates at a time of crop movement. But Miller disagreed and insisted that higher rates would have resulted in reduced call loans and that the credit released by this action would have resulted in lower customer rates. In Hamlin's view there was no reasoning with Miller, whose stance was due to his "supreme contempt for the rest of the board."[12]

In the meantime Miller prepared a draft of a letter to the Federal Advisory Council requesting its advice and assistance in controlling or eliminating call loans in the securities market. On March 11 the letter was submitted to the board for consideration. But there it quickly ran into the objections of Secretary of the

---

8. Mark Sullivan, undated manuscript, in Mark Sullivan File, PPI, HHPL.

9. *Commercial and Financial Chronicle*, January 2, 1926, p. 1.

10. Hamlin Diary, January 8, 1926.

11. Ibid., January 13, 1926.

12. Ibid., March 2, 1926. Hamlin had made an entry in his diary a year earlier that Miller apparently believed that only political *Economist*s were fit to be Federal Reserve governors. Hamlin Diary, January 26, 1925.

Treasury Andrew Mellon who argued that if word leaked out that such a radical control over stock exchange operations was being contemplated, it would threaten the extension of Federal Reserve bank charters then under consideration. Hamlin also objected. He was not opposed to seeking advice from the Council concerning the board's ability to control the excessive use of Federal Reserve funds in the call loan market. But the proposed letter, he thought, by stating that the board was in the process of developing a procedure to "check or altogether eliminate" the abuse of such funds, seemed to imply that the board had the power to do this and that this was a questionable point of law. A bank, he also noted, when it borrowed from a Reserve bank, made good its net reserves rather than the reserve against a specific loan, whether agricultural, commercial, or speculative, and it was therefore prudent for the board to determine carefully how far the diversion of credit into speculative ventures could be corrected by applying direct pressure on borrowing institutions before resorting to so drastic a measure as refusing rediscounts, even if the latter was legal. Miller's letter, Hamlin feared, would be construed as an attempt to destroy the call loan market and should therefore be tabled, at least until the Reserve bank charter extensions had been granted, and on this the majority of the Reserve Board concurred.[13]

After the board adjourned, Hamlin discussed the matter with Mellon, arguing further against sending such a letter and reminding Mellon of Miller's speech before the Commercial Club in Boston in late November, where he had stated that the Federal Reserve Act contained specific provisions that precluded the use of Federal Reserve credit for speculative purposes and that it was the duty of Reserve banks to carry out these provisions. If the letter were sent, Hamlin thought, word of it would leak out, since there appeared to be, although he could not prove it, a pipeline running from the board. Mellon concurred and stated that he was certain that they had the same persons in mind, Hoover and Miller.[14]

The matter was further complicated by the fact that the Stock Exchange, for the first time in its history, issued a statement showing that as of January 30 its members had borrowed $3.5 billion. This created a good deal of discussion, not so much because of the amount borrowed by members of the Stock Exchange, as because that seemed to be only a fraction of the credit involved in stock speculation. When the borrowings of non-member bankers and brokers for Wall Street's speculative and investment activities were added, it was estimated that the total would amount to nearly $5 billion.[15]

Meanwhile, stock prices had turned down, and Strong believed that the FRBNY's rate hike had provided a needed check. He had disliked taking the action, he told Norman, but the FRBNY had been going through a difficult time with the stock market, and it was much better to have it over with. By late

13. Hamlin Diary, March 11, 1926.
14. Ibid.
15. "Wall Street's Speculative Borrowings," *American Review of Reviews* 73 (January-June 1926): 242.

March he maintained that the big boom in stocks was undoubtedly over and that there was "little likelihood of its recurrence."[16] The only question in his mind was whether the decline would "continue at such a rate as to have a dampening effect upon business."[17] He hoped that it would not.

Hoover, for one, did not believe that this would be the case. He held that in spite of the flurries on Wall Street and the collapse of the Bull Market, prosperity was still the "prevailing note in American business." Speculative values, he argued, were bound to fluctuate, and intermediate movements on the stock exchange were not necessarily a reflection of the domestic financial situation. Conditions were still good and there was no reason why production should not continue as it had. His only concern was that reckless optimism and speculation be avoided if the high level of prosperity were to continue.[18]

The Open Market Investment Committee report to the Governor's Conference on March 22 also noted the "wholesome" diminution of speculative activity. Movements, it held, had been orderly, and there appeared to be no untoward consequences, even though it was not yet possible to determine how far the liquidation would go or whether speculation, with all its inherent dangers, might start up again. The consensus on the Committee, was that in all probability "the peak of speculative and business expansion [had] been passed,"[19] and like Strong the Committee was concerned about the effects on business if the liquidation went too far. Strong wanted to limit the debts of banks in New York City to $50 million and thought it prudent to apply the same restriction to Chicago banks. And finally, at Strong's urging, the Open Market Committee favored a prompt purchase of additional securities if it appeared that a further recession in business activity was taking place and especially if there was no further liquidation in the outstanding amount of Federal Reserve credit.[20]

At a joint meeting of the Federal Reserve Board and the Governor's Conference on March 24, Strong again raised the issue of "business liquidation." He argued that a "business recession had started in all over the country," that no one could tell if it would continue, and that the system should therefore be prepared "to cope with it if it continued."[21] Miller, though, argued that this was a specious argument, aimed at justifying the retention of low rates. As far as he was concerned the "talk about business recession was all rot"; that the real motive

16. Benjamin Strong to Montagu Norman, March 27, 1926, in Strong Papers, FRBNY.

17. Ibid.

18. *Staunton News Leader*, March 21, 1926; *New York Herald Tribune*, March 5, 1926.

19. Open Market Investment Policy Excerpts, p. 68, in Adolph Miller Personal File, CP, HHPL.

20. Ibid., p. 71.

21. Hamlin Diary, March 20, 1926.

was to help the stock market. If the board approved the request, he said, it would "within a week be hauled before Congress and severely catechized."[22]

Undaunted by such criticisms, Strong repeated what he claimed was a unanimous request by the Open Markets Investment Committee that it be authorized to "purchase additional securities if and as soon as it may be apparent that conditions justify."[23] He was especially concerned that New York City banks were still heavily indebted to the FRBNY, that discounts, in other words, had not decreased and movements in the money market had not been reduced to normal. He was unable, however, in Mellon's absence to get the measure approved by the board, the result being a tie vote. Miller claimed that if Strong had submitted only a written report, he would have voted to approve the request. But after the ensuing discussion he was convinced that Strong was absolutely wrong. He also claimed that one of the members of the Open Market Investment Committee had told him that he disagreed with Strong's conclusions, but that Strong had a way of suppressing dissent within the Committee.[24]

On March 25, with Mellon presiding, the board reconsidered the request, and this time, with Mellon casting the deciding vote, gave its approval. Miller remained strongly opposed, arguing that he did not believe that an emergency existed or would exist. A reliable source, he said, had told him that the problem in New York was due to the fact that certain banks "were loaded up with new issues of securities which they could not place."[25] He refused, however, to divulge his source, and Crissinger, who suspected that the source was Hoover, stated that he would not pay any attention to information from an unnamed source. Winston and Mellon were also convinced that Hoover was the power behind Miller. During the course of a private conversation, Winston told Hamlin that he and Mellon had evidence that Miller supplied Hoover with information about board action, evidence, he said, that greatly disturbed Mellon.[26] Among those present, Strong also thought that Hoover had inspired Miller's claim, but in his view Hoover was getting his information from Winston who was apt to leak.[27]

---

22. Ibid., March 24, 1926.

23. Open Market Investment Policy Excerpts, pp. 71-72, in Adolph Miller Personal File, CP, HHPL.

24. Hamlin Diary, March 27, 1926.

25. Ibid., March 25, 1926.

26. Hamlin Diary, March 29, 1926.

27. Ibid., March 25, 1926. Hamlin also wrote that Strong claimed the real facts were that a California oil company wanted to sell out to an eastern oil company in which Mellon had an interest, but that Mellon refused to buy. A group of New York bankers then agreed to place the stock, but it was rumored that the group could not carry out the undertaking because of the large amount of money involved. Strong felt it was his duty to investigate the rumor. He found that the bankers had been able to raise the money and did in fact place the stock. According to Strong, Mellon was present at the meeting when Miller made his charge, was familiar with the entire situation, and knew that the charge was totally and absolutely false.

Meanwhile, debate about Federal Reserve policy had also resumed in the financial and business press. Writing in the *Economic World* in early 1926, W.F. Gephart, Vice-President of the First National Bank of St. Louis, questioned the ability of the system to govern the economic situation. He agreed that the uses to which credit was being put needed to be closely watched. But he also believed that many people, perhaps too many, had made a fetish of the Reserve System and were laboring under the delusion that it was a "panacea for all . . . financial problems," and that due to the existence of the system the country was "largely freed from the requirements which formerly were essential to a sound banking structure."[28]

The presence of the Federal Reserve System, according to Gephart, did not actually alter any of the primary functions or requirements of commercial banking. It was basically intended not to fund "speculative ventures in commodities, real estate or the securities market, but to supply essentially the necessary liquid capital for the day to day commercial transactions" through "short term self-liquidating loans."[29] Hence, the time to call attention to the problems arising from speculation was before the diversion of commercial credit had gone too far in that direction. It must be checked before it went beyond the point where it was possible to guarantee "that the volume of long-term credits" could be safely carried by the banking structure.[30]

Henry Chandler of the National Bank of Commerce in New York also took note of the credit situation and the doubts that it had raised in the minds of some, especially about the wisdom of the actions taken by the Reserve System during the latter part of 1925. Some of the speculative aspects "of the business situation," he thought, were clearly unfortunate and "should have been prevented [had] it been practicable to do so."[31] Had the system faced nothing more than an excess of easy money producing excessive speculative activity, it should have taken decisive action to tighten credit conditions during the last quarter of 1925.[32] But the problem was that the system was also confronted by the need to aid in European currency stabilization, the restoration of the gold standard, and the improvement of international trade. The latter was crucial if the gold standard was to be maintained, and it called for a good deal of financial assistance

28. *Economic World*, January 2, 1926, p. 5.

29. Ibid.

30. Ibid.

31. *Economic World*, January 9, 1926, p. 43. The decision, however, had been made to stay with low discount rates and, as H. Parker Willis points out, this continued to be the desired course of action. "In the autumn of 1926 a group of bankers, among whom was one with a world famous name, were sitting at a table in a Washington hotel. One of them had raised the question whether the low discount rates of the System were not likely to encourage speculation. 'Yes,' replied the conspicuous figure referred to, 'they will, but that cannot be helped. It is the price we must pay for helping Europe.'" H. Parker Willis, "The Failure of the Federal Reserve," *North American Review* 227 (May 1929): pp. 547-557.

32. *Economic World*, January 9, 1926, p. 43.

from the United States. It offered a great opportunity for this country "to be of service to the world" and to greatly benefit the United States in the long run.[33] And aid was being provided, both through the Federal Reserve System and from commercial banks and private investors, that was making it possible to achieve monetary stability abroad, check and reverse the influx of gold into the United States, and thus lay the basis for further trade expansion.[34]

In Chandler's view, however, a good deal still remained to be done in Europe before all countries there could return to the gold standard or stability in other countries could be assured. The crux of the credit dilemma was London. Great Britain was still dependent on the United States, while Europe in general, was dependent on both Britain and the United States. Credit movements affecting London were also felt in other European countries. In short, European financial conditions were held hostage to credit operations in the United States, and Federal Reserve policy had to be formulated accordingly. Since domestic requirements were not the same as international requirements, Reserve banks were confronted with the question of how much weight they should give to either in formulating their policies. This involved considerations such as raising or lowering of rediscount rates, the relation of discount rates to other rates, and open market operations. The challenge for the system was to steer the clearest course possible between the short term domestic requirements, such as the need to curb speculation, and long-term domestic and international credit requirements. And in Chandler's view, this should involve a resumption of conservative banking practices, which would go a long way towards halting the march of speculation and in doing so would avoid complicating the problems confronting the Reserve System in the international arena.[35]

On this issue, Chandler was taking a position at odds with the one staked out by Miller and Hoover. While they also recognized the importance of European economic recovery, they were not ready to foster it in ways that they believed would stimulate speculation in the United States. In his 1926 report, Hoover continued his warnings about reckless optimism, remained convinced that an increase in interest rates could be an effective check against speculation, and cited the importance of proper Federal Reserve management in moderating the business cycle and establishing "policies leading to maintained stability." Most businessmen, he was also convinced, believed "that the Federal Reserve should [not] be so managed as to result in stimulation of speculation and overexpansion."[36]

As for Strong, public discussion of Federal Reserve policy, particularly when it involved European stabilization and the gold standard, made him increasingly nervous. Writing to Norman in late March of 1926, he noted that there had again been a drift "into a period where unadvised and possibly ill tempered discussion of all sorts of questions . . . seem to be stirring up bad feelings

33. Ibid.

34. *Economic World*, February 13, 1926, p. 223.

35. Ibid.

36. U.S. Department of Commerce, *Annual Report*, 1926, pp. 12-13.

again."[37] He feared that this would not help the gold standard, and he was concerned that American investors might become "distrustful of European conditions . . . [and] button up their pocketbooks," in which case it would "be hard for everybody."[38]

Also related to the discussion of Federal Reserve policy was a continuing discussion of foreign loans. Administration policy in regard to these remained unaltered from agreements reached earlier.[39] But the policy was being criticized in the Senate by Democrats and radical Republicans,[40] and this was of great concern to Strong and Mellon. The latter feared that such criticism would retard the reestablishment of sound fiscal systems in Europe, would hamper American exports, and would threaten domestic prosperity.[41]

The criticism from overseas was also sharp. According to the Italian finance minister Giussepi Volpi, for example, "the United States had a mistress, and like a true gentleman, although he did not bow to her in public places, he slept with her at night." This mistress was Wall Street, which had formed an international club whose members were Norman and Strong along with "a servant named Schacht," who had been accorded membership privileges.[42] And the result was both an American stranglehold on credits and a foolish and shortsighted policy of collecting war debts, which required that money be pumped back into Europe by Wall Street in the form of enormous loans.

In addition, Strong was concerned about the congressional inquiry that had been authorized in the wake of the 1925 credit arrangement between the FRBNY and the Bank of England.[43] By late March of 1926, the House Banking and Currency Committee had begun hearings on a proposed Amendment to the Federal Reserve Act introduced by Representative James K. Strong of Kansas. And Benjamin Strong, ever mindful of the attitude of the agricultural bloc towards the Federal Reserve System, was deeply concerned that the persisting depression in agriculture would lead farm groups to attempt once again to lay the blame for their misfortunes on the Federal Reserve, just as they had in 1921. Specifically, Congressman Strong's bill proposed:

---

37. Benjamin Strong to Montagu Norman, March 27, 1926, in Strong Papers, FRBNY.

38. Ibid.

39. Harold Stokes to Grosvenor Jones, June 18, 1925, Memorandum, in State Department General Correspondence file, HHPL.

40. Garrard Winston to Benjamin Strong, February 12, 1926, in Strong Papers, FRBNY. Winston thought that the Ku Klux Klan was at the bottom of it all.

41. Andrew Mellon to Calvin Coolidge, February 10, 1926, in Strong Papers, FRBNY.

42. Garrard Winston to Benjamin Strong, February 12, 1926, in Strong Papers, FRBNY.

43. J.F. Fowler to W. Randolph Burgess, June 1, 1925, in Bank of England Revolving Credit File, FRBNY.

To establish from time to time, subject to review and determination of the Federal Reserve Board, a minimum rate of discount to be charged by such bank for each class of paper, which shall be made with a view to accommodating commerce and promoting a stable price level for commodities in general. All of the powers of the Federal reserve system shall be used for promoting stability in the price level.[44]

The bill's objective was to stabilize commodity prices. But as the hearings progressed, various other aspects of Federal Reserve policy also came under scrutiny, among them the participation of the FRBNY in England's return to the gold standard, its relationship with the German Reichsbank, Federal Reserve policy as it applied to speculation, and the FRBNY's repurchasing policy.

In the eyes of Benjamin Strong, Congress was now attempting to alter the Federal Reserve Act. But as Representative Strong saw it, this was "simply an effort to renew the various attempts that [had] been suggested to carry out the direction of the Constitution wherein Congress was authorized 'to coin money and regulate the value thereof.'"[45] Congress, he argued, had made an effort to regulate the value of money when it first enacted the Federal Reserve Act in 1913. But the act's provisions had been used in the interest of bankers rather than in the interest of stabilizing the purchasing power of American money and had thus contributed to detrimental speculative activities.

The Reserve System, according to Representative Strong, had the power to increase or decrease the volume of money and to regulate its rental or cost value. It also had at its disposal "powers of publicity," which, to his thinking, should be "used to better regulate the stability of the price level of commodities."[46] However, he feared that there were those who had "come to believe that the Federal Reserve System . . . had become a sacred thing" that Congress should not attempt to change or improve upon,[47] and that those who held this view would likely attempt to mobilize opinion against his proposal by arguing that it would fix prices or stabilize individual prices such as those of agricultural products. In reality, he said, nothing of the sort was contemplated. Individual commodity prices would continue to be determined by the law of supply and demand.

According to Congressman Strong, moreover, both domestic and foreign conditions were favorable to the kind of stabilization that he was advocating. They were such that stabilization would not only benefit the agricultural sector but would also be helpful to the United States and the world at large. The time had come to take the "money question out of politics or any special class,"[48] and

---

44. House Committee on Banking and Currency, *Stabilization, H.R. 7895*, 69th Cong., 1st sess., 1926, p. 1.

45. Ibid.

46. *Stabilization Hearings*, p. 2.

47. Ibid.

48. Ibid. p. 5. Strong pointed out that farmers had just gone through their sixth year of declining prices, but the cost of credit remained high.

the way to do it was to have Congress instruct Federal Reserve officials to take appropriate action.

Despite these claims of benefiting all sectors, however, the fact remained that the bill was proposed by a member of the farm bloc and reflected all its enmity towards and distrust of the eastern banking establishment that was already working hand in glove with the Federal Reserve System. George Shibeley, the Director of the Research Institute of Washington, D.C., brought this sectional conflict into the open when he insisted that after six years of declining prices farmers had become a submerged group, and that this had begun to affect bankers and other creditors who, with the exception of monied interests in the East, had joined with farmers in a political revolt. Shibeley, like Representative Strong, argued that the time was "ripe" to enact legislation that would bring about stabilization in the price level and end permanently the deflation "brought about by the Government's agent, the Federal Reserve Board."[49] The system's duty, in Shibeley's view, was to regulate the money supply with a view toward accommodating commerce and business, which meant "the largest possible stability in the value of money" after such a drop in the price level as had been experienced in the preceding six years.[50] The problem, as he saw it, was that the return of the Republicans to power had been accompanied by a return of those who had supported the Aldrich plan, and the result was a Federal Reserve Board that was now using its power to control the upward trend in prices in collusion with bankers and speculators.[51]

Irving Fisher, Professor of Economics at Yale University, agreed in principle with Shibeley. The Genoa Resolution of 1922, he argued, recommended the very thing proposed in the Strong bill and the same way of achieving it. It called for stabilizing the internal purchasing power of currency through central banks that would control their gold reserves and exercise credit control to prevent undue inflation or deflation. And this, Fisher maintained, would be good policy for the United States.[52] It needed a stabilized dollar to prevent economic injustices and to avoid the secondary evils that came from misunderstanding, fault-finding, and accusation during periods of monetary instability. When inflation prevailed corporations and bankers were accused of profiteering from the losses of others, and when there was deflation the farmers blamed the Rockefeller, Morgan, and other Wall Street interests for troubles that were actually caused by impersonal forces. The result was ill feelings, class warfare, and at times bloodshed, and the Strong bill, he thought, was admirably suited to preventing class warfare and avoiding the kind of trouble experienced in Russia.

The woes of the agricultural sector, Fisher went on to explain, were not the result of any malevolent scheme of either bankers or the Federal Reserve System, but were more than anything else, the "left-overs of the deflation of 1919 and 1920." Farmers had been hit hardest by that deflation and were the slowest

49. *Stabilization Hearings*, p. 7.
50. Ibid.
51. Ibid.
52. Ibid., p. 57.

to recover from its effects, a view with which Hoover also agreed.[53] At present, at least 50 percent of their difficulties stemmed from that experience. The important thing now was to make sure that whatever steps were taken to achieve stabilization not be viewed as class legislation and designed to help only agricultural interests at the expense of everyone else. Such action must be for the general good.

More specifically, Fisher, like Hoover and Miller, thought that a raise in the rediscount rate would be an effective way to check inflation. He did not believe that open market operations, which Crissinger favored, would be as effective since it was not possible to contract too far ahead when it came to the securities held by banks in their portfolios. Once they were gone, moreover, banks were out of ammunition, which happened to be the case in 1926. And the potential in such a situation was for inflation unless the Federal Reserve System used great wisdom and discretion.

Finally, Fisher echoed the concerns of the time that English influences had been brought to bear, particularly by those who were seeking through inflation to reduce the burden of war debt payments. During his 1921 trip to Britain, Fisher recalled, he had heard a number of economists say that it would serve the United States right if a large amount of gold was shipped to America in order to foster inflation. He was confident, though, that the Federal Reserve System would not go along with any such plan but would instead feel "insulted and resent it."[54]

One who did not share Fisher's confidence in the Reserve Board was Western Starr of the National Committee of the Farmer-Labor Party. Expressing deep concerns about the effects of England's return to gold on America's domestic economy, Starr argued that Norman and Strong had reached a gentlemen's agreement so as to permit gold to stay in England and strengthen the pound. England's interests had counted for more than those of the United States, and the result had been an inflationary situation in America.[55]

Representative Louis McFadden, a member of the House Banking Committee, also questioned the legality, terms, and reasonableness of Federal Reserve participation in England's return to gold. He wondered whether any institution that was allowed to invest "in a foreign credit of this kind" could also

---

53. Ibid.; U.S. Department of Commerce, *Annual Report*, 1926, pp. 12-13.

54. *Stabilization Hearings*, p. 73.

55. Ibid., p. 239. Starr did not have a very high regard for the Federal Reserve System or its members. He had a particular disdain for former board member Warburg, who he claimed originated the idea of the Reserve System and put it over on the American people. According to Starr, bankers came on board only with the push for the Aldrich bill, and it took five more years of pressure to put the scheme across. The way farmers viewed it was that the "Federal Reserve Act was passed, and they put one of the men that had been denounced as a criminal. . . . Paul Warburg . . . on the board to run it." *Stabilization Hearings*, p. 227.

serve as the maintainer of America's bank reserves in periods of emergency.[56] And the implication was that he thought not.

George Seay, however, who was currently Governor of the Federal Reserve Bank Richmond, saw nothing wrong with the transaction, legal or otherwise. Nor did Reserve Board member George James. He endorsed the action as well, although in doing so he did point out that the system had not extended any loan to Great Britain, as McFadden had stated. It had only made an arrangement that allowed Great Britain, if the necessity arose, to avail itself of a loan.[57]

Adolph Miller then pointed out that the entire transaction had been undertaken by the FRBNY and only later approved by the Reserve Board.[58] Subsequently, Benjamin Strong admitted that the FRBNY had been the initiator and actor in the situation. Unlike Miller, however, he did not point out that the agreement had been discussed by the board in January, but only retroactively approved in April.

In his later testimony, Miller was sympathetic to the aims contained in the Strong bill and critical of a number of aspects of the systems operations, particularly its rediscount policies. He also brought out a part of the internal clash over the use of Federal Reserve credit, a clash that previously had been confined to acerbic interchanges during board meetings, limited attacks through proxies in trade journals, or carefully crafted letters to the Federal Reserve Board. Miller now spoke directly and on the record about what he thought were the shortcomings of the system and what steps should be taken to remedy them. As one might expect, the concern about speculative loans that he and Hoover had expressed through Lenroot and which, according to Miller, was shared by other board members became the focal point of his testimony.

Miller was especially concerned about what he considered to be the board's responsibility to keep a "close guard over the direction in which Federal Reserve credit flowed."[59]   One possible solution to this problem, he thought, was to amend the Federal Reserve Act to provide that reserve banks extend only such discounts, advances, and accommodations to member banks as could be safely made, as were required to meet the operating needs of their customers, and as were to be used in trade, industry, and agriculture.[60]   The suggestion greatly disturbed Andrew Mellon.[61]   But Representative Otis Wingo thought that such restrictions already applied to Federal Reserve discounts, and wondered what the Federal Reserve had done the previous fall. Had it done anything, and if not, was this because it believed that it did not have the authority to intervene?

---

56. Ibid., p. 274.
57. Ibid., p. 281.
58. Ibid., p. 284.
59. Ibid., p. 673.
60. Ibid., p. 857.
61. According to Hamlin the Comptroller of the Currency reported that Mellon was very much disturbed by Miller's proposal and believed that he had made a mistake in recommending Miller for reappointment in 1924. Hamlin Diary, May 14, 1926.

Some action, Miller said, had been taken. The rediscount rate had been raised, and banks that had borrowed from reserve banks to make security loans or to maintain an existing volume of such loans had been admonished. But Wingo thought this insufficient and asked Miller whether the Reserve Board or Federal Reserve banks had the authority to deny loans along the lines of Miller's proposal. In his view, Miller replied, they did not, but it was clearly important, he added, for them to keep informed of the credit operations and borrowings of member banks.[62] Miller's testimony, said Representative McFadden, was evidence that the "Federal Reserve System had been lending credit, in spite of itself, for speculative purposes."[63] This, he thought, could be remedied by amending Article 4 of the Act, as Miller had suggested.

In addition, Miller criticized the system's open market operations, at least as they had been conducted up to that time. The Reserve Board, he thought, needed more power over these, and at a Reserve Board meeting in late March he and James had expressed the view that if there was any doubt about the board's authority to regulate such purchases, it should go to Congress and secure a grant of such power. At the same time, Miller had stated that it was his intention to bring the matter before the House Banking and Currency Committee.[64]

Accordingly, Miller now suggested that Section 14 of the Act be amended so as to give the board a plenary power of review over open market operations. These, he argued, were both a system matter and "a matter of great consequence in handling the general credit situation." The board needed the power to supervise them since they involved the investment of the legal reserves of Reserve banks and since they were much more conducive to Federal Reserve resources being employed in speculation than was reserve expansion "through the rediscount and borrowings by member banks."[65] It was evident, Miller maintained, that the Reserve System's operations had not been confined to the legitimate needs of commerce, industry, and agriculture, as contemplated under the Act. They had contributed to speculation, although he admitted that it was difficult to determine just which funds were employed in that way.[66]

Miller also went on to point out that if the board disapproved purchases, the Reserve banks simply proceeded to operate in the open market on their own. He stopped short, however, of indicting Strong for aggravation of this problem, as he would do two years later.[67] Nor did he publicly accuse Strong, as he had done in front of other board members and Mellon, of being influenced by the needs of the stock market in determining open market policies. And Strong, for his part, did not bring up the issue of stock market influence as he had threat-

62. *Stabilization Hearings*, p. 858.

63. Ibid., p. 869.

64. Hamlin Diary George, March 29, 1928.

65. *Stabilization Hearings*, p. 869.

66. *Stabilization Hearings*, p. 919.

67. House Committee on Banking and Currency, *Stabilization, H.R. 11806*, 70th Cong., 1st sess., 1928, p. 126.

ened to do earlier when he stated that "he would bring Miller out in the open and that there would be a sensation before the Committee on Banking and Currency."[68] That he was dissuaded from voicing his grievance was apparently due to Hamlin, who feared that this would only show the divisions within the board.[69]

Miller's successor as a witness was Randolph Burgess, the Assistant Reserve Agent at the FRBNY, who was confronted with the various criticisms and suggestions that Miller had offered. The committee wanted to know his views on open market operations, and it was particularly interested in the system's repurchase policy that allowed banks in need of short-term loans to "sell" government securities to Federal Reserve banks and then to "repurchase" them at the same price and pay only the interest borne by the bond. This was quite legal, Burgess insisted. But Representative Wingo was not certain that it was and requested that the Federal Reserve Board be instructed to provide a statement for the Committee spelling out what authority the FRBNY had to carry out such transactions. He also wanted an opinion from the bank's attorney or the Attorney General, if one had been obtained.[70]

In response to Wingo's requests, Daniel Crissinger asked George Harrison of the FRBNY to prepare a memorandum detailing the development of the bank's repurchase agreement and to bring it to Washington personally, for a discussion of the purpose, scope, and legality of the scheme. According to Harrison it was also agreed that the memorandum was to be inserted into Strong's testimony,[71] which it subsequently was. It was important, Strong subsequently advised Harrison, always to present a constructive rather than a defensive attitude where doubts such as those over the legality of the repurchase agreement arose. The bank, he thought, should always take the position that it had the power to do whatever it was doing. For if the power were denied, this would injure not only the banks but "the country and the system."[72] He noted that the committee reacted well to such suggestions when he appeared in front of it, and that he was certain that it always would because it was in a constructive frame of mind and would be helpful.

While appearing before the committee, Miller was also critical of the FRBNY's decision on April 23 to reduce its rediscount rate from 4 to 3 1/2 percent. It was premature, he thought, and had he been at the Reserve Board

68. Hamlin Diary, April 13, 1926.

69. During the same conversation Hamlin stated that Miller "perhaps unconsciously was a rabid deflationist." Strong answered that "Miller, Dr. Welles, and the New York Commercial and Financial Chronicle were all leagued together in the cause of radical deflation, and that he certainly would have something to say about the . . . Chronicle before he finished his testimony." Hamlin Diary, April 13, 1926.

70. *Stabilization Hearings*, p. 934.

71. George Harrison to Benjamin Strong, May 18, 1926, in George Harrison Papers, Butler Library, Columbia University.

72. Benjamin Strong to George Harrison, June 11, 1926, in George Harrison Papers, Butler Library, Columbia University, New York.

meeting where it was approved, he would have opposed it. On this as on other matters, his position was duly noted by Harrison and then passed along to Strong, who at the time was in Britain testifying before a Royal Commission on the possible adoption of the gold standard in India. Strong would be interested, Harrison thought, since he might want to make supplementary remarks about the issue when he appeared before the committee again.[73]

Harrison was not overly concerned when Miller, Representative Strong, and Governor Harding came to New York to speak on the Strong bill at a dinner given by the Stable Money Association. On the contrary, Harrison saw nothing improper in attending. He arranged to get a table and then proceeded to take advantage of Representative Strong's presence in New York to invite him to breakfast and ask him to spend May 5, the day of the dinner, at the FRBNY.

Harrison later noted that Congressman Strong was really impressed with the building, its simplicity and businesslike appearance, and the immense amount of work conducted there. The visit, he said, had been an eye opener to him. After lunch the two men also visited the Stock Exchange and, according to Harrison, "had a most satisfactory day of it."[74] He learned that from Representative Strong's point of view, the hearings in Washington were progressing satisfactorily and were likely to continue until everyone had ample opportunity to be heard, which meant that while he regretted further delay he did believe that action on his bill would be taken before the next session. In addition, Harrison came away with the impression that when all the hearings were concluded, all evidence compiled, and all arguments presented, the sponsors of the bill hoped to take the suggestions given by Benjamin Strong and others and draft a new measure that would be in line with them. This new bill, Harrison thought, would not run the risk of altering the Federal Reserve Act, something that Benjamin Strong had feared if the original bill were enacted.[75]

Harrison also learned from Representative Strong that some members of the Committee were sympathetic to Miller's recommendations for restrictions on Federal Reserve credit. In writing to Benjamin Strong, however, he discounted this threat, noting that in his testimony Miller had conceded that it would be next to impossible to trace the ultimate use of Federal Reserve credit. What Harrison was more concerned about was Miller's testimony "to build up in the minds of the committee an idea of the importance and influence of the Federal Reserve Board in contrast to the power and influence of the individual banks." He had, for example, claimed that rate changes in the past had, for the most part, resulted from the "study and suggestion of the Reserve Board" because it had a much broader perspective than individual Reserve banks did,[76] and he had made

---

73. George Harrison to Benjamin Strong, April 30, 1926, in George Harrison Papers, Butler Library, Columbia University, New York.

74. George Harrison to Benjamin Strong, May 7, 1926, in George Harrison Papers, Butler Library, Columbia University, New York.

75. Ibid.

76. George Harrison to Benjamin Strong, April 30, 1926, in George Harrison Papers, Butler Library, Columbia University, New York.

a number of statements, some subtle, others more blatant, saying that he, "more than any one else in the system," studied the statistics, charts, and records available to the board, and used them as a foundation upon which to base his judgment and decisions about rate policies and open market operations. Miller, moreover, had claimed that he was apt "to be guided by a more traditional knowledge of these matters than [was] possible to others in the System" who did not use these materials to the extent that he did.[77]

Yet, Harrison admitted that Miller had not made any specific charges that "could properly start a fight." Instead, he had cleverly created "an opportunity" for the Committee to "see the power and influence and the effectiveness of the Federal Reserve Board." And in some ways , Harrison thought, this was not at all bad. It might, after all, help to allay the fears of the radicals in Congress who thought that the system was really being dominated by Wall Street. Everything considered, Harrison concluded, Miller's testimony was unlikely to prevent the majority of the Committee from seeing the FRBNY's "true relation to the whole system."[78]

Benjamin Strong, though, was deeply disturbed by Miller's testimony, and in a subsequent letter to Harrison he argued that attempting to place limitations on the speculative use of Federal Reserve funds was a futile and foolhardy undertaking and that the implications of such limitations could spell disaster for the bank. He was also annoyed by the proposal to give complete control over market operations to the board. This, he argued, could "only be answered by a request to the Committee to consider the competence of the board, not only intellectually but geographically and in every other way, to exercise such control."[79] As he saw it, these suggestions were directed not at improving the service provided by the reserve banks, but at enlarging the powers of the board. They were an example of the maxim that "all impotent bodies seek to cure their disabilities by enlargement of their powers."[80] However, he concluded, he was not sure that much could be done about it. He would have to read more of what Miller had to say.

Writing again shortly thereafter, Strong stated that to him Miller's testimony amounted to a wearisome document giving strong indications of his beliefs that "the board must have a large hand in operations" and that the directors and officers of the Reserve banks had too much influence in arriving at major decisions.[81] Miller, he thought, had been disingenuous in giving the impression that the Reserve Board "had a much greater comprehension of the system's problems" than "the people at the FRBNY knew it had." Moreover, Miller had committed the "natural error" of stating his views as though they were repre-

77. Ibid.

78. Ibid.

79. Benjamin Strong to George Harrison, May 5, 1926, in George Harrison Papers, Butler Library, Columbia University, New York.

80. Ibid.

81. Benjamin Strong to George Harrison, June 11, 1926, in George Harrison Papers, Butler Library, Columbia University, New York.

sentative of the board as a whole. And most irritating of all, he had divulged the number and detailed specifics of the FRBNY's foreign account.[82] Strong, in Europe at the time, asked Parker Gilbert about the propriety of public discussion, such as Miller had conducted, on the position and status of the Reichsbank account and of disclosing the bank's foreign balances. The latter, he was told by Gilbert, were not only carefully guarded in bank statements but the law prohibited the full disclosure even to the bank's directors. The object was to give the bank the freedom to deal with foreign exchange accounts and their reserves in order to ensure the greatest possible protection to the exchange value of the mark. Miller's disclosure, Strong insisted, was such a serious matter that it should be eliminated from the record, though he decided to leave the method of its removal up to Harrison.[83]

Harrison was properly sympathetic. He suggested that such details as Miller had discussed should be eliminated from future reports and that he had already changed the report he was going to submit to the directors of the FRBNY; instead of specifics it would provide only a summary of the bank's deposits and investments in foreign banks. The fact that Miller had made the amount of the FRBNY's Reichsbank account public, he thought, would be a valid excuse for raising the question with the Reserve Board and the governors of the other Reserve banks. He would, he promised, take the matter up with Crissinger, so that he could determine what information the board really needed, and would see if that portion of Miller's testimony pertaining to the FRBNY's Reichsbank account could be deleted from the transcript, if it were not already too late to do so.[84] To what extent he discussed the matter with Crissinger is not known, but he was determined to find a way to have Miller's comments about the Reichsbank's account stricken from the official record.

Indeed, he had already made some preliminary attempts along this line, specifically by taking up the matter with Dr. Emanuel Goldenweiser, who was one of those in charge of editing the record and who remembered the remarks in question as having been already deleted from the galley proof. Harrison had then asked Goldenweiser to make sure that this was the case, and the latter, who "understood" the situation, had agreed to keep Harrison's name out of any action that he took regarding the editing of Miller's testimony.[85] The official transcript of Miller's testimony did not contain the disclosures of the Reichsbank's account with the FRBNY.[86]

The possibility for future breaches continued to exist, and because of this Harrison adopted a policy of going over each statement and report issued by the

82. Ibid.

83. Benjamin Strong to George Harrison, July 29, 1926, in George Harrison Papers, Butler Library, Columbia University, New York.

84. George Harrison to Benjamin Strong, August 5, 1926 in George Harrison Papers, Butler Library, Columbia University, New York.

85. George Harrison to Benjamin Strong, August 25, 1926 in George Harrison Papers, Butler Library, Columbia University, New York.

86. *Stabilization Hearings*, p. 833.

FRBNY's foreign department, whether to other divisions in FRBNY, the Federal Reserve Board, or other Federal Reserve banks. A number of these, he said, had been eliminated. But this could only go so far. It would be impossible for bank officials to accomplish what they wanted as far as other Federal Reserve banks or even the board were concerned until they had an opportunity to discuss it with the governors.[87]

Another matter on Harrison's mind at the time was Representative Strong's request for input in redrafting his bill. The congressman had sent a circular to the reserve banks requesting their input but was disappointed with the results, in part perhaps because the FRBNY had refused to provide guidance for the other banks for fear that this would be seen as making propaganda or exerting undue influence. In any event, Representative Strong stated that with the exception of Benjamin Strong, representatives of the Reserve System "all seemed to take a rather blind and unhelpful attitude towards any proposal to amend the Federal Reserve Act."[88] This was the feeling he got from Norris's testimony and others who had written him.[89] Harrison thought that while the attitude on the part of other officials was easy enough to understand, it was too bad that they had given this impression because the Strong bill was too serious "to deal with by wholly uncompromising denials." The FRBNY's governor, he added, had struck the right note, and he only wished that other governors had found a way to do the same.[90]

87 George Harrison to Benjamin Strong, August 25, 1926 in George Harrison Papers, Butler Library, Columbia University, New York. The evidence available does not indicate the extent to which this matter was discussed either with the Federal Reserve Board or the governors of the other reserve banks.

88. George Harrison to Benjamin Strong, July 16, 1926, in George Harrison Papers, Butler Library, Columbia University, New York.

89. See, for instance, former Reserve Board member Paul Warburg's reaction to the proposed scheme. "My dear Strong: I thank you for your letter of March 19 inclosing [sic] a copy of HR 7895, introduced by yourself, and a copy of the Congressional Record bearing upon that bill. While of course, I share your view that price stability is a thing devoutly to be wished for, I regret to say that I am not in sympathy at all with the amendment that you propose. No banking system, to my mind at least, can undertake to provide a stability of prices, and I believe it would be dangerous to place the Federal reserve system in a position when the responsibility for extreme fluctuations in the price level, could be laid at its door. Naturally those in charge of the Federal reserve system should always watch most carefully fluctuations in the price level and fashion the policy of the system as far as it is practicable so as to combat excesses of inflation or deflation; but the powers of the central banking system in this regard are distinctly limited. Interest rates may be a contributing factor in affecting price levels, but to my mind they are only one of the many factors of all the world-wide economic forces at play which in the end determine price levels." Paul Warburg to James Strong, May 22, 1926, printed in *Stabilization Hearings*, p. 223.

90. George Harrison to Benjamin Strong, July 16, 1926, in George Harrison Papers, Butler Library, Columbia University, New York.

Benjamin Strong was disturbed by the attitude of his peers and argued that the issue was not whether one agreed with Congressman Strong, but that the sincerity with which he had approached an extremely difficult problem entitled him to the best help members of the system could provide. Benjamin Strong insisted that he would do his best to assist the Congressman, at least up to the point where he would be forced to sacrifice some honest convictions which he would not do. A formula, he believed, could be devised, which would express the objectives of the system without being deceptive as to what the banks could not do, and in that process he would like to have a role.[91]

In addition, Harrison worried about rumors that Louis McFadden, the Chairman of the Banking and Currency Committee, was interested in being appointed to the board. The real purpose of the hearings, he speculated, might be to embarrass some of the members of the board by asking questions that might "evidence their ignorance or incompetence rather than to procure helpful testimony." "Heaven forbid," he added, that McFadden should be appointed,[92] but the possibility existed in view of the fact that Hamlin was up for reappointment and Cunningham and Crissinger were seriously ill.[93]

Then there were the continuing problems with Miller. There was fear that in going to France, he would "tumble unwittingly into a hornet's nest."[94] In addition to his criticism of open market operations and of the FRBNY's rediscount policy, there were his charges that the New York bank had undermined the effectiveness of the Reserve Board's research division by hiring away one of Miller's abler assistants and absorbing much of the research work that the board should be doing. According to Hamlin, this had produced strains not only between Miller and Strong but also between Miller and Crissinger. The latter saw nothing improper in the action and "got very angry" with Miller, stating that his trouble was that he was "too damned jealous" and that he acted as if he, rather than Crissinger, were Governor of the Federal Reserve Board.[95] Miller's chief support on the episode came from James, who thought Strong had taken similar action in the past and was out to cripple the board.[96]

One problem, as Strong and Winston saw it, was that Crissinger was simply unable to do his job. He was in Marion, Ohio, ill with kidney trouble and in no condition to undergo any operations because of the condition of his heart. He would, Harrison thought, be forced to resign sooner or later, and this might provide an opportunity for a "realignment of the board's personnel," something that

---

91. Benjamin Strong to George Harrison, August 3, 1926, in Benjamin Strong Papers, FRBNY.

92. George Harrison to Benjamin Strong, May 18, 1926, George Harrison Papers, Butler Library, Columbia University, New York.

93. George L. Harrison to Benjamin Strong June 18, 1928 in George Harrison Papers, Butler Library, Columbia University, New York.

94. Ibid.

95. Hamlin Diary, April 20, 1926.

96. Hamlin Diary, May 22, 1926.

Mellon was unlikely to do anything about until a vacancy occurred.[97] Or as Winston suggested, if Crissinger did not resign, nature might soon lend a helping hand. In the meantime, he asked Strong to provide him with the names of desirable members. "We all sit around and criticize," he said, but it was "awfully hard to make constructive suggestions."[98]

Strong clearly wanted something done about his relations with the board, and in June expressed his fear to Pierre Jay that the directors of the FRBNY did not understand how serious he was about wanting to resolve the situation.[99] Harrison, though, insisted that both he and Jay understood quite well how serious Strong was and that he had emphasized this point in every discussion he had had with the directors of the Bank.[100] The problem, Harrison argued, was that not much could be done given the situation in Washington. Crissinger's health, and the possibility of his resignation, was the reason for inaction there, and besides, Mellon was scheduled to go overseas during July, and this meant that nothing would be done until after his return, even if Crissinger should resign during his absence. In all probability, there would be no appointment until after the election, which meant that Strong would return from abroad with little if anything changed.[101]

The only alternative, Harrison thought, was to make Mellon aware of the situation and point out that Strong would resign if relations with the board were not made more tolerable. This, though, had already been discussed with the directors of the FRBNY, and they had taken the position that this would be a questionable course to follow and would accomplish little other than to embarrass Mellon and Strong. They wanted to wait for Crissinger to retire, which was now a real possibility, and in the meantime to begin thinking about a possible successor. He hoped, Harrison said, that someone could be found who would "grip the board with some force and determination."[102]

Two weeks later, Harrison again wrote Strong, saying that the bank's directors recognized that something had to be done to improve relations with the board, if for no other reason than Strong's health. They had taken to discussing the subject at nearly every meeting, and while they did not want "to serve Mel-

97. George L. Harrison to Benjamin Strong, June 18, 1928, in George Harrison Papers, Butler Library, Columbia University, New York.

98. Garrard Winston to Benjamin Strong, June 16, 1926, FRBNY.

99. George L. Harrison to Benjamin Strong, June 18, 1928, in George Harrison Papers, Butler Library, Columbia University, New York. Harrison refers to one of Strong's letters to Jay in which he expressed his concern about his relations with the Federal Reserve Board.

100. Strong was seriously considering resigning his position if relations with the board [Miller] could not be settled. As far as his belief that neither Harrison nor Jay understood his intentions, he cited as evidence the fact that they continued the lease on Strong's apartment; see, for instance, George L. Harrison to Benjamin Strong, June 22, 1926, in Strong Papers, FRBNY.

101. Ibid.

102. Ibid.

lon with anything savoring of an ultimatum 'Strong or Miller,'" James Alexander and Pierre Jay were trying to impress upon Secretary Mellon how serious Strong was and that this was largely on account of his health.[103]   Again, the problem was that Mellon was at a loss about what to do in the absence of a resignation and preferred to temporize "rather than to force an open fight," especially in view of the illness of Crissinger and Cunningham. On the whole, Harrison thought, everything possible had been done, and attention should now be focused on who should succeed Crissinger in the event of his resignation. The task ahead was to "get some Governor who [could] keep A.C. Miller within bounds."[104]   Within a short while, though, Crissinger recovered, and resumed his functions on the board.

Harrison also attempted to find allies in Congress who might take a more favorable view of the Federal Reserve System, particularly among those representing silver interests. In conversations with officials of the U.S. Smelting, Refining and Mining Company, Harrison pointed out that the first step toward European usage of silver in subsidiary coinage was monetary stabilization because no country could "use any metal in coinage of a real bullion value so long as it did not know how far its currency was going to slide."[105]   The company's interest in the matter, he thought, would be most helpful in obtaining sentiment in the West for reestablishing stability in Europe and for the participation of the Federal Reserve System and American bankers in the process. In addition, Senators like Reed Smoot of Utah were apprised of how much Benjamin Strong had done for the silver interests by his testimony in England against India's being allowed to adopt the gold standard. Had India departed from silver currency it would have seriously depreciated the value of silver, and in the event it had actually entered on the gold standard it would have permanently cheapened silver, thus affecting silver, copper, zinc, and lead mines in the United States.[106]

Strong's testimony abroad, however, while pleasing to the silver interests, caused yet another row with members of the Reserve Board, who had been notified of it only after it had taken place and then only with Mellon's insistence that he did not want it publicly known.[107]   Subsequently, Mellon sent an expense voucher to cover Strong's appearance before the Parliamentary Commission, stating that the matter was a fiscal agency one. But this was not accepted without a debate, during which Crissinger and James bitterly criticized Mellon for his failure to consult with the board before asking Strong to testify. Crissinger

103. George L. Harrison to Benjamin Strong, July 6, 1926, in George Harrison Papers, Butler Library, Columbia University, New York.

104. Ibid.

105. George Harrison to Benjamin Strong, July 17, 1926, in George Harrison Papers, Butler Library, Columbia University, New York.

106. George Harrison to D.R. Crissinger, July 15, 1926, in George Harrison Papers, Butler Library, Columbia University, New York. Garrard Winston had a lengthy discussion with Senator Reed Smoot and informed him about all Strong had done to protect his silver interests.

107. Hamlin Diary, June 22, 1926.

had heard of the trip before, but was put out because the information had come to him from someone other than Mellon.[108]

During his stay in Europe, Strong had also visited France in order to gain a better understanding of economic conditions there. This irked James, who sponsored a resolution calling for an explanation of the authority under which Strong went there and demanding a detailed report of his activities.[109]   Strong later insisted that the object of his trip had been fully explained to Mellon and Crissinger and had been fully approved by them.[110]   Yet, as noted earlier, Crissinger claimed that his information about Strong's trip had come from outside sources. Moreover, Harrison feared that the bitter attitude towards Strong on the part of some board members, particularly James, might cause problems if an offer for assistance with a French credit were submitted to the board, especially if Miller returned from abroad with a "bad reaction."[111]

To everyone's surprise, however, Miller was strongly in favor of Federal Reserve assistance with credits to France. As for Strong, he responded to his critics by arguing that one could not expect them to grasp so complicated a situation, assimilate the information, and act appropriately when they had "none of the atmosphere" and knew none of the people. If they wanted to take a constructive attitude, Strong thought, they had to realize that unless they were willing to undertake the job themselves, they would have to trust someone else to do it.[112]

In the meantime, the Open Market Committee had met again, with Crissinger, James, and Comptroller of the Currency Joseph McIntosh in attendance. At the meeting, Harrison submitted a report for the FRBNY, which stated that since the committee had met in June the business atmosphere had improved and that business was now being carried forward at a very active pace because of an optimistic outlook about the future. Mirroring the optimism of earlier reports, it stated that 1926 would establish new records in production, building, freight car loadings, and other phases of business activity, all of which was particularly good news since past periods of relatively easy credit had usually been followed by over-production, over-speculation, and a decline in business activity.[113]   This time, the report said, there was little evidence of overdoing business prosperity. Although there was some overbuilding and a continued slump in the textile industry, businessmen in general were continuing their affairs in a conservative and orderly manner, and except for some decline in farm prices the

---

108. Hamlin Diary, July 20, 1926.

109. George Harrison to Benjamin Strong, July 16, 1926, in George Harrison Papers, Butler Library, Columbia University, New York.

110. Hamlin Diary, August 18, 1926. Hamlin also claimed that James' antagonism was motivated by his jealousy of Strong.

111. George Harrison to Benjamin Strong, July 16, 1926, in George Harrison Papers, Butler Library, Columbia University, New York.

112. Benjamin Strong to George Harrison, August 3, 1926, in George Harrison Papers, Columbia University, New York.

113. Open Market Committee Report, p. 78.

commodity markets had been remarkably steady. The principle example of "speculative" activity was in the stock market, but the "higher prices and active trading" there appeared to "reflect not only heavy professional operations, but large earnings and an increasing public interest."[114]

The report did point out that member banks had lent about one billion dollars more than the previous year, but this, it held, was not unusual considering the country's growth and the expansion of bank investments. It was no cause for alarm, although for the immediate future it would be wise to pursue a policy of caution and conservatism and to make some sales from the special investment account so that a larger portion of the outstanding Federal Reserve credit could be converted into discounts. Such action, it argued, would make discount rates more effective in getting member banks to shoulder their responsibilities and subject their extensions of credit to closer scrutiny. Again, this was a policy that should be exercised with caution. There was no need for "drastic or precipitate action in the sale of securities which might disrupt the financing of fall trade and agriculture."[115]

Crissinger, though, disagreed with Harrison's assessment and argued, rather vehemently, that the system should sell all of its holdings before October 1. He had serious misgivings, he said, about the stock market, which had got itself into the "rottenest situation" in some time, and was now "honeycombed with pool operations on the part of people who were booming stocks to unload before election when they anticipated a democratic victory." The system, he insisted should not be a party to providing funds for such operations.[116]

In writing to Strong, Harrison noted that Crissinger had called him earlier, stating that the FRBNY should raise its rediscount rate and sell $75 million of its holdings. However, any action had been postponed until a clearer picture of business activity emerged and outside interest rates and conditions improved. Besides, Harrison and others at the bank wanted to consult Strong before making any changes, either in the rediscount rate or the bank's holdings. Crissinger had then met with the board, which by a vote of three to one had supported his proposal, the lone dissenter being Hamlin who reserved judgement until he had a recommendation from the FRBNY.[117] When the bank did not act immediately to change its rate Crissinger and James became angry, and the result had been Crissinger's statement at the Open Market Investment Committee meeting. It was a matter of "pique" that the bank had not followed the express wishes of the board, and it was enough to cause one to loose all patience with the situation. As Harrison saw it, not one of the board members could have made "a decent argument for the raise at the time they expressed a willingness to approve an increase."[118]

---

114. Ibid. p. 78.

115. Ibid. p. 79.

116. George Harrison to Benjamin Strong, August 20, 1926, in George Harrison Papers, Butler Library, Columbia University, New York.

117. Ibid.

118. Ibid.

The FRBNY had raised its rate from 3 1/2 percent on August 12, but Crissinger continued to express his conviction that the FRBNY should have sold some of its holdings as far back as June. According to Harrison, Crissinger had never made this known to him in any conversations until August 3. This was unwarranted criticism, Harrison thought, and the explanation probably was that someone had been talking to Crissinger about the stock market, had given him quite a scare, and had got him to dropping remarks about pool operations, member bank speculation, and the need to prohibit directors of Federal Reserve Banks from dealing in the stock market. One bright note, from Harrison's standpoint, was that Crissinger had become disenchanted with his position on the board and was entertaining an offer to accept the presidency of a new indemnity company. Harrison hoped that this would materialize because it would solve a number of problems, or "at least offer the opportunity for their solution."[119]

In the end, though, the hopes of Harrison and Strong were again frustrated. Crissinger chose to remain as governor, and the divisions within the board and the enmity of some of its members towards the FRBNY continued. Mellon was greatly disturbed but could do little about James's and Miller's lack of confidence in the FRBNY and their seeming determination to deny its requests.[120] Repeatedly, Hamlin noted, they seemed bent on thwarting the New York Reserve Bank, an attitude that he attributed to hatred and jealousy.[121]

Credit expansion also continued, despite warnings about it in financial circles. Benjamin Baker, in his business column in the *Annalist,* stated that continued credit inflation for purposes other than commerce and industry would increase the possibility of a dangerous crisis in the event that there was a heavy recall of European capital "hiding" in the United States.[122] According to the *Monthly* of the Cleveland Trust Company, it would be dangerous for businessmen to attempt to stimulate business back to the level it was during the spring. The dangers, it argued, were "at the top where credit is granted rather than among the ultimate consumers where it is used."[123] This was an analysis with which both Hoover and Miller agreed.

---

119. George Harrison to Benjamin Strong, September 1, 1926, in George Harrison Papers, Butler Library, Columbia University, New York.

120. Hamlin Diary, October 5, 1926.

121. Hamlin Diary, December 15, 1926. Hamlin noted that among other things Miller vigorously opposed a salary increase for Randolph Burgess at the New York bank. In the end Miller compromised on a figure less than a fourth of that recommended by the bank. Mellon was evidently shocked by Miller's attitude. See Hamlin Diary, December 22, 1926. In another instance Miller moved to remove Carl Snyder, the statistician of the FRBNY, from the rolls of the Federal Reserve Agent, this despite the fact that his work was widely quoted. Hamlin Diary, December 28, 1926.

122. Adolph Miller to Herbert Hoover, November 29, 1926, in Banks and Banking file, CP, HHPL. Benjamin Baker wrote a weekly leader on The Business Outlook in the Annalist. Miller repeated Baker's comments in his note to Hoover.

123. Adolph Miller to Herbert Hoover, November 29, 1926, in Banks and Banking file, CP, HHPL.

The Federal Reserve System had begun the year 1926 mired in a controversy over speculation and its control initially spawned by the Hoover-Lenroot correspondence of the previous year. The debate did not remain confined to the system, as bankers, economists, and other officials were soon participating, congressmen became interested in amending the Federal Reserve Act, and those suffering from the agricultural depression again tried to blame their misfortunes on monetary managers who were allegedly more concerned with foreign than with domestic economic conditions. Steering a proper course between curbs on speculation and long-term international credit requirements was proving to be a major challenge, and as efforts to do so continued the House Banking and Currency Committee began hearings on the system's performance, its relationship to agricultural prosperity, and what it might do to bring about price stabilization. As it turned out, they achieved little other than to provide an opportunity for friends and foes of the Reserve System to present their views, but they did prove to be timely for Adolph Miller, who had not been able to make much headway with the board but now had the opportunity to air his objections about system policies directly to Congress. Whether change would come remained to be seen, since the system was still handcuffed by internal divisions on the board, conflict and a struggle for power between the board and the FRBNY, and congressional reluctance to resolve the situation through legislative action. The system ended the year as it began it, encumbered by strife, plagued by the connection between European stabilization and domestic speculation, and pulled in different directions by the thinking of Benjamin Strong and that of Adolph Miller and Herbert Hoover.

Chapter 6

Easy Money

The 1927 easy money policy was initiated by the New York Reserve bank to encourage domestic business and strengthen European exchanges. The policy was successful in achieving these objectives, but it gave a dangerous impetus to stock market speculation.

Adolph Miller[1]

The difficulties between the Federal Reserve Board and Benjamin Strong, especially between Strong and Adolph Miller, continued in 1927. Strong was not well and at the December 4 board meeting had been granted a leave of absence from the FRBNY until April 1, 1927. But if he thought that tensions between Washington and the FRBNY would abate during his absence he was mistaken. Miller continued his efforts to effect the sale of Government securities as a way of reducing bank reserves, and while some shared his thinking on the matter, he still lacked the support to effect a change in the system's holdings.[2] In addition and more seriously, he continued his efforts to strengthen the board's control over the system.

This chapter examines the continuing struggle for domination of the Federal Reserve System. It focuses in turn on attempts to centralize control in Wash-

---

1. Adolph Miller, "Federal Reserve Policies: 1927-1929," *American Economic Review*, 25 (September 1935): p. 442.

2. See, for instance, Hamlin Diary, February 9, 1927, and D.R. Crissinger to Adolph Miller, February 12, 1927, in Adolph Miller File, Federal Reserve Board of Governors, CP, HHPL.

ington, on the Chicago rate controversy, on the policy adopted in the autumn of 1927, and on Adolph Miller's subsequent testimony before the House Banking and Currency Committee. In addition, it examines the ongoing clash between board members over the use of open market operations and the discount rate to check speculation. All of these contributed in some degree to the inability of the system to develop a coherent Reserve policy that could provide the regulatory instrumentality that the nation needed.

In November 1926, when Pierre Jay resigned as Chairman and Federal Reserve Agent of the FRBNY, Adolph Miller saw this as an opportunity to bring the New York bank under the Reserve Board's control. This would be achieved by appointing a chairman who would be a dominant type and who would recognize that he was an official of the Reserve Board first, and an officer of the FRBNY second. The directors of the FRBNY had suggested that J. Herbert Case, George Harrison, or W. Randolph Burgess, all intimates of Strong, be considered for the job. Harrison and Case did not want the job, the latter saying that he would accept it only as a matter of duty. As for Burgess, whom the directors really wanted, Miller thought that he would be a good Federal Reserve Agent, but that as Chairman he would be dominated by Strong. Miller urged the appointment of Paul Warburg instead.[3]

There was no argument about Warburg's qualifications, but Charles Hamlin and others feared that he would not co-operate with Strong. Under the Federal Reserve Act, the Chairman was the principal officer of the Reserve bank, but at the FRBNY, where Strong was a potent factor, a special status had been created by Jay's willingness to defer to Strong, and Warburg, it was argued, would attempt to dominate Strong and would on account of his lack of tact create problems from the outset.[4] Actually, there was probably never any real possibility of Warburg's accepting such an offer because, as he later stated, he would not have accepted the position of Federal Reserve Agent for a million dollars if Miller was to be his boss.[5] However, Hamlin was initially concerned, worrying particularly about Strong's likely reaction. Burgess, so Hamlin wrote in his diary, was the best man for the job. He was "a good . . . and a growing man," and one that Strong would cooperate with and not try to dominate.[6]

Another possibility was Gates McGarrah, but again Hamlin and others, including Andrew Mellon, feared that this might not be the best appointment because McGarrah and Strong would not pull together.[7] McGarrah, to be sure, held Strong in high esteem, but he also thought that Strong had dominated Pierre Jay. And hence, he was interested in accepting the position only if the board

---

3. Hamlin Diary, December 3 and 4, 1926.

4. Ibid., December 4, 1926.

5. Ibid., March 21, 1927.

6. Ibid., March 4, 1927. Hamlin was particularly concerned that no one offensive to Strong be appointed to the job. And while he did not think that Warburg would be offensive, he did, nevertheless, believe that it would throw the directors of the FRBNY into confusion and cause Strong to resign.

7. Ibid., January 6, 1927.

defined his duties in such a way as to make it clear to everyone that he was the ranking officer and that Strong understood that the Chairman was to be the dominating officer in the bank. Hamlin worried that Strong would never agree to this condition, and if by chance he did, he would resign within a short time.[8]

Miller, who was determined to bring the FRBNY under board domination, then tried to create the impression in McGarrah's mind that the duties of the Chairman would be defined in such a way that he rather than the governor was the dominant officer of the bank. On February 7, he succeeded in getting a new Federal Reserve Board by-law stating that henceforth the Chairman was to preside at meetings of the Executive Committee of the FRBNY in place of the Governor.[9] In addition, he argued that the duties of Chairman and Federal Reserve Agent should be separated and that in the future only the most capable bankers should be appointed as Chairman. Though Hamlin, for one, did not think that this could be done under existing law.[10]

Shortly thereafter, McGarrah was appointed on the understanding that he would take office in May, and a few days later the *Wall Street Journal* carried an article in which it claimed that "far reaching changes in the fundamental theory of administration of the Federal Reserve System [were] impending."[11] The foundations had already been laid, the article said, for a policy designed to centralize control in the board and restrict the powers of the individual banks. This would be done by appointing the best available individuals as Class C or public directors of the individual banks and then using them to develop a disciplined organization in which Reserve Board policies would be administered uniformly by individual banks, and the board would guide the system's actions rather than being compelled "to follow the lead of a few of the Reserve banks."[12] The appointment of McGarrah as Chairman and Owen Young as a class C director of the FRBNY, the article continued, represented a first step in this direction, one that would be followed by similar appointments intended to overturn the policy dictatorships exercised by the governors of the individual banks. In the offing, in other words, was an impending power struggle between the chairmen of the reserve banks and the governors, and if the former could win, then "virtually complete control" would pass to the board since the chairmen were responsible to it. In that case, it would finally be in a position to require greater uniformity in discount and open market operations and to formulate policies from "the standpoint of national administration" rather than having policy determined by individual banks that could see the national aspect only through local eyes.

Writing to Owen Young on March 6, Strong took issue with the arguments in the article. The idea, he argued, would not work because the board, except in the case of McGarrah, had never been able to attract the type of individual required to carry out such a scheme successfully. No one of stature and ability

---

8. Ibid., January 11, 1927.

9. Ibid., February 7, 1927

10. Ibid., January 11, 1927.

11. *Wall Street Journal*, February 25, 1927, p. 12, col. 3.

12. Ibid.

wanted to accept its domination, and none of the Governors had done so.[13] Trying to implement the scheme, moreover, would only drive out some of the best people that the system had. And if this were to happen and the remaining people became mere agents of the board, it would be almost impossible to stem a tide of centralization that would be contrary to the convictions and desires of those who understood the system and had a keen interest in its welfare. He hoped the trend could be resisted but wondered whether he could or should play any further role in the process.[14]

In his letter to Young, Strong also argued that the "unsatisfactory" relationship between the board and the reserve banks was one outstanding weakness of the Federal Reserve System. It resulted, he maintained, from an inherent defect in independent agencies, namely their inability to attract good men because of small salaries and, more importantly, the fact that when such men were appointed they became timid and inefficient and unconsciously subordinated their real convictions "to their fears lest they may not be reappointed or might encounter criticism."[15] Such bodies, Strong said, tried to cure their inefficiency by grabbing for more power, and in the case of the board there had been a systematic effort to accumulate greater powers than the laws allowed in order to control the operations of individual reserve banks from Washington. This was something to be feared, for once such power was obtained the chances were that it would not be wisely and intelligently used and would impair the efficient operation of the system.[16]

In addition, Strong feared that a body such as the Federal Reserve Board, located in Washington a great distance from the money markets, could not govern the system effectively when all of its information was second hand, by word of mouth, or from written reports based on a few limited sources. At the same time, he argued that if the executive and administrative direction of the system were gradually assumed by the reserve board, its decision making would be subject to fear of political consequences and this would preclude any possibility of arriving at clear-cut, decisive, and courageous policies. There had, he argued, been ample evidence of this time and again.[17] But, ironically, much of Strong's decision making had been guided by his fear of congressional reaction, so that in his case distance from Washington had not proven to be a barrier to political pressure on the decision making process.

Another point in the *Wall Street Journal* article was that the chairmen of the respective reserve banks were not members of the open market committee and were therefore in no position to insure the uniform policy for open market purchases and rediscount rates that the system was supposed to have. As a result, there had been instances when one bank had forced the rest of the system to follow its lead. And while the article did not specifically name the FRBNY as

---

13. Benjamin Strong to Owen Young, March 6, 1927, in Strong Papers, FRBNY.
14. Ibid.
15. Ibid.
16. Ibid.
17. Ibid.

the bank in question, there can be no doubt from the tenor of the article, especially its conclusion, that it was the one in question. In the conclusion it was stated that:

> The board would reject any suggestion that Benjamin Strong, governor of the New York Bank, overshadowed the rest of the system as a national figure, and hence exercised an influence which made the Federal Reserve Bank of New York looked upon internationally as the representative of the entire system. But it is realized that Mr. Strong can not be the perpetual governor of the New York bank, even though the charter of that institution has been made indefinite. Thus the board has sought to place in the New York bank a chairman who can eventually take over the controlling hand there, just as other chairmen to be named through the coming years are to be expected to assume the helm in other Federal Reserve banks.[18]

Besides, the article pointed out, the Federal Reserve Act did not provide for the position of governor in any of the twelve banks. Instead, it specifically established the office of chairman and intended for it to be the central point of authority.

In important respects the article set views similar to those of Adolph Miller, and among his critics there was strong suspicion that he had inspired it. The discussions with McGarrah concerning the status of chairman, it was noted, had been privileged, which meant that the information concerning it could only have been divulged by a member of the board.[19] In addition, Hamlin questioned whether McGarrah would react kindly to the article or that he would permit himself to serve as the board's rubber stamp in New York. In Congress, Senator Carter Glass was irritated by the contents of the article and was among those who suspected Miller of being behind it.[20] He intended, Glass said, to inform Secretary Mellon that if the *Journal* article accurately reflected the Reserve Board's views and intentions, he was sorry that he had ever voted to extend the charters of the Federal Reserve banks and would take appropriate action at the next session of Congress.[21] He did not suggest what that action would be, but Harrison thought that the article might have been a blessing in disguise because the scheme set forth afforded the opportunity "to 'smoke out' its proponents."[22]

There was clearly an interest in finding out where the inspiration for the article came from, and before long Miller provided an opportunity for the question to be raised during a Reserve Board meeting. The occasion came on March 17, when Miller expressed anger about his vote against a new branch bank in Charlotte, North Carolina having been revealed in the press and asked each

18. *Wall Street Journal*, February 25, 1927, p. 12, col. 3.

19. George Harrison to Benjamin Strong, March 15, 1927, in Strong Papers, FRBNY.

20. Hamlin Diary, March 7, 1927.

21. George Harrison to Benjamin Strong, March 15, 1927, in Strong Papers, FRBNY.

22. Ibid.

board member "to answer, directly or indirectly," whether he had leaked the information.[23] Hamlin then said that he had discussed the matter with Senator Furnifold Simmons, who had already known about the vote, apparently from Daniel Crissinger or Edmund Platt. And during the discussion, he said, he had told the Senator that Miller thought the request had merit, and had opposed it only because of his record against all branch applications. At this point Miller exploded, stating that he did not care to hear what Hamlin had said and demanding that an old board circular be read regarding the disclosure of information,[24] whereupon Hamlin replied that if Miller was so keenly interested in the conduct of board members in giving out information, he wished to call formal attention to the article in the *Wall Street Journal*.

Hamlin then proceeded, as Miller had done on the Charlotte branch matter, to ask each member whether they were "directly or indirectly" aware of or responsible for the article or had provided any information on which it could have been based.[25] He got denials, but when the question was put to Miller, he looked worried and, according to Platt, turned ashen pale. He insisted that he had not seen "Sergent [the writer of the article] for months," but he did not give an unqualified denial as the others had done.[26] A few days later Walter Eddy of the Reserve Board spoke with the author of the article, who conceded that he had had a great deal of difficulty in writing it and that he received help from "some quarter." He would not divulge his source, but he thought that Eddy could guess who it might be. This, Hamlin thought, pointed to Miller.[27]

Meanwhile, Strong, who was still on leave in Biltmore, North Carolina, had expressed satisfaction that Hamlin and Glass were determined to get to the bottom of the matter. This, he said, would be difficult, given the inertia in the Reserve banks and the general unwillingness to start a row. But if Glass was willing to pursue his intention of taking the matter up with Mellon or making it the subject of an inquiry in Congress, then something might be accomplished.[28]

---

23. Hamlin Diary, March 17, 1927.

24. Ibid. Crissinger and Platt saw no impropriety in having discussed the matter with Senator Simmons. Moreover, he could at any time have obtained the minutes of the Federal Reserve Board through his senate committee. On March 16 Miller had informed the board that he had met with the German Ambassador and informed him of the board's decision to allow McGarrah to remain on the Reichsbank Advisory Committee and that he was very anxious to see how the Reichsbank would view this. After the flair-up on March 17, Hamlin wondered how Miller could deny the right of a board member to speak with Senator Simmons concerning System matters, and yet divulge confidential board decisions to the German Ambassador.

25. Hamlin Diary, March 17, 1927.

26. Ibid. Hamlin noted that Miller cooled down after this.

27. Hamlin Diary, March 21, 1927.

28. Benjamin Strong to George Harrison, March 17, 1927, in Strong Papers, FRBNY.

As for himself, he was "too weary and crippled to have much punch left,"[29] even though it irritated him a great deal that "some of those folks in Washington" were able to get "some shrewd licks" in during his absence,[30] especially in their effort to give the impression that he was too ill to return to the FRBNY and that McGarrah would be the dominant figure at the bank. He was determined, he told Hamlin, that he would govern the FRBNY as long as he remained its Governor, and McGarrah, he said, was agreeable to this.[31] Nor did he intend to ignore what had happened in his absence. Writing to Montagu Norman on May 1, he noted that the reaction had been "a petard for the bomber" and now that he was fully in the harness again he would smoke out the offender, something that was long overdue.[32]

Strong also continued to defend the independence of the Reserve banks, arguing, in particular, that since domestic requirements were not the same as foreign economic requirements, a uniform policy laid out by the board could undermine the continued maintenance of the gold standard. The board, he said, lacked an international perspective that would take into account the complications brought about by the entanglement of reparations, debts, and exchange. And since the New York money market was the primary source for foreign loans, unstable conditions in Europe could mean a loss of American investments. In 1919, he had contested the board's power to impose a rate on the system because he thought its policies were leading to inflation, and he remained willing to initiate proceedings that would again test this power.[33] At the time he did not realize that he would soon find himself in the uncomfortable position of having to rely on the board to force the Chicago Reserve bank to implement a rate change.

Strong's concern with the international situation was also enhanced by a new threat to the gold standard inherent in the French policy of trying to peg the exchange rate on sterling between 120 and 125 francs.[34] To do so, the French Central Bank had purchased large amounts of foreign currencies, including marks, dollars, and sterling.[35] But such purchases had stimulated speculation on the franc with money obtained at low rates of interest in foreign money markets.

---

29. Benjamin Strong to Montagu Norman, March 25, 1927, in Strong Papers, FRBNY.

30. Ibid.

31. Hamlin Diary, May 4, 1927.

32. Benjamin Strong to Montagu Norman, May 1, 1927, in Strong Papers, FRBNY.

33. Hamlin Diary, May 4, 1927. Strong also stated that he had a legal opinion in support of his position and that John W. Davis once told the Reserve Board that it had this power only if a Federal Reserve bank proved to be recalcitrant.

34. Montagu Norman to Benjamin Strong, June 4, 1927, Outgoing Cable No. 49, Bank of England.

35. See Chandler, *Benjamin Strong*, p. 371. The largest purchase was of sterling. The net purchase of foreign exchange amounted to £5.3 million by the end of December 1926; £20 million by February 1927; and $100 million by May 1927.

The French had then countered by withdrawing gold deposits from London and Berlin and threatening further withdrawals unless the Bank of England raised its discount rate.[36] To Norman it appeared that foreigners had taken charge of the franc and that the French were trying to save the situation by wreaking havoc in London.[37] They were, moreover, causing the European demand for dollars to fall exclusively on the London market, which led to a fall in the dollar-sterling exchange rate, an export of British gold, and a reduction in British gold reserves.[38] Their actions were capricious and difficult to explain, and this was especially true since the speculative loans they were concerned about did not originate in London but had been obtained in Germany and the Netherlands.[39]

The British reaction to the French threats was to offer a bit of accommodation but nothing like the rate increase that the French desired. In May of 1927 the Bank of England had raised its rate from 3 5/8 to 4 1/8 percent, well below the 5 1/2 that the French wanted,[40] while also taking the position that a further advance would seriously threaten the gold standard and have an adverse effect upon international trade.[41]

In New York it was argued that much of the money involved consisted of French owned foreign currencies and that the amount of these could be reduced by removing the embargo on the export of French capital. In addition, it was suggested that readily convertible foreign investments in French governmental securities be discouraged.[42] But Strong also recognized the negative effects that the French actions could have on Central European bank reserves,[43] and he was even more worried about the negative effects that could flow from the French policy of shipping the gold they had withdrawn from the Bank of England to the United States and depositing it in the FRBNY and other Reserve banks.[44]

On May 12 the Federal Reserve Board considered the latter problem, voted that the gold not be counted as part of the banks' gold reserves, and approved Strong's recommendation against making any further sales from the system's holdings of government securities in order to offset the arrival of gold from

---

36. Montagu Norman to Benjamin Strong, May 22, 1927, Strong Papers, FRBNY.

37. Ibid.

38. Ibid. The Bank of France "refused to sell devisen but continued to buy at its fixed rates."

39. Ibid.

40. Montagu Norman to Benjamin Strong, May 24, 1927, Outgoing Cable No. 38, Bank of England.

41. Benjamin Strong to Montagu Norman, June 3, 1927, Incoming Cable No. 74, Bank of England.

42. Benjamin Strong to Montagu Norman, May 24, 1927, Incoming Cable No. 63, Bank of England.

43. Benjamin Strong to Montagu Norman, Incoming Cable No. 69, Bank of England.

44. Open Market Policy Investment Excerpts, 1923-1928, pp. 109, in Adolph Miler Personal File, HHPL.

abroad. Instead, the system would gradually acquire additional short-term government obligations.[45] and additional purchases of this sort were recommended by Mellon at the June 13 Reserve Board meeting.

Miller was opposed. He had argued against expansion of the open market account in May, and he now took the position that no additional purchases could be made without board approval, and since the majority of the board was out of town he could not see how authorization to do so could be granted. Mellon was irritated by Miller's stance. He argued that the board ought to have some confidence in the Open Market Investment Committee,[46] and the majority of the board members present seemed to agree. They were concerned about the U.S. and European economic situation, the exchange situation, and the gold standard, and they now interpreted the action taken in May as authorizing the Open Market Investment Committee to make further purchases.[47] Miller's objections were ignored.

In the meantime, Strong was seeking a way to stabilize the European monetary situation. For some time he had been hoping for a meeting with Norman, Hjalmar Schacht, and Emile Moreau of the Bank of France, and in early May he had offered to go to Europe if his presence there would be beneficial. He also issued an invitation to Norman and Schacht to meet with him in July in New York, and Norman then countered by suggesting that Moreau and Charles Rist, the Deputy Governor of the Bank of France, be invited as well.[48] It was essential, he thought, to help the Bank of France out of its dilemma in order to remedy the general economic situation and especially to ensure the maintenance of the gold standard.

Moreau did not want to undermine the conservative government in Britain or endanger the stabilization of sterling and agreed to send Rist to New York to meet with Strong, Norman, and Schacht. In the meantime, Strong sold the Bank of France $60 million of earmarked gold in order to ease the drain on the Bank of England's gold reserves. The meeting took place in early July, and as a result of it a scheme was developed under which the French agreed to lessen the stress on London and to shift French gold purchases from there to New York, as did the German Reichsbank.[49]

While Norman, Rist, and Schacht were in the United States they also called separately on members of the Federal Reserve Board and were guests at a

45. Ibid., p. 111.

46. Hamlin Diary, June 23, 1927.

47. Ibid., p. 125.

48. See, for instance, Benjamin Strong to Hjalmar Schacht, May 18, 1927, in Benjamin Strong Papers, FRBNY; Benjamin Strong to Montagu Norman, May 18, 1927, in Strong Papers, FRBNY; Benjamin Strong to Montagu Norman, June 2, 1927, Incoming Cable No. 73, Bank of England; Montagu Norman to Benjamin Strong, June 4, 1927, Outgoing Cable No. 49, Bank of England; Montagu Norman to Benjamin Strong, June 7, 1927, Outgoing Cable No. 51, Bank of England.

49. Benjamin Strong to Montagu Norman, June 3, 1927. Incoming Cable No. 74, Bank of England.

luncheon in Washington's New Willard Hotel hosted by Governor Crissinger. The luncheon, however, was mostly a social occasion, at least in the eyes of Adolph Miller. He attempted to talk with the European bankers after lunch but found them to be evasive and came away with the impression that they really did not want to discuss matters with him. Hamlin also left with a similar feeling and thought that they did not want to take the board into their confidence.[50]

Such discussion as Miller was able to have with Norman convinced him that the latter was quite concerned about the gold standard. During the discussion, Norman went into a lengthy account of the problems confronting the Bank of England, tried to impress upon Miller the importance of assisting the bank, and got Miller to say that easing things for the bank, even if this were the only result, "would be one of the greatest central banking achievements in history."[51] Following this concession, however, Miller pointed out the effects that such assistance could have on speculation and brokers' loans in the United States. And when Norman replied that at least they could agree on the importance of saving the gold standard, Miller thought that this was missing the point, which was that there was no real gold standard. If there were, they would not be sitting together talking about how best to prop it up.[52] Miller then proceeded to discuss the call rate, at which point Strong came in, said that Miller always had the call rate on his mind, and asked Norman if the Bank of England paid as much attention to brokers' loans in his country. Norman said it did not, whereupon Miller pointed out that this was the difference between New York and London. "We," he said, "have to pay attention to them."[53]

The conversation with Norman left Miller with the impression "that he was in such a 'jittery' state of mind, with reference to the gold standard . . . that he was in no state of mind to advise on the matters of Federal Reserve policy without prejudice and passion."[54] Miller was also convinced that any such action as selling the gold being held in the Bank of England to the Bank of France and taking a sterling credit in its place would create an "awful mess."[55] And he remained skeptical of the European argument that an easy money policy in the United States was necessary to counter the deflationary effects of actions abroad. The only one, according to Miller, who did not feel this way was Schacht, who preferred to have the bank rate in the United States adjusted with sole regard to the domestic situation.[56]

---

50. Hamlin Diary, July 7, 1927.

51. Mark Sullivan, undated manuscript, Mark Sullivan Papers, HHPL.

52. Ibid.

53. Ibid.

54. Adolph Miller to Herbert Hoover, October 31, 1934, in Adolph Miller File, PPI, HHPL.

55. Hamlin Diary, July 13, 1927.

56. House Committee on Banking and Currency. *Stabilization*, 70th Cong. 1st sess., (Washington, DC: Government Printing Office, 1928), pp. 217-218.

In any event, both Strong and the European bankers regarded the Washington gathering as little more than a courtesy call. The important meeting was held subsequently in New York, where Norman, Rist, and Schacht met with the officers of the FRBNY and the members of the Open Market Committee. This was a meeting, moreover, of which the Federal Reserve Board members were not even informed. Crissinger, to be sure, was in attendance, as was the Comptroller of the Currency, though, they did know that there was to be such a conference until they arrived in New York with the European bankers. Hamlin thought that it was shortsighted of Strong to ignore the board and that Strong showed poor judgement by not discussing with the board the questions that were discussed with Norman, Schacht, and Rist in New York.[57] And a similar observation was later made by Congressman James Strong when the House Banking and Currency Committee resumed its hearings on the Strong Stabilization Bill.[58]

According to Crissinger, Norman opened the New York meeting by stating that the Bank of England was in a critical position regarding gold and that it would be forced to raise its rates, to the detriment of business and commerce, unless the FRBNY reduced its rate.[59] Those at the conference were sympathetic, and at the July 27 meeting of the Open Market Investment Committee, attended by the Federal Reserve Board and representatives of two Midwestern banks, Strong did his best to make a case for lower rates in the United States. Money rates in Europe, he said, had risen vigorously, and the result had been pressure on international trade and prices that was likely to have an unfavorable impact on trade and prices in the United States. Additionally, there had been a reduction in business activity, some congestion in the bond market, and reduced industrial payrolls that in turn were causing a reduction in credit and currency demand. Moreover, the autumn demand for funds could tighten money conditions, and this could put increasing pressure on the world money market, possibly force the Bank of England and a number of European banks to raise their discount rates, and thus lead to actions that would accentuate the tendency towards reduced business activity in the United States.[60]

The situation, Strong thought, called for measures that would prevent a seasonal increase in money rates and make for easier money. This, he argued, would ease the pressure on world money markets and have a favorable reaction on world trade; it would facilitate the marketing of crops at favorable prices; and it would encourage business enterprise by removing credit pressure. The danger was that it could encourage speculation in securities, but this could be dealt with by actions to localize the effects of easier money conditions.[61] The consensus of those present was that money rates should be kept at as low a level as could be

---

57. Hamlin Diary, July 7 and 25, 1927

58. House Committee on Banking and Currency. *Stabilization*, 70th Cong. 1st sess., (Washington, DC: Government Printing Office, 1928), p. 220.

59. Ibid., July 25, 1927.

60. *Open Market Investment Policy Excerpts*, 1923-1928, pp. 126-127, in Adolph Miller Personal File, HHPL.

61. Ibid., pp. 127-128.

safely attained, and that this could now be done without any harm and with "reasonable expectations of beneficial results."[62] The "possibility" that it could fuel speculation "should not stand in the way of the execution of an otherwise desirable policy,"[63] but should be seen instead as the risk that had to be taken in helping Europe.[64]

The consensus, then, was that the time had arrived for the discount rate at the FRBNY and the other reserve banks to be reduced. Only the two Midwestern bankers who were present objected, arguing that conditions in some of the interior districts indicated that there was an adequate supply of credit at the prevailing rate.[65] Adolph Miller would have objected had he been there, but he had left during the middle of July for a two-month trip to California.

Before departing, though, Miller had written a memorandum in which he stated his preference for lower discount rates over open market operations as a way of easing money and then went on to express views similar to those of the Midwestern bankers. There was, he said, no need for lowering rates at this time because agriculture would have a billion dollars more of purchasing power from the sale of its products. While he was away, he also wired the board suggesting that rates not be reduced and asking that any rate change be held in abeyance until September because immediate action could prove an unhealthy stimulus to speculation.[66] Unlike Strong, he was not willing to risk a rise in speculative activity in order to aid European stability.

In the end Strong's views prevailed and the board could do little other than to give its approval to the scheme to which the FRBNY had now committed the system. Not everyone, however, viewed the new rate policy favorably. The Chicago, Minneapolis, Philadelphia, and San Francisco banks refused to lower their rates, and there was some question, at least in Hamlin's mind, whether Miller was in any way responsible for the stand taken by these banks.[67] In any event, a showdown now loomed, and Strong was in the somewhat awkward position of having his leadership ignored yet being reluctant to request a board action that would force the dissenting banks into line. He was, after all, committed to the view that the board did not have such a power, and he now tried to avoid the issue by advising the board not to "issue anything which might be construed as

---

62. Ibid., p. 129.

63. Ibid.

64. H. Parker Willis, "The Failure of the Federal Reserve," *North American Review* 227 (May 1929): p. 553.

65. *Open Market Investment Policy Excerpts*, 1923-1928, pp. 129-130, in Adolph Miller Personal File, HHPL.

66. Hamlin Diary, July 13, 1927.

67. Hamlin Diary, September 16, 1927. Hamlin at a later date brought up that Miller had been opposed to any rate reduction and that when he went west he had stopped over at the Chicago, Minneapolis, and San Franciso banks, all of which refused to lower their rates.

an order" and by undertaking campaigns of persuasion aimed at each of the recalcitrant banks.[68]

In his attempts to persuade Governor George Norris of the Philadelphia
Reserve Bank, Strong argued that the rate policy was justified irrespective of
any effect it might have on stock speculation. That orgy, he insisted, would always be present, and if the Federal Reserve System were to be run "solely with a
view to regulating stock speculation" rather than to benefit industry and commerce, its policy would degenerate to "regulating the affairs of gamblers." He
had no patience, he said, with such a view of the system's role.[69] He also attempted to sway James McDougal of the Chicago bank, one of the two bankers
who had voiced his opposition to a rate reduction at the July 27 meeting of the
the Open Market Investment Committee and who in Strong's eyes had acted
selfishly in doing so.[70] To McDougal he sent a letter similar to the one he had
written Norris, but the Chicago banker was not convinced. Chicago, he replied,
would reduce its rate "if and when it seemed expedient to do so." [71]

Meanwhile, Strong was reporting to Crissinger that the FRBNY had lost
$120 million of its reserves in part because of the seasonal demand for funds in
the interior, but also because of "the failure of Chicago and Philadelphia to reduce their discount rates."[72] At the same time, he also reported, the Open Market Investment Committee had taken advantage of the increasing strength in the
sterling rate to dispose of its sterling balances and to offset these sales had increased the system's holdings of government securities. [73]

On August 26 Strong wrote to McDougal once more about lowering the
Chicago rate. He admitted that local conditions alone were no justification for a
reduction in the Chicago district. This, though, was not simply a Chicago or
New York question. It was a national question bearing upon American markets
in Europe and therefore an international question as well. The rate reduction, he
added, would benefit agriculture in McDougal's and other districts by making it
possible for farmers to market their surplus crops in Europe.[74]

Again, though, the Chicago bank was unconvinced and continued to insist
that local conditions did not warrant a reduction in its rate and that, contrary to
Strong's claims, a lower rate would injure agricultural interests in the Midwest.
Moreover, the Chicago directors could see no connection between a lower rate
in the seventh district and the value of the pound. It was, they insisted, the heavy

---

68. Hamlin Diary, July 27, 1927.

69. Benjamin Strong to George Norris, August 18, 1927 in Strong Papers, FRBNY.

70. Hamlin Diary, July 27, 1927.

71. James McDougal to Benjamin Strong, August 24, 1926, in Strong Papers,
FRBNY.

72. Open Market Investment Policy Excerpts, 1923-1928, p. 134, in Adolph Miller
Personal File, HHPL.

73. Ibid.

74. Benjamin Strong to Walter McDougal, August 26, 1927, in Strong File,
FRBNY.

open market purchases in New York, not the lowering of the New York discount rate, that had stimulated large purchases of sterling and in the process improved its position.[75] And they intended, despite Strong's arguments, to remain with their 4 percent rate.

On August 30 the Federal Reserve Board rejected the Chicago decision to remain with the higher rate. The Chicago bank then asked that it be allowed to remain with the 4 percent rate until a scheduled meeting of the directors on September 9, but the board promptly rejected this request and recommended that the rate be lowered on September 2. On that day the Chicago directors failed to act, and on September 6 the board voted to lower the Chicago rate at once. Miller, who had pushed for a uniform rate policy and greater system control by the board, might logically have been ecstatic. But he was actually opposed. He did not favor lower rates, and he and Hamlin thought it extraordinary to force a 3 1/2 per cent rate on September 6 when the Chicago directors seemed likely to implement it on September 9.[76] Later, he said that he would have voted for a decrease if the Chicago directors had not lowered the rate on September 9.[77] But clearly his principles of centralization and curbs on speculation were at odds with each other as he considered the Chicago case.[78]

The board's action resulted in a good deal of controversy, with the Federal Advisory Council objecting to its method but refusing to question the wisdom of the action. Much unfortunate and misleading publicity, Strong thought, had been paid to the incident. He also thought that the significance of the matter could become greatly exaggerated, especially the apprehensions expressed by some members of the press that this would result in a serious controversy throughout the country. For thirteen years the system had been able to escape serious controversy on this point, and he hoped that it could "continue to do so without litigation or amendment to the Act." He hoped, too, that when Congress reconvened, discussion could be minimized, and he doubted that the controversy would lead to any material changes in the Federal Reserve Act or in the system's policies.[79]

The Chicago bank complied with the board's directive and immediately implemented the lower rate, and by September 13 the Minneapolis, Philadelphia, and San Francisco Reserve banks had adopted the 3 1/2 percent rate as well. Still, the directors of the Chicago bank objected to the forced rate reduction, and there was talk that the bank might test the powers of the Federal Reserve Board in court or even ask Congress to clarify the act by amendment. Strong claimed that he was not happy with the board's action and that he had sought to delay it. His bank, he insisted, "had not wished to intervene in the controversy" and had

75. *New York Times*, September 9, 1927, p. 34; September 10, 1927, p. 3; September 14, 1927, p. 41; September 16, 1927, p. 10; September 17, 1927, p. 19.

76. Hamlin Diary, September 6, 1927.

77. Ibid., September 16, 1927.

78. Ibid.

79. Benjamin Strong to Montagu Norman, September 21, 1927, in Strong Papers, FRBNY.

"scrupulously refrained from doing so from the very beginning."[80]   His only involvement had come when Crissinger, responding to his report concerning the Chicago situation, had told him that the board was thinking about using force. At that point he had told Crissinger that he did not favor such a move and had then spoken to Secretary Mellon, who had sought to have the matter delayed until he returned to Washington and had asked Strong to relay this request. This he had done.[81]   But according to Hamlin, Crissinger never mentioned the conversation with New York to the board. As Hamlin saw it, Crissinger had "deliberately withheld the information . . . in order to jam through the Chicago rate"[82] and in doing so had been disloyal both to Mellon and the board.[83]   One outcome was that both Strong and Miller suggested a new by-law providing for five affirmative votes for rate initiations,[84] although Miller would not apply this when a Federal Reserve bank established a rate and the board decided to put in a different one.[85]   The proposal did not carry.

It is questionable, however, whether Strong was truly at odds with the board's action. The only concern he might have had was that the board had exercised its power to impose the lower rate and that it might do so again. This would explain his move for five affirmative votes in future cases of this nature. There is also a question about the timing of his message to Crissinger. If it came during the noon hour, as seems likely, it probably arrived after action on the Chicago rate had been taken. And raising further doubts is·Strong's correspondence with John Mitchell of the Illinois Merchants Trust Company. In this he defended the rate reduction, arguing that when the New York rate was reduced a certain amount of borrowing shifted from Chicago to New York because banks that had connections in both markets wanted to go with the cheaper rate, and that the effect of this was to induce withdrawals from New York, affect market rates for money, and thereby make the New York rate less effective.[86]

---

80. Benjamin Strong to William Harding, September 19, 1927, in Strong Papers, FRBNY.

81. Hamlin Diary, September 9, 1927.

82. Ibid., September 20, 1927.

83. Ibid.

84. Ibid., September 26, 1927; September 27, 1927.

85. Ibid., September 27, 1927.

86. Benjamin Strong to John J. Mitchell, October 4, 1927, in Strong Papers, FRBNY. New York experienced withdrawals that amounted to $109 million between August 3 and September 7, when Chicago reduced its rate. The majority of the loss went to those banks which had remained with the 4 percent rate. As a result borrowing by banks in the New York district increased about $75 million. It looked as though there would be even larger borrowings and this made it necessary to purchase $50 million of securities during August. Had this action not been taken, money rates would have increased and the purpose of the new policy would have been defeated. Open Market Investment Policy Excerpts, p. 145. This argument reflected the same concerns he had expressed to Crissinger on August 19, a little more than a week before the Board began pressing Chicago to reduce its rate.

Another individual incensed by the board's handling of the Chicago rate case was Senator Carter Glass, author of the Federal Reserve Act and former Secretary of the Treasury. Yet, as Hamlin took pains to remind him, Glass had once been on the other side of the issue, especially when he acted in 1919 to uphold the board's authority to force Strong and the FRBNY into line with that period's easy money policy. He had to make a distinction, and he did so by noting that Strong's aggressive stubbornness had provoked him into making "a case for the board" and that even though he considered the matter to be one of "immediate grave exigency," he had not advised "the board to exercise the power in question nor did the Federal Reserve Board, as such, assert or exercise the power of 'establishing' a rediscount rate for the New York or any other Federal Reserve Bank."[87] In his opinion, nothing that had happened in 1919 could be used to justify the board's utterly capricious action in the Chicago case. It had clearly overstepped its bounds, and he was truly amazed that the board would deliberately precipitate an issue that would "involve the bitterest kind of agitation" and would ultimately "subject the board and the Federal Reserve System to injurious criticism, if not unwise attempts to radically alter the Act itself."[88]

The case also came in for a good deal of discussion in the press. *World's Work,* for example, noted that the authority, which had been affirmed by the Attorney General in 1919, was little known and had not been used until this particular instance. Yet it seemed to be of immense practical importance.[89] In addition, the press speculated about the fact that Crissinger, who had cast the deciding vote, resigned his position shortly after the incident took place. In reality, the resignation had no relation to the controversy, and those in the know, such as Strong, had been aware that it was coming for over a month.[90] But when President Coolidge appointed Roy Young of Minneapolis to succeed Crissinger as Governor of the Reserve Board, the press saw the action as one designed to prevent a "political clash based on sectional prejudices and fears," especially the traditional fears in the South and the West of the money power concentrated in the East.[91]

It is quite likely, moreover, that sectional prejudice did play a role in the decision of the Chicago directors not to fall in line with the new rate policy. The Middle West at the time entertained strong anti-foreign feelings and tended to favor financial isolationism, while New York, on the other hand, had become an important international financial center.[92] This was not lost on Glass, who told Hamlin that if he would read the September issue of the *London Banker* he

87. Carter Glass to Charles S. Hamlin, September 12, 1927, in Charles S. Hamlin Papers, Manuscript Division, Library of Congress, Washington, D.C.

88. Ibid.

89. *World's Work,* 55 (November 1927): p. 10.

90. Benjamin Strong to Montagu Norman, September 21, 1927, in Strong Papers, FRBNY.

91. Ibid.

92. Elisha Friedman, "The Federal Reserve Fight," *Nation* 125 (October 12, 1927): p. 360.

would see the assumption against which Glass had warned him some time ago, namely that the FRBNY was being regarded "as the central bank of the Reserve System with the other eleven banks merely branches."[93]

It seems plausible, then, that in appointing Crissinger's successor, Coolidge considered the fact that the most violent opposition to the new rate policy came from the Midwest and that the Minneapolis Reserve Bank had been the last to lower its rate. Young's appointment, one commentator noted, "acted as salve" in a situation where even the Eastern bankers thought that the board had needlessly precipitated the issue, had used powers that it should have reserved for times of national emergency, and had taken steps that might lead to political domination of the system by elevating presidential appointees over people chosen by member banks and in the end amount to more government in business.[94] Political control, as Strong had pointed out to Owen Young earlier in the year, had been a fear from the beginning.[95] This was especially true, economist Elisha Friedman pointed out, when the political dimension was considered not in terms of partisan cleavages but in terms of sectional antagonisms and the demagoguery of those advocating "panaceas and utopias."[96] As Friedman analyzed the "fight" in the *Nation*, he stressed the need to vary rates to fit the conditions of each region, to keep England on the gold standard, to assist in the restoration of England's financial and industrial soundness,[97] and to do something about the large invisible credits received by the United States on the payment of inter-allied debts. Eliminating the debts completely, he thought, would lessen the amount of gold coming into the United States.[98] But according to the Harvard Economic Service, this was unlikely. So long as the United States continued to lend the money required to fund the debts, it noted, the readjustment of international trade would be postponed, and the longer it was postponed the greater would be the difficulty of ultimate readjustment.[99]

Neither Friedman nor the public commentators, however, had much to say about the possibility that easy money might give impetus to yet another round of speculation. Nor did Herbert Hoover, who only two years prior to this had caused a great deal of difficulty for the Reserve Board when he thought that the speculative orgy had been allowed to go too far. In September 1927 he merely stated that money rates were low, that this would invariably stimulate business,

---

93. Carter Glass to Charles Hamlin, September 29, 1927, in Charles S. Hamlin Papers, Manuscript Division, Library of Congress, Washington, D.C.

94. *World's Work*, November 1927, p. 11.

95. Benjamin Strong to Owen Young, March 6, 1927, in Strong Papers, FRBNY.

96. Elisha Friedman, "The Federal Reserve Fight," *Nation*, 125 (October 12, 1927): p. 359.

97. Ibid. See also Samuel Crowther, "Can we plan on easy Money," *Magazine of Business*, (October 1927): pp. 388-391, 434, 436.

98. Friedman, "The Federal Reserve Fight," *Nation*, p. 360.

99. Harvard Economic Service letter of July 23, 1927 as found in Friedman, "The Federal Reserve Fight," *Nation*, p. 360.

and that the outlook for the ensuing five or six months was good.[100] It was not until April and May of 1928 that he would issue further warnings to guard against inflation.[101]

Behind the scenes, to be sure, Hoover continued to discuss Federal Reserve policy with Miller, and some of those on the board continued to believe that Miller spoke for him. But in 1927 he removed himself from the kind of debate that had put him at odds with Mellon, Strong, and other members of the system in 1925. To some extent, he may have lost interest, as he tended to do in other debates in which he became involved as Secretary of Commerce. And there was also the fact that he now aspired to the Republican presidential nomination and would be running on a platform of Republican prosperity. Edward Hunt later argued that Hoover "could not repeat the Lenroot inquiry" because the Senate was not in session. A more important reason for Hoover's inaction, according to Hunt, was that Hoover was "completely absorbed in the Mississippi flood rescue work" at the time the policy was formulated.[102]

Still, the concern about speculation was anything but a dead issue among Federal Reserve policy makers. McDougal and Norris continued to express apprehension,[103] and in November Strong admitted that a less favorable result of the new policy, though one which was anticipated, had been some stimulation on the stock exchange. He did not, however, see this as any great danger. Although gains in stock prices totaled $336 million, there was, he thought, no way of knowing how much of this advance could be attributed to excessive speculation and how much of it represented a gradual adjustment of values due to increased industrial efficiency, larger profits, higher commodity prices, and a lower basic interest rate.[104] In his judgement, the price level of stock market prices was less abnormal than a casual examination of it would suggest and any problem could if necessary be taken care of by temporary open market operations.[105]

It was Miller who again took the opposing position. At the board meeting in December, he raised the question as to whether it might not be time for rediscount rates to advance. Edward Cunningham also showed an interest in the matter and after the meeting asked Governor Young whether he saw anything in the situation that justified an increase at that particular time. Young said he did not, with the possible exception of the stock market; and he hoped that it would crack of its own weight before it was necessary for the Reserve banks to raise rates and be blamed for any break that might occur in the market. The situation,

100. Economic situation, Press Release, September 24, 1927, in Public Statements File, HHPL.

101. *Stabilization Hearings*, p. 337.

102. Hunt, Edward, Hoover Memos, 1933, 1935, in Edward Eyre Hunt Papers, Hoover Institution on War, Revolution and Peace, Stanford, CA.

103. Open Market Investment Policy Excerpts, p. 137, in Adolph Miller Personal File, HHPL.

104. Ibid., p. 147.

105. Ibid., p. 155.

he thought, could be controlled through open market operations, and because securities purchases by banks had lagged so far behind the gold movement he thought that most members of the board were also satisfied with this approach. Even Miller, the sharpest critic of the system's open market policy, had little criticism of the way the account had been handled since November. And accordingly, matters were left as they were and any further discussion of rate changes postponed until after the turn of the year.[106]

Strong in the meantime had sailed for Europe to participate in discussions of Italian stabilization. Before leaving, however, he was pleased to note that gold flows into the United States had been reversed, that money conditions abroad were easier than they had been for some time, and that large volumes of foreign loans were being floated in the American market. He had hopes now that the improved economic situation would hold and that European monetary stability could be achieved.[107]

By early 1928, though, the board was hearing renewed complaints about the difficulty of floating foreign loans. German issues had become a particularly worrisome problem, which if not solved might seriously threaten the continued operation of the Dawes Plan. And again, Miller was calling for an end to the policy that had not worked. Money, he said, had been made cheap for international reasons, and the result was speculative inflation that would help big manufacturers crush their smaller rivals. Hamlin, however, reminded Miller that if rates had not been reduced, gold would have continued to pour into New York and this would have led to inflation.[108]

Also provoking further discussion was an expanding volume of brokers' loans, stimulated by a drop in call money rate from 5 1/2 to 4 percent. In response to this situation, the Open Market Investment Committee decided on January 9 to sell $50 million in securities from the Special Investment Account.[109] Yet it did so at a time when there were also worries about a slump in production and wholesale distribution. Both were off, but this, it was thought, was due to temporary circumstances, particularly to Henry Ford's shutdown for retooling, the after effects of the Florida land boom collapse and the 1927 floods, the impact of the coal strike, and the decrease in orders for new railroad equipment. They were not indicators of a downturn that required any change in monetary policy. For those wanting to expand production there was ample credit available at reasonable rates.

---

106. George Harrison to Benjamin Strong, December 15, 1927, in George Harrison Papers, Butler Library, Columbia University, New York.

107. Strong's thoughts on the international situation are reflected in the the Open Market Investment Committee Excerpts, November through December 1927, in Adolph Miller Personal File, HHPL. See also Strong-Norman Correspondence, in Strong Papers, FRBNY, September 1927 through December 1927.

108. Hamlin Diary, January 9, 1928.

109. Open Market Investment Policy Excerpts, pp. 166, 170, in Adolph Miller Personal File, HHPL.

The discussion of the recession, then, did not lead to any immediate changes in policy. Some of the discussants, to be sure, noted the greater freedom of the system to deal with the domestic situation, primarily because the threat to European monetary stability was no longer as great. But the decisions were merely to monitor the business situation and if it changed in ways that required corrective action to provide this primarily through open market operations rather than rate changes.[110] These were decisions, moreover, that were consensual. Not even Miller disagreed.[111]

Within weeks, however, the concern about speculative activity had led to rate increases. In late January a number of the Reserve Banks decided to raise their rediscount rate to 4 percent, and during the first week in February the FRBNY raised its rate to the same figure. This was an action supported by Miller, who was again taking the position that the sale of government securities could not control the situation.[112] Strong was again ill and was not directly involved in the decision. But according to Harrison, he had for some time expected that it might have to be taken.[113]

In practice the higher rates proved effective in checking further increases in speculative credit. Loans on stocks and bonds decreased, while those for commercial purposes increased. This improvement, however, turned out to be short-lived. By early March speculation was on the rise again and along with it the total volume of credit. Strong conceded this at the March 26 meeting of the Open Market Investment Committee. Yet he also recommended that the policy adopted in January should remain in effect and that in the absence of further deterioration in the situation any further intervention should be through changes in open market operations.[114]

In April stock prices and brokers' loans reached higher levels than ever before. Those doing the borrowing, it was said, believed that the increased cost of money was seasonal and that it would soon decline.[115] To curb such loans, the Boston Reserve Bank proposed an increase in its rediscount rate from 4 to 4 1/2 percent, and the result was another debate among members of the Federal Reserve Board. Miller initially supported the request, but he later reversed himself, argued that it would adversely affect business,[116] and expressed the view that approving such a request would amount to a declaration that the board was in favor of controlling speculation by manipulating discount rates. Instead, he argued, the Boston bank ought to refuse discounts for member banks carrying

---

110. Ibid., pp. 172-175.

111. Hamlin Diary, January 11, 1928.

112. Hamlin Diary, January 23, 1928.

113. George Harrison to Montagu Norman, January 23, 1928, Bank of England File, FRBNY.

114. Open Market Investment Policy Excerpts pp. 185-187, in Adolph Miler Personal File, HHPL.

115. Ibid., p. 193.

116. Hamlin Diary, April 16 and 18, 1928.

speculative loans.[117]   Hamlin then reminded Miller that back in 1925 he had supported an advance in the New York rate in order to control speculation even though the FRBNY had argued that the situation was being kept under control through direct action. Miller's arguments, he said, would have greater force if there was a central bank in Washington with a branch at Boston. But this was not the case, and the Boston bank had to protect itself "against unduly increasing rediscounts and falling reserves," which had decreased to 57 percent, the lowest in the system.[118]

Miller was not persuaded and voted against the motion. But within hours he had changed his mind again, primarily because he had learned from J. Herbert Case, the Deputy Governor of the FRBNY, that money was pouring into New York, and that at least $50 million came from Boston. The request for a rate increase was put to a second vote and this time it passed with Miller supporting the measure. Subsequently, Miller also supported the board's decision to approve similar rate increases in the Chicago, Richmond, and St. Louis districts,[119] and on May 18 the FRBNY advanced its rate to 4 1/2 percent even though Strong had urged that this not be done until all other banks had raised their rates to 5 percent. He had hoped in this way to draw out-of-town funds away from New York and to divert borrowing to the New York market,[120] but he was unable in this instance to have his way.

In these actions Miller made it clear that he did not have a very high regard for his fellow policy makers, an attitude that was also reflected in his testimony before the House Banking and Currency Committee, which in March had resumed hearings on the Strong Stabilization Bill. In his testimony in 1926 he had been favorably disposed toward the bill. But he now argued that it would give too much power to an institution that lacked sufficient people of creative judgement to administer it properly and tended to thwart the use of what "native ability they might have."[121]

There were, Miller said, a considerable number of amateur economists in the system, which for him constituted a dangerous element. Benjamin Strong, he said, was one of them. He was an able man but not an economic statesman of the kind that the Stabilization Bill contemplated. It called for "exercise of power of analysis, of power of foresight, that is very unusual in any group of men anywhere, no matter what their experience or training," and he doubted that the system's members, including Strong, could measure up to these requirements.[122] Miller gave the impression that he was the only board member who could ana-

---

117. Ibid., April 17, 1928.

118. Ibid., April 18, 1928.

119. Ibid., April 18, 19, and 23, 1928.

120. Chandler, Benjamin Strong, p. 455. See also George Harrison to Montagu Norman, April 25, 1928, Incoming Cable No. 98/28, Bank of England.

121. Stabilization Hearings, p. 187.

122. Ibid., pp. 213-215.

lyze system matters correctly and properly,[123] and who maintained "an attitude of relative calm about situations in which there [was] a danger of an unconscious hysteria developing."[124]

During the course of his testimony, Miller touched on a number of areas, including the deflation of 1920-21, England's return to the gold standard, and the policy of rate reductions in support of European stabilization during the autumn of 1927. About each of these he voiced various concerns, but he was especially critical of the way open market operations had been carried out in support of easy money. Limitations, he thought, should be put on the open market powers of the system because the decisions made in the fall of 1927 amounted to a misadventure in Federal Reserve policy. The intended effect had been to bring about a lowering of money rates. But the one market that apparently had an insatiable appetite for credit was the securities market, and the low money rates, in his view, had been particularly effective in stimulating the "remarkable speculative movement" underway by March 1928.[125] What he did not tell the Congressmen was that back in January he had favored the use of open market operations over discount rates to check speculation,[126] and that on April 28, in opposing the request of the Boston Reserve Bank, he had declared that he would never vote to increase rates in order to check speculation.[127] His position had vacillated more than he implied, although it now seemed to be emphatic. By July he was saying the if the system continued to operate in the open market the Board "should and ought to be hauled over the coals by Congress."[128]

Among the members of the House committee, there was a good deal of interest in how the open market policy decisions during the second half of 1927 had been made. Congressman Strong wondered if sectional forces were at play, especially since the committee controlling open market operations was composed primarily of eastern men. But as Miller saw it, the most important influence in the Open Market Investment Committee was exercised by the representative of the FRBNY. New York was the largest open money market in the United States, and this meant that the attitude of the FRBNY was the most important influence in shaping the recommendations of the committee "no matter what its geographical representation."[129] Miller pointed out that the committee consisted of five banks that were represented through their governors, but that it

123. Ibid., p. 161.
124. Ibid., p. 163.
125. *Stabilization Hearings*, p. 188.
126. Hamlin Diary, January 11, 1928.
127. Ibid., May 1 and 29, 1928.
128. Ibid., July 18, 1928.
129. Ibid., p. 126. New York, Miller argued, was the banking center of the world, and the result was that men who came to the fore in New York as bankers were men who belonged to the master class in banking, and usually "put their ideas over upon those of less prestige and experience." Ibid., p. 127.

was very likely that a majority of one, meaning Benjamin Strong, determined the open market policy for the system.[130]

Miller was referring in particular to the events of July 1927, when Strong met with Norman, Schacht, and Rist, and later persuaded the Open Market Investment Committee and the board in Washington to pursue a cheap money policy to facilitate monetary stabilization in Europe. In response, Congressman Otis Wingo expressed the view that board policy should be controlled by business needs, not what might take place in the stock market.[131] But Miller insisted that the board had to be concerned about what became of the credit that it had created. In his opinion, a tight control was needed to prevent the diversion of Federal Reserve credit into any kind of speculative loan,[132] and he was convinced that the speculative situation in the United States should have had more of a bearing on reserve policy than the international situation.[133] He also expressed a lack of enthusiasm about central bank cooperation. The United States, he said, should not be overzealous in extending its hand to "any country or group of countries."[134] There were already too many American innocents abroad and too many violations of the principle that the United States, particularly the Federal Reserve System, should be "represented by men who [knew] what it [was] all about."[135]

Miller's testimony offended fellow board member Hamlin, and when the latter appeared before the Committee he did his best to contradict what Miller had stated during his appearance before it.[136] Miller, he thought, had made an unfavorable impression upon the Committee,[137] and Secretary Mellon, disturbed by some of Miller's remarks, was wondering how the administration could have reappointed him to the Reserve Board.[138]

Miller also continued to be irritating in other ways. In early May, for example, he demanded that Vice-Governor Case of the FRBNY call all the presidents of the large New York banks together and admonish them to bring speculative excesses under control. Yet in the ensuing discussion, he reportedly shouted, "and what will they say to you when you call them in! They will say you are responsible for the condition of things because of the cheap money policy!"[139] A bit later, moreover, he argued against such an action.[140] And in July, after the

130. Ibid.
131. Ibid., p. 118.
132. Ibid., p. 121.
133. Ibid., p. 117.
134. Ibid., p. 235.
135. Ibid., p. 237.
136. Hamlin Diary, May 23, 1928.
137. Ibid., May 24, 1928.
138. Ibid., May 25, 1928.
139. Ibid., May 1, 1928.
140. Open Market Policy Investment Excerpts, 1923-1928, p. 216, in Adolph Miller Personal File, HHPL.

Open Market Investment Committee had recommended it, he was still opposed to having the board request it. He thought that a more practical way could be found to prevent the leakage of Federal Reserve credit into speculative markets.[141] But when Hamlin asked him how this could be done, his only suggestion was that individual banks should be studied, and if it was determined that any bank had gone beyond its percentage of normal call loans, it should then be admonished.[142] Hamlin wondered whether a similar inquiry should not be made about real estate and other kinds of speculative loans but Miller did not think so. Call loans, he said, should be regulated first.[143]

In the meantime, the bull market continued to advance, and on July 11 the Federal Reserve Bank of Chicago raised its rediscount rate from 4 1/2 to 5 percent. Similar advances were then made by the FRBNY on July 13, the Atlanta Reserve Bank on July 14, and the Boston and St. Louis Reserve Banks on July 19.[144] Strong, though, was opposed to the hike in the New York rate. It was, he wrote to Cecil Lubbok, a mistake and would have grave foreign and domestic consequences.[145] About the same time the board recommended the adoption of preferential rates for agricultural acceptances, bankers' acceptances, and trade bills—the very policy, in other words, that Strong had fought to end in 1919 and which at that time had brought him into conflict with Treasury officials. After a detailed discussion, the motion to establish preferential rates was defeated.[146]

Strong did not take part in these discussions. He had been ill a good part of 1928 and therefore spent little time at the bank or on system matters. During the year he chaired only one meeting of the Open Market Investment Committee, and while he did appear before the House Committee on Banking and Currency on March 19, his testimony was confined to that one day. He did not, as requested, return to give further testimony in May or June. On May 12 he sailed for Europe to assist with stabilization there, and when he returned in August he was exhausted and informed Harrison that he would have to retire immediately. The directors of the FRBNY were reluctant to accept his retirement and persuaded him to put it off until the end of the year. But in October he died, thus removing from the system what his biographer called a "center of enterprising and acceptable leadership." According to his analysis, the Federal Reserve Board, which had determined that the FRBNY should no longer play a leadership role, was not capable of assuming it "in an enterprising way."[147]

---

141. Hamlin Diary, July 18, 1928.

142. Ibid.

143. Ibid.

144. Open Market Policy Investment Excerpts, 1923-1928, p. 216, in Adolph Miller Personal File, HHPL.

145. Benjamin Strong to Cecil Lubbok, August 20, 1928, in Strong Papers, FRBNY.

146. Open Market Policy Investment Excerpts, 1923-1928, pp. 229-233, in Adolph Miller Personal File, HHPL.

147. Chandler, Benjamin Strong, p. 465.

Because of his illness and lengthy absences, then, Strong's influence on Federal Reserve policy had been a rapidly diminishing one in the months preceding his death. Decisions were made, both in Washington and New York, that he regarded as mistakes, and the period witnessed no further exchanges with Miller or Hoover. Early in the year, however, he did come into possession of some information, which, if acted upon could have caused a good deal of trouble for Miller. Miller, it appeared, had loaned $300,000 on the call market through a New York banker. If this became known publicly, Strong believed, Miller would be driven from office, and when Hamlin was informed about it he wondered what the public's reaction would be if it became known that Miller was "feeding stock exchange speculation which was fast becoming a menace to business."[148] An opportunity apparently existed to remove Miller from the board, but in the end nothing was done.

The year 1927 had begun with a continuing struggle for domination of the Federal Reserve System. Miller and others actively sought to centralize authority in the hands of the board, something that Benjamin Strong was determined to resist. But International developments led Strong to pursue policy changes that were not acceptable to all Reserve banks and therefore had to be imposed upon them by the Federal Reserve Board. Although he sought to prevent centralization in the hands of the board, the policy changes initiated by the FRBNY during July and early August 1927 provided an opportunity for the board to move in that direction.

In addition, the new policy gave an impetus to speculation that was hard to contain. It therefore drew a good deal of criticism from Miller, who thought that domestic considerations should have been paramount in formulating Reserve policy. Internationally, the situation improved, but speculation continued to be a problem for the system and during 1928 a combination of open market operations and rate adjustments were employed in efforts to contain it. This, however, led to yet another round of debates, both in Congress and at Federal Reserve Board meetings, over the wisdom of relying on open market operations to curtail speculation, and by early fall speculative activity in the securities market was reaching new highs with stock prices advancing higher than ever before. Consequently, the debate continued, with those involved unable to say with assurance when the movement would culminate, to what degree it had a sound economic basis and to what extent it reflected a boom psychology. The system was about to encounter its greatest test, but all indications were that the conflicts between the board and individual Reserve Banks and the divisions within the board itself would militate against the development of a coherent Reserve policy that would curtail speculation and still meet the needs of industry, commerce, and agriculture. Neither the Strong version of coherence nor the Hoover version of it had established itself in ways that could provide the regulatory instrumentality that the nation needed.

---

148. Hamlin Diary, January 9, 1928.

Chapter 7

Conclusion

[In 1926] a group of bankers, among them . . . one with a world famous name were sitting at a table in a Washington hotel. One of them had raised the question whether the low discount rates of the system were not likely to encourage speculation. "Yes" replied the conspicuous figure referred to, "they will, but that can not be helped. It is the price we must pay for helping Europe."

H. Parker Willis[1]

Speculation plagued the Federal Reserve System throughout the 1920s, and the failure to agree upon a coherent policy, especially during the second half of the decade, contributed to the collapse of the securities market in 1929. Since that time a number of theories have been advanced about the causes of that collapse and claims have been made about how it could have been prevented. Herbert Hoover, for example, later claimed that he led the opposition to the board's easy money policies, which, he insisted, plunged the world into inflation, and led to the collapse of the stock market and the ensuing depression. Others insisted that if Benjamin Strong had not died in 1928 he would have reversed the easy money policy before it had gone too far and thus averted the financial collapse of 1929. This chapter attempts to assess the impact and significance of the policy incoherence and the validity of the claims that Hoover and others would later make regarding the coming of the depression.

---

1. H. Parker Willis, "The Failure of the Federal Reserve," *North American Review* (May 1929): p. 553.

Beginning in 1920 Hoover issued warnings about European economic stabilization and the tangle of reparations and interallied debts. But he was satisfied that a practical solution to these problems had been found with the establishment of the Dawes plan and England's return to the gold standard. Hoover praised both events and recognized that American participation was required to ensure their successful operation. Yet within a short time he began to criticize the easy money policies that the Reserve System had developed to aid both in European monetary stabilization and in England's successful return to gold.

During the autumn of 1925 Hoover began to issue warnings about speculation and credit expansion, arguing that speculative excesses would result in a financial crisis. On this issue he and Adolph Miller were on one side while Benjamin Strong and the majority of the Federal Reserve Board were on the other. But after 1926 Hoover appears to have given less attention to the matter and removed himself from the kind of debate in which he had been involved in late 1925. By 1927 and 1928 he was enmeshed in presidential politics and the celebration of Republican prosperity, and he remained very much in the background even when Miller undertook new initiatives to curb speculation and strengthen the powers of the board over the Reserve banks. After 1925 his design for policy coherence persisted, but he did relatively little to push it and it was never implemented.

As for the view that Benjamin Strong would have taken corrective action had he not died in 1928, skepticism seems warranted. By 1928 Strong's influence at the FRBNY and within the Federal Reserve System had already been greatly reduced. And in the eyes of various contemporaries, Strong's background and previous performance were not such as to equip him to deal with the situation that developed in 1929. Eugene Meyer, for example, would concede that Strong had turned the position of Governor into the dominant position at the FRBNY, something that was clearly not intended by those who had initially maneuvered him into the governorship in order to keep him from becoming president of the Bankers Trust Company. But in later discussions with Mark Sullivan, Meyer strongly disputed the ability of Strong to provide the kind of leadership that could have stayed the economic collapse beginning in 1929.[2]

At the same time it should be recognized that the problems with which Norman and Strong wrestled were built into the system from its beginning. The decision was not to establish a central bank with uniform policies throughout the country, but rather to create semi-autonomous regional banks that would allow for rate and policy changes based on regional economic conditions. Nor did the war experience, which had turned the system into an instrument for financing both the American and Allied war efforts and by doing so had contributed to the post-war boom and bust, alter the structure in permanent ways. The power remained with the Reserve Banks and especially with the one that had been the strongest from the beginning, the Federal Reserve Bank of New York. It became the government's fiscal agent, and it remained at the center of the system's ma-

---

2. Mark Sullivan to Herbert Hoover, Mar 24, 1949, in Mark Sullivan File, PPI, HHPL.

chinery for carrying on open market operations, acting as the agent of the other banks in the New York money market[3] and dominating the Open Market Committee that brought together the Governors of the Boston, Chicago, New York, and Philadelphia Reserve Banks.[4]

It was the FRBNY that handled the investment account set up by the Open Market Investment Committee in 1923. And, while changes in Reserve banks holdings were theoretically subject to approval by the Federal Reserve Board, Adolph Miller was essentially correct when he said that if the board did not approve of purchases, "the board of directors of the Reserve Bank would go ahead on their own and operate in the open market."[5] Nor was Miller much off the mark when he said that Benjamin Strong, the man who dominated the FRBNY, also constituted a "majority of one" on the Open Market Investment Committee.[6] Something approaching a "central bank" seemed to be evolving, but in New York rather than Washington, and in a way that still allowed for much resistance to its conception of national needs and sound policy. In particular, a farm bloc in Congress, regional interests in other Federal Reserve districts, and a group of would-be economic managers in the Commerce Department resisted the kind of balance between international and domestic requirements that Strong envisioned and tried to implement.

During his early years at the FRBNY, Strong was greatly concerned with speculation and sought every means to curtail it. In November 1919, he advocated that the screws be turned on the speculator by raising the rediscount rate. And in 1923 he supported Hoover's claim that the "Federal Reserve System as an organization [had] the responsibility for checking undue expansion by credit control."[7] At the time, Strong agreed that the seed for depression was sown by over-expansion and inflation during periods of prosperity. Therefore, if anything was to be done towards controlling the business cycle, the control had to be applied during the period of prosperity. He stated in 1923 that the country was in a period of prosperity and that "fortunately the report of [Hoover's] committee, begun in a period of depression, has been issued at just the right time."[8] It could lead to actions that would determine "the extent and nature of the period of depression which is to follow."[9] At the time, moreover, he considered Hoover's

---

3. This began in 1915. See Annual Report of the Federal Reserve Bank of New York, 1915, p. 20.

4. In 1923 the Governor of the Federal Reserve Bank of Cleveland was added to the committee.

5. House Committee on Banking and Currency. *Stabilization*, 69th Cong. 1st Sess., (Washington, DC: Government Printing Office, 1926), p. 866.

6. House Committee on Banking and Currency. *Stabilization*, 70th Cong. 1st Sess., (Washington: Government Printing Office, 1928), p. 126.

7. Hoover stated this in a report on the President's Committee on Unemployment, of which he was chairman.

8. Benjamin Strong, Memorandum on Credit Policy, April 18, 1923, FRBNY.

9. Ibid.

conclusions about credit control to be sound and thought it reasonable to expect the Federal Reserve System to protect the credit resources of the country from exploitation.

Later, however, Strong became more deeply concerned with the international aspects of the problem, especially with the possible consequences of continued monetary instability in Europe. Britain's return to the gold standard became essential to future economic well-being, at least in Strong's mind. And to facilitate this, he was now willing to subordinate concerns about domestic speculation and keep rediscount rates in the New York district as low as possible for as long as possible. In 1927 and 1928, moreover, Strong continued to believe that the United States had done "the right thing to get Europe back on its feet financially," even though "we may have to pay a high price for it." These were the sentiments conveyed to Walter Wyatt, who in retrospect thought that the New York bankers had rendered a great disservice to the United States in making money conditions too easy, that their actions contributed to the inflation in both the stock market and the country as a whole, and that this inflation was aided by Strong's determination to get Europe back on its feet financially.[10]

One way to arrest speculation while retaining easy money would have been to regulate the demand for stock exchange loans by increasing margin requirements. This was a method that the period's policy makers understood, especially since it had been successfully applied in September 1918 when an alarming speculation in stocks had been curbed by increasing margin requirements from 20 to 37 1/2 percent on loans collateralled wholly by industrial stocks.

This course of action had been suggested by the Money Committee (a subcommittee of the Liberty Loan organization), composed of Strong as chairman and eight top officials of New York City banks. The Federal Reserve Board had then acted on the suggestion, and Strong's Committee had become the regulatory agency responsible for implementing the requirements. Yet despite the success, there was no talk of doing something similar during the speculative crisis of the later 1920s. Instead, Strong seemed willing to let speculators take their chances.

The difference in Strong's attitude may be explained by the different contexts in which speculation was taking place. In 1918 it threatened to interfere with the floating of the Victory Loan, which was at the time Stong's chief concern. But in 1925 and 1927 it did not materially threaten the stabilization of sterling. On the contrary, the cheap money policy that made speculation possible also promised to keep sterling afloat. Still, it seems possible that if Strong had requested the power to set margins from Congress and had taken the same approach with the stabilization of the pound that he had taken with the Victory Loan—that is, to keep money rates low for foreign borrowing but to increase the margin on stock purchases—he might have found a way to curtail the speculative orgy that eventually got out of hand. Congress, however, would have had to act, or at least other institutions would have had to cooperate. It was not until the

---

10. Oral History, Walter Wyatt, conducted by James R. Sargent, May 1970, Oral History Research Office, Columbia University, New York.

passage of the Securities Exchange Act of 1934 that the Federal Reserve Banks were specifically authorized to set margin requirements.

Strong, to be sure, was loath to seek changes in the Federal Reserve Act that would open the system to undue interference by Congress or the President. Yet in a larger sense he acted in ways that negated the notion that the system was apolitical, and almost from the beginning administration officials brought political pressure to bear on Federal Reserve policy makers. This was reflected early in the clash between Strong and Glass and later in his clashes with Hoover.

During the first episode, the administration manipulated Federal Reserve policy in an effort to provide a favorable position for the Liberty Loans, both during and after the war, and when Strong sought to level the playing field by doing away with preferential rates for Treasury and government obligations, the Secretary of the Treasury balked and argued that the Federal Reserve Board, of which he was an ex-officio member, had the right to nullify such action. Had he been simply a member of the board, that action might have been understandable. But since he was also a member of the administration, it amounted to political interference.

During the 1920s Herbert Hoover continuously sought to influence Federal Reserve policy formulation, especially in regard to the floating and control of foreign loans, the stabilization of the money supply, and the curbing of speculative activity. He was quick to offer advice when he deemed it necessary, and in the early 1920s he regarded the Federal Reserve output as being generally satisfactory and credited it with improving economic performance and helping to prevent a severe depression. Initially, moreover, he got along well with Strong, was a supporter of the latter's European stabilization policies, and was not among those calling for Strong's resignation. It was only in the mid-1920s that he began to find fault with a policy output increasingly dominated by Strong and to seek ways of altering it through the strengthening of the Federal Reserve Board and the mobilization of pressures from Congress. In these endeavors, Adolph Miller became his close ally and representative on the board, so much so that a number of the board members believed that whenever Miller said something he also spoke for Hoover.[11]

After 1926 Hoover was less overtly involved, but Miller, sometimes speaking for Hoover, was persistent in challenging Strong and other members of the board. Much of the time, Miller was a minority of one. But on some occasions James and others sided with him, and he did articulate a critique that kept Strong worried and the board often in an uproar.

Miller's critique began with the contention that Strong's policies had not established a "real gold standard" but only one that Federal Reserve policy had to keep propping up. In addition, he was disturbed because the board appeared to pay more attention to European considerations than domestic ones, which meant that the easy money policies developed in support of the artificial gold standard were contributing materially to speculation in the securities market. And thirdly, Miller was concerned about alleged abuses in open market opera-

---

11. Charles Hamlin makes entries in his diary to this effect beginning in 1925.

tions. These, he said, needed to be curbed, but as the system was currently structured the board was powerless to control the Open Market Investment Committee and the market operations undertaken by the individual Reserve banks.[12]

In effect, as Miller, Hoover, and some congressional critics analyzed it, the Federal Reserve Act had never been successful in dismantling the old financial system. Monetary policy making was still concentrated in New York, which through the FRBNY and the Open Market Investment Committee operated as a central bank and, under the leadership of Benjamin Strong, set the system's policies. Hence, it was a fundamental flaw in the way that the system was started and had developed that had allowed a man like Benjamin Strong to gain control over the policy apparatus and make it reflect his preoccupations with European monetary stabilization, inter-allied debts, war reparations, the restoration of the gold standard in European countries, and the solidification of Wall Street's position as the world's financial center. It was a flaw, they believed, that needed fixing, somewhat along the lines subsequently undertaken in the Banking Act of 1935, but their efforts to redistribute powers within the system had little success.

As far as Strong's relations with Hoover were concerned, the problem could also be viewed from the standpoint of Hoover's meddlesomeness and the resentments it aroused. During the period Hoover involved himself in almost every facet of the administration, much to the consternation of other Cabinet members and appointed officials. And while it may have irked Hoover that he was not able to exert more influence on Federal Reserve Board decisions than he did, his attempts to exert such influence certainly irked Strong. Both men were strong-willed individuals, and it appears that neither was willing to listen to the other when they disagreed.

At the same time, Hoover labored under the misconception that Strong was being dominated by Norman, a charge that he repeated years later when he sought to explain the failed policies of the twenties. He was sure, he told Adolph Miller in 1934, that Norman was the one who pulled the strings.[13] Miller also believed that Strong was influenced by Norman, an assessment that was most likely based on Strong's close friendship with Norman, their frequent contacts, and the seeming willingness of Strong to go along with Norman's wishes in 1927 and maintain low discount rates for the purpose of aiding European monetary stabilization. What neither Hoover nor Miller recognized was that Strong had already decided to stay with lower rates prior to his meeting with Norman in July 1927. Nor was the man whom we can now see revealed in the Strong-

12. As noted previously Miller stated this during the 1926 and 1928 hearings on the Strong Bill before the House Banking and Currency Committee.

13. Herbert Hoover to Adolph Miller, October 17, 1934, in Adolph Miller Individual File, PPI, HHPL. Hoover's memory was not accurate about the order of events, and in his memoirs he linked his protests in the fall of 1925 with the policy developed in late 1927.

Norman correspondence the kind of puppet that Hoover and Miller believed him to be.[14]

Strong, it seems clear, had his own agenda in mind. England's stabilization was, to Strong, the cornerstone of European financial reconstruction. The latter could not be accomplished without the former, and both were required if the involvement of the American banking community in international finance and debt settlements was to yield the current and future returns that it gave promise of yielding. If Strong acted for anyone's interest, it was as the Italian Finance Minister Giuseppe Volpi stated, for his mistress "Wall Street." The ultimate beneficiary was not supposed to be the Bank of England, as Hoover and Miller insisted, but the bankers in the world's leading money market located in lower Manhattan, in the second Federal Reserve District.

---

14. Strong had decided as far back as 1919 to aid the Bank of England. This was not based on any coercion by Norman but was done on his own volition. At the time he wrote to Montagu Norman, "If at any time I can personally or officially, or in any way, be of service to you as Governor of the Bank of England, I want the opportunity to do so." Benjamin Strong to Montagu Norman, December 8, 1919, in Strong Papers, FRBNY.

Glossary

The individuals listed in this in one way or another contributed to monetary policy formulation or debates over the formulation of monetary policy during the 1920s.

Aldrich, Nelson   U.S. Senator from Rhode Island; proposed legislation to consider a central banking system in the United States

Beckhart, Benjamin   Professor of Economics at Columbia University

Campbell, Milo D.   Farmer; Member FRB

Capper, Arthur   U.S. Senator, Kansas

Chandler, Henry   National Bank of Commerce New York

Crissinger, Daniel   Governor FRB 1922-1927

Crosby, Oscar T.   Assistant Secretary of the Treasury during the Wilson Administration

Dawes, Charles G.   Member of the second committee of experts of the Allied Reparations Commission objective was to arrive at a settlement of Germany's WW I debts and reparations

Edmonds, Richard   Editor Manufacturer's Record

Fisher, Irving   Professor of Economics at Yale University

Gilbert, S. Parker   Assistant Secretary of the Treasury under Secretary Mellon

Glass, Carter   Congressman later Senator from Virginia, proposed the bill which ultimately became the Federal Reserve Act;

	Secretary of the Treasury 1918-1920
Hamlin, Charles	Member FRB; inveterate diarist kept a daily diary of the Board's activities.
Harding, W.P.G.	Governor FRB until 1922; appointed Governor FRBB in 1922
Harrison, George L.	Deputy Governor FRBNY under Benjamin Strong. Assumed the governorship FRBNY upon Strong's death.
Harrison, Leland	First Assistant Secretary of State under Secretary Hughes and Secretary Kellog
Hoover, Herbert	Head U.S. Food Administration during the Wilson Administration; Secretary of Commerce during the Harding and Coolidge Administrations; President U.S. 1929-1933
Hughes, Charles E.	Secretary of State 1921-1925
James Logan	State Department Representative, member of the First Committee of Experts at the Paris conference on German debt settlement
Jay, Pierre	Chairman FRBNY
Jones, Grosvenor	Chief of Finance and Investment Division Commerce Department
Kent, I.E.	Vice-President Bankers trust Company New York
Keynes, Maynard	British economist opposed England's return to the gold standard
Lansing, Robert	Secretary of State during the Wilson Administration
Leffingwell, Robert	Assistant Secretary of the Treasury during the Wilson Administration
Lenroot, Irvine	U.S. Senator Wisconsin
McAdoo, William	Secretary of the Treasury 1913-1918
McDougal, James	Governor FRBC
McGarrah, Gates	Succeeded Pierre Jay as Chair FRBNY
Mellon, Andrew	Secretary of the treasury under the Harding, Coolidge, and Hoover Administrations
Miller, Adolph	Economist; Member FRB
Mitchell, Charles E.	President National City Bank New York
Norman, Montagu	Governor Bank of England
Norris, George	Governor FRBP
Roberts, George	Vice-President National City Bank New York
Schacht, Hjalmar	President of the German Reichsbank
Seay, George	Governor of the Federal Reserve Bank Richmond
Shibeley, George	Director Research Institute Washington D.C.
Stewart, Walter	Director of Research FRB
Strong, Benjamin	Governor FRBNY 1913-1927
Strong, James K.	Congressman from Kansas; proponent of amending the Federal Reserve Act to promote price stability
Vissering, Gerard	Governor of the Dutch National Bank

Warburg, Paul	Banker; member FRB during the Wilson Administration
Winston, Garrard	Undersecretary of the Treasury 1923-1927
Young, Owen	Chairman of the second committee of experts of the Allied Reparations Commission objective was to arrive at a settlement of Germany's WW I debts and reparations
Young, Roy	3rd Governor FRB appointed 1927

Bibliography

MANUSCRIPT COLLECTIONS

Bank of England, Correspondence with Federal Reserve Bank of New York, photocopies, Herbert Hoover Presidential Library, West Branch, Iowa.

Glass, Carter. *Carter Glass Papers.* University of Virginia, Charlottesville, Va.

Hamlin, Charles. *Charles Hamlin Papers.* Manuscript Division, Library of Congress.

Harrison, George L. *George L. Harrison Papers.* Butler Library, Columbia University, New York, New York.

Hoover, Herbert. *Herbert Hoover Papers.* Herbert Hoover Presidential Library, West Branch, Iowa.

Hoover, Herbert. *Herbert Hoover Papers.* Hoover Institution on War, Revolution and Peace, Stanford, Ca.

Hunt, Edward Eyre. *Edward Eyre Hunt Papers.* Hoover Institution on War, Revolution and Peace, Stanford, Ca.

Lenroot, Irvine. *Irvine Lenroot Papers.* Manuscript Division, Library of Congress.

Miller, Adolph. *Adolph Miller Papers.* Manuscript Division, Library of Congress.

Strong, Benjamin. *Benjamin Strong Papers.* New York Federal Reserve Bank.

PUBLISHED GOVERNMENT DOCUMENTS

Federal Reserve Bank of New York. *Annual Report.* 1915, 1925, 1926, 1927, 1928, 1929.

Federal Reserve Board. *Annual Report.* 1925, 1926, 1927, 1928, 1929.

Federal Reserve Board. *Bulletin.* 1919, 1920, 1925, 1926, 1927, 1928, 1929.

Great Britain. *Parliamentary Papers* (Commons). "Report of the Committee on the Currency and Bank of England Note Issues," 1925.

U.S. Congress. *Congressional Record,* 1913, 1922, 1930.

U.S. Congress, *Joint Commission on Agricultural Inquiry.* 3 vols. 67th Cong. 1st Sess. Washington, DC: Government Printing Office, 1921, and 1922.

U.S. Congress, *Report of the Joint Commission on Agricultural Inquiry.* 67th Cong. 1st Sess. Washington, DC: Government Printing Office, 1922.

U.S. Congress. House. Committee on Banking and Currency. *Stabilization.* 69th Cong. 1st Sess. Washington, DC: Government Printing Office, 1926.

U.S. Congress. House. Committee on Banking and Currency. *Stabilization.* 69th Cong. 1st Sess. Washington, DC: Government Printing Office, 1927.

U.S. Congress. House. Committee on Banking and Currency. *Stabilization.* 70th Cong. 1st Sess. Washington, DC: Government Printing Office, 1928.

U.S. Congress. Senate. Committee on Banking and Currency. *Operation of the National and Federal Reserve Banking System.* 71st Cong. 3rd Sess. Washington, DC: Government Printing Office, 1931.

U.S. Department of Commerce. *Annual Report of the Secretary of Commerce,* 1924-1928. Washington, DC, 1924-1928.

BOOKS AND NEWSPAPERS

Alchon, Guy. *The Invisible Hand of Planning, Capitalism, Social Science, and the State in the 1920s.* Princeton: Princeton University Press, 1985.

Bach, G.L. *Federal Reserve Policy Making.* New York: Alfred Knopf, 1950.

Barber, William J. *From New Era to New Deal: Herbert Hoover, the Economists and American Economic Policy 1921-1923.* New York: Cambridge University Press, 1976.

Beckhart, Benjamin. *Federal Reserve System.* New York: Columbia University Press, 1972.

_____, ed. *The Discount Policy of the Federal Reserve System.* New York: Henry Holt, 1924.

_____, ed. *The New York Money Market* Vols. 2-4. New York: Columbia University Press, 1932.

Boyle, Andrew. *Montagu Norman.* New York: Weubright and Talley, 1967.

Brandes, Joseph. *Herbert Hoover and Economic Diplomacy: Department of Commerce Policy, 1921-1928.* Pittsburgh: University of Pittsburgh Press, 1962.

Burgess, W. Randolph. ed. *Interpretations of Federal Reserve Policy in the Speeches and Writings of Benjamin Strong.* New York: Harper and Brothers, 1930.

_____. *The Reserve Banks and the Money Market.* 3rd ed., New York: Harper & Row, 1946.

Burner, David. *Herbert Hoover A Public Life.* New York: Alfred A. Knopf, 1979.

Case, Josephine Young, and Everett Needham Case. *Owen D. Young and American Enterprise.* Boston: David R. Godine, 1982.

Chandler, Lester V. *American Monetary Policy 1920-1941.* New York: Harper & Row, 1971.

_____. *Benjamin Strong Central Banker.* Washington: Brookings Institution, 1958.

_____. *The Economics of Money and Banking.* New York: Harper & Brothers, 1948.

Clark, Lawrence E. *Central Banking Under the Federal Reserve System.* New York: Macmillan, 1935.

Clarke, Stephen V.O. *Central Bank Cooperation, 1924-1931.* New York: Federal Reserve Bank of New York, 1967.

Clay, Sir H. *Lord Norman.* London: St. Martins, 1957.

Cleveland Plain Dealer, April 1, 1925.

Clifford, A. Jerome. *The Independence of the Federal Reserve System.* Philadelphia: University of Pennsylvania Press, 1965.

Cohen, Warren I. *Empire Without Tears.* Philadelphia: Temple University Press, 1987.

Bibliography 169

Commercial and Financial Chronicle. 1923, 1924, 1925, 1926.

Costigliola, Frank. *Awkward Dominion.* Ithaca, N.Y.: Cornell University Press, 1984.

Edie, Lionel D. *The Stabilization of Business.* New York: Macmillan, 1923.

Financial World. 1925, 1926, 1927, 1928, 1929.

Fleisig, Heywood. *Long Term Capital Flows and the Great Depression: The Role of the United States, 1927-1933.* New York: Arno Press, 1975.

Friedman, Milton and Anna J. Schwartz. *A Monetary History of the United States, 1869-1960.* Princeton: Princeton University Press, 1963.

Galbraith, John Kenneth. *The Great Crash, 1929.* Boston: Houghton Mifflin, 1954.

Glass, Carter. *An Adventure in Constructive Finance.* Garden City, NY: Doubleday, Page, 1927.

Greider, William. *Secrets of the Temple: How the Federal Reserve Runs the Country.* New York: Simon and Schuster, 1987

Grigg, Sir James. *Prejudice and Judgement.* London: Jonathan Cape, 1948.

Harding, W.P.G. *The Formative Period of the Federal Reserve.* Boston: Houghton Mifflin, 1925.

Hawley, Ellis. *The Great War and the Search for a Modern Order, 1917-1933.* New York: St. Martins Press, 1979.

Hogan, Michael J. Informal Entente: *The Private Structure of Cooperation in Anglo-American Economic Diplomacy, 1918-1926.* Columbia: University of Missouri Press, 1977.

Hoover, Herbert. *The Memoirs of Herbert Hoover.* 3 vols. New York: Macmillan, 1952.

Horvitz, Paul M. *Monetary Policy and the Financial System.* Englewood Cliffs, NJ: Prentice Hall, 1963.

Hughes, Charles Evans. *The Pathway to Peace.* New York: Harper and Brothers, 1925.

Huthmacher, Joseph J., and Warren I. Sussman, eds. *Herbert Hoover and the Crisis of American Capitalism,* 1973.

Karl, Barry. *The Uneasy State.* Chicago: University of Chicago Press, 1983.

Kemmerer, Edwin, W. *Gold and the Gold Standard: The Story of Gold Money, Past, Present and Future.* New York: McGraw Hill, 1944.

Kettl, David F. *Leadership at the Fed.* New Haven, Conn.: Yale University Press, 1986.

Kindleberger, Charles. *The World in Depression.* Berkeley: University of California Press, 1973.

Leffler, Melvin. *The Elusive Quest: America's Pursuit of Stability and French Security, 1919-1933.* Chapel Hill: University of North Carolina Press, 1979.

Literary Digest. 1926.

Maier, Charles S. *Recasting Bourgeois Europe: Stabilization in France, Germany and Italy in the Decade after World War I.* Princeton: Princeton University Press, 1975.

McCoy, Donald R. *Calvin Coolidge, The Quiet President.* Lawrence: University Press of Kansas, 1967.

McNeill, William C. *American Money and the Weimar Republic.* New York: Columbia University Press, 1986.

Meyer, Richard. *Bankers' Diplomacy: Monetary Stabilization during the 1920s.* New York: Columbia University Press, 1970.

New York Times. 1921, 1922, 1923, 1924, 1925, 1927.

New York Herald Tribune, March 5, 1926.

Parini, Carl P. *Heir to Empire: United States Economic Diplomacy, 1916-1923.* Pittsburgh: University of Pittsburgh Press, 1969.

Pentzlin, Heinz. *Hjalmar Schacht.* Berlin: Ullstein, 1980.

Rosenberg, Emily. *Spreading the American Dream: American Economic and Cultural Expansion 1890-1945.* New York: Hill and Wang, 1987.

Rothbard, Murray. *America's Great Depression.* Princeton: Van Nostrand, 1963.

Sayers, R.S. *The Bank of England,* 1891-1944. Cambridge: Cambridge University Press, 1976.

_____. *A History of Economic Change in England 1880-1939.* Cambridge: Cambridge University Press, 1967.

Schacht, Hjalmar. *Stabilization of the Mark.* New York: Adelphi Co., 1927.

Schlessinger, Arthur Maier, Jr. *The Age of Roosevelt: Crisis of the Old Order, 1919-1933.* Boston: Houghton Mifflin, 1957.

Seay, George J. *The Course of the Federal Reserve Banks Before and During the Price Crisis Readjustment.* Address before the North Carolina Bankers' Convention, April 26-28, 1922. Published by Federal Reserve Bank of Richmond, May 1922.

Soule, G. *Prosperity Decade: From War to Depression, 1917-1929.* New York: Holt, Reinhart & Winston, 1947.

Staunton News Leader, March 21, 1926.

Toma, Mark. *Competition and Monopoly in the Federal Reserve System 1914-1951: A Microeconomic Approach to Monetary History.* Cambridge: Cambridge University Press, 1997

Van Petten, Donald R. "The European Technical Advisor and Post-War Austria 1919-1923." Ph.D. dissertation, Stanford University, 1943, pp. 358-365, 583-590.

Wall Street Journal, February 25, 1927.

Warburg, Paul. *The Federal Reserve System.* 2 vols. New York: Macmillan, 1930.

West, Robert Craig. *Banking Reform and the Federal Reserve, 1863-1923.* Ithaca, NY: Cornell University Press, 1977.

Wheelock, David C. *The Strategy and Consistency of Federal Reserve Monetary Policy 1924-1933,* Cambridge: Cambridge University Press, 1991.

White, Eugene. The Regulation and Reform of the American Banking System, 1900-1929. Princeton: Princeton University Press, 1983.

Wicker, Elmus. *Federal Reserve Monetary Policy, 1917-1933.* New York: Random House, 1966.

Wilson, Joan Hoff. *American Business and Foreign Policy, 1920-1933.* Lexington: University Press of Kentucky, 1971.

JOURNALS

American Review of Reviews 73 (January-June 1926): 242.

Annalist. 1923, 1925, 1926.

Banker. 1926, 1927, 1928.

Braeman, John. "American Foreign Policy in the Age of Normalcy: Three Historiographical Traditions," *Amerika Studien* 2 (1981): 152-158.

_____. "The New Left and American Foreign Policy During the Age of Normalcy: A Re-examination," *Business History Review* LVII (Spring 1983): 73-104.

Bryan, William Jennings. "My Forecast on Next Year's Election," *Hearst's International Magazine* (November 1923): 23.

Crissinger, D.R. "The Federal Reserve System," *Congressional Digest* 5 (March 1926): 81-82.

Crowther, Samuel. "Can We Plan on Easy Money," *Magazine of Business* 52 (October 1927): 388-391.

Daiger, J.M. "Did the Federal Reserve Play Politics?" *Current History* 37 (October 1932): 25-32.

Economic World. 1925, 1926, 1927, 1928, 1929.

Economist. 1922, 1923, 1925, 1926, 1927, 1928, 1929.

Fisher, C.O. "American Banking Fallacy." *American Economic Review* 16 (December 1926): 663-665.

Friedman, Elisha M. "The Federal Reserve Fight." *Nation* 125 (October 1927): 359-360.

Logan, Walter S. "Amendment to the Federal Reserve Act." *Annals of American Academy of Political and Social Science* 99 (January 1922): 114-121.

London Economist. 1923, 1925.

Manufacturers Record 1921, 1922, 1923, 1924, 1925, 1926.

Miller, Adolph C. "Federal Reserve Policies: 1927-1929," *American Economic Review* 25 (September 1935): 442-458.

_____. "Federal Reserve Policy," *American Economic Review* 11 (June 1921): 177-206.

_____. "The Federal Reserve System: Looking Ahead" *Economic World*, New Series 12 (November 1916): 588-592

Mills, Ogden L. "An Explanation of Federal Reserve Policy" *American Review of Reviews* 78 (September 1928): 251-260.

Roberts, George E. "Federal Reserve Control of the Money Market." *Economic World* (December 19, 1925): 868.

Toma, Mark. "The Policy Effectiveness of Open Market Operations in the 1920's." *Explorations in Economic History* 26 (January 1989): 99-116

Warburg, Paul M. "Political Pressure and the Future of the Federal Reserve System." *Annals of American Academy of Political and Social Science* 99 (January 1922): 70-74.

Welton, A.D. "The Federal Reserve Action Its Implicit Meaning." *Annals of American Academy of Political and Social Science* 99 (January 1922): 56-62.

Wheelock, David C. "The Strategy, Effectiveness, and Consistency of Federal Reserve Monetary Policy, 1924-1933." *Explorations in Economic History*, 26 (October 1989): 453-476.

Willis, H. Parker. "The Discount Rate Controversy in the United States." *Banker* 4 (November 1927): 408-416.

_____. "The Failure of the Federal Reserve." *North American Review* 227 (May 1929): 547-557.

World's Work 55 (November 1927): 10-11.

Young, Owen D. "Recent Federal Reserve Policy." *American Review of Reviews.* 78 (September 1928): 252-255.

Index

About the Author

SILVANO A. WUESCHNER is Assistant Professor of History at William Penn College.